Florida History and Culture Series

d by Raymond Arsenault and Gary R. Mormino

t's Florida: Snowbirds, Sand Castles, and Self-Rising Crackers, by Al Burt (1997)

Miami in the Twentieth Century, by Marvin Dunn (1997)

men: Gator Hunters, Moonshiners, and Skiffers, by Glen Simmons and Laura Ogden (1998)

to My Sunland": Letters of Julia Daniels Moseley from the Florida Frontier, 1882–1886, by Julia
nifred Moseley and Betty Powers Crislip (1998)

during Seminoles: From Alligator Wrestling to Ecotourism, by Patsy West (1998)

ment in the Sunshine State: Florida since Statehood, by David R. Colburn and Lance
Haven-Smith (1999)

rglades: An Environmental History, by David McCally (1999), first paperback edition, 2001

s, Stowes, and Yankee Strangers: The Transformation of Florida, by John T. Foster Jr. and Sarah
itmer Foster (1999)

ic of Cracker, by Al Burt (1999)

ng Evils Judiciously: The Proslavery Writings of Zephaniah Kingsley, edited and annotated
Daniel W. Stowell (1999)

Soldiers in the Sunshine State: German POWs in Florida, by Robert D. Billinger Jr. (2000)

za: The South's Oldest Spiritualist Community, edited by John J. Guthrie, Phillip Charles Lucas,
Gary Monroe (2000)

epper and Ed Ball: Politics, Purpose, and Power, by Tracy E. Danese (2000)

during the Civil War: A Thorn in the Side of the Confederacy, by George F. Pearce (2000)

the Sand: The Life and Times of Carl Graham Fisher, by Mark S. Foster (2000)

S.A., by Helen Muir (2000)

d Growth in Twentieth-Century Tampa, by Robert Kerstein (2001)

ble Empire: The Ku Klux Klan in Florida, by Michael Newton (2001)

Brim: Early Poems and Ponderings of Marjory Stoneman Douglas, edited by Jack E. Davis
)

ecture of Leisure: The Florida Resort Hotels of Henry Flagler and Henry Plant, by Susan R.
n (2002)

pace Coast: The Impact of NASA on the Sunshine State, by William Barnaby Faherty, S.J.

of Hurricane Andrew, by Eugene F. Provenzo Jr. and Asterie Baker Provenzo (2002)

A Most Disorderly Court

THE FLORIDA HISTORY AND CULTURE SERIES

UNIVERSITY PRESS OF FLORIDA

Florida A&M University, Tallahassee
Florida Atlantic University, Boca Raton
Florida Gulf Coast University, Ft. Myers
Florida International University, Miami
Florida State University, Tallahassee
New College of Florida, Sarasota
University of Central Florida, Orlando
University of Florida, Gainesville
University of North Florida, Jacksonville
University of South Florida, Tampa
University of West Florida, Pensacola

Florida's Farmworkers in the Twenty-first Century, text by Nano Riley and photographs by Davida Johns (2003)

Making Waves: Female Activists in Twentieth-Century Florida, edited by Jack E. Davis and Kari Frederickson (2003)

Orange Journalism: Voices from Florida Newspapers, by Julian M. Pleasants (2003)

The Stranahans of Ft. Lauderdale: A Pioneer Family of New River, by Harry A. Kersey Jr. (2003)

Death in the Everglades: The Murder of Guy Bradley, America's First Martyr to Environmentalism, by Stuart B. McIver (2003)

Jacksonville: The Consolidation Story, from Civil Rights to the Jaguars, by James B. Crooks (2004)

The Seminole Wars: The Nation's Longest Indian Conflict, by John and Mary Lou Missall (2004)

The Mosquito Wars: A History of Mosquito Control in Florida by Gordon Patterson (2004)

The Seasons of Real Florida, by Jeff Klinkenberg (2004)

Land of Sunshine, State of Dreams: A Social History of Modern Florida, by Gary Mormino (2005)

Paradise Lost? The Environmental History of Florida, edited by Jack E. Davis and Raymond Arsenault (2005)

Frolicking Bears, Wet Vultures, and Other Oddities: A New York City Journalist in Nineteenth-Century Florida, edited by Jerald T. Milanich (2005)

Waters Less Traveled: Exploring Florida's Big Bend Coast, by Doug Alderson (2005)

Saving South Beach, by M. Barron Stofik (2005)

Losing It All to Sprawl: How Progress Ate My Cracker Landscape, by Bill Belleville (2006)

Voices of the Apalachicola, compiled and edited by Faith Eidse (2006)

Floridian of His Century: The Courage of Governor LeRoy Collins, by Martin A. Dyckman (2006)

America's Fortress: A History of Fort Jefferson, Dry Tortugas, Florida, by Thomas Reid (2006)

Weeki Wachee, City of Mermaids: A History of One of Florida's Oldest Roadside Attractions (2007)

City of Intrigue, Nest of Revolution: A Documentary History of Key West in the Nineteenth Century, by Consuelo E. Stebbins (2007)

The New Deal in South Florida: Design, Policy, and Community Building, 1933–1940, edited by John A. Stuart and John F. Stack Jr. (2008)

Pilgrim in the Land of Alligators: More Stories about Real Florida, by Jeff Klinkenberg (2008)

A Most Disorderly Court: Scandal and Reform in the Florida Judiciary, by Martin A. Dyckman (2008)

UNIVERSITY PRESS OF FLORIDA

Gainesville
Tallahassee
Tampa
Boca Raton
Pensacola
Orlando
Miami
Jacksonville
Ft. Myers
Sarasota

A Most Disorderly Court

Scandal and Reform
in the Florida Judiciary

MARTIN A. DYCKMAN

Foreword by Gary Mormino and Raymond Arsenault

13 12 11 10 09 08 6 5 4 3 2 1

Library of Congress Cataloging-in-Publication Data
Dyckman, Martin A.
A most disorderly court: scandal and reform in the Florida judiciary / Martin A. Dyckman;
foreword by Gary Mormino and Raymond Arsenault.
p. cm.—(The Florida history and culture series)
Includes bibliographical references and index.
ISBN 978-0-8130-3205-4 (alk. paper)
1. Judicial corruption—Florida. 2. Courts—Florida—Corrupt practices. 3. Florida. Supreme
Court.
I. Title.
KFF525.5.D5D93   2008
347.759'01—dc22   2007034583

The University Press of Florida is the scholarly publishing agency for the State University
System of Florida, comprising Florida A&M University, Florida Atlantic University, Florida
Gulf Coast University, Florida International University, Florida State University, New College
of Florida, University of Central Florida, University of Florida, University of North Florida,
University of South Florida, and University of West Florida.

University Press of Florida
15 Northwest 15th Street
Gainesville, FL 32611-2079
www.upf.com

To the memory of

Richard Tilghman Earle Junior

Patriot

Contents

Foreword

A *Most Disorderly Court* is the latest volume of a series devoted to the study of Florida history and culture. During the past half-century, the burgeoning population and increased national and international visibility of Florida have sparked a great deal of popular interest in the state's past, present, and future. As a favorite destination of countless tourists and as the new home for millions of retirees and transplants, modern Florida has become a demographic, political, and cultural bellwether. Florida has also emerged as a popular subject and setting for scholars and writers. The Florida History and Culture Series provides an attractive and accessible format for Florida-related books. From killer hurricanes to disputed elections, from tales of the Everglades to profiles of Sunbelt cities, Florida is simply irresistible.

The University Press of Florida is committed to the creation of an eclectic but carefully crafted set of books that will provide the field of Florida studies with a new focus that will encourage Florida writers to consider the broader implications and context of their work. The series includes standard academic monographs as well as works of synthesis, memoirs, and anthologies. And while the series features books of historical interest, authors researching Florida's environment, politics, literature, and popular or material culture are encouraged to submit their manuscripts as well. Each book offers a distinct personality and voice, but the ultimate goal of the series is to foster a broad sense of community and collaboration among Florida scholars.

Like a Greek chorus or a plot twist in a Shakespearian tragedy (or comedy, depending upon one's politics), the Florida Supreme Court's 2000 judgment in *Gore v. Harris* boldly rushed onto the stage. In his new book, Martin A. Dyckman eloquently recounts the compelling story of a Florida Supreme Court under fire and facing reform-minded politicians and officials.

In *A Most Disorderly Court*, Dyckman masterfully demonstrates his talents as a historical detective, investigative journalist, and political analyst. The era between the 1950s and early 1970s serves as the setting, a period in which the author covered state politics for the *St. Petersburg Times*. In the 1950s and 1960s, the Florida Supreme Court justices' relationships with powerful interest groups had earned that body a notorious reputation. Justices such as B. K. Roberts, Glenn Terrell, and John E. Matthews Sr. embodied the old order, symbolized by conservatism, racism, and indifference to corruption. In the 1960s, the U.S. Supreme Court rocked Florida's rural-dominated "Pork Chopper" legislature with a series of landmark decisions. By the early 1970s, Reubin Askew, Lawton Chiles, and Bob Graham represented a vanguard of talented and idealistic reformers who brought sunshine (literally and figuratively) to Florida's solons and courts. By the end of the decade, the Florida Supreme Court was almost unrecognizable, so sweeping were the changes in the composition and character of that branch of government. Dyckman's study suggests the power of determined individuals to bring about positive change. It is a story of republican virtue and democratic rights.

Gary R. Mormino and Raymond Arsenault
Series coeditors

Chronology/Cast of Characters

August 1967: Governor Claude R. Kirk Jr. appoints David L. McCain to the Fourth District Court of Appeal.

November 1968: McCain loses Supreme Court race to James C. Adkins Jr. Vassar B. Carlton defeats appointed justice Wade Hopping. Joseph A. Boyd elected to vacancy.

February 1970: McCain's Fourth District opinion dismisses aggravated assault conviction of Nancy Wakeman, who will claim she contributed to his 1968 campaign.

November 1970: Justice Campbell Thornal dies.

December 1970: Kirk appoints McCain to Thornal vacancy over opposition of Florida Bar. David Smith, former McCain supporter, alleges wrongdoing in 1968 campaign.

January 1971: Dade Grand Jury refers McCain matter to Judicial Qualifications Commission (JQC).

August 1971: Supreme Court Justice Hal P. Dekle lobbies Circuit Judge W. L. Fitzpatrick regarding a campaign supporter.

September 1971: Governor Reubin Askew establishes nominating commissions for midterm judicial vacancies.

March 1972: Voters ratify amendment incorporating nominating commissions into constitution.

July 1972: McCain, running for reelection, telephones Judge Joseph McNulty at Second District Court of Appeal on behalf of Richard Nell, campaign supporter appealing criminal conviction. McNulty informs Second DCA colleague Robert T. Mann.

September 1972: Second DCA affirms Nell conviction; Nell appeals. McCain visits union hall for campaign speech and private meeting with Nell.

October 1972: Fitzpatrick recuses himself after Dekle's telephone call concerning campaign supporter.

February 1973: Fitzpatrick responds to inquiry from JQC. McCain satisfies second mortgage with $9,4340 in $10 and $20 bills.

April 1973: Nell lobbyist Robert May meets with McCain at Supreme Court. McCain votes to reverse Nell conviction and dismiss case. McNulty and Mann report McCain to JQC.

May 1973: JQC notifies Dekle of investigation.

June 1973: Supreme Court hears *Gulf Power v. Bevis*, a major tax case. Boyd assigned to write majority opinion favoring utility.

July 1973: Boyd tells law clerk Roger A. Schwartz to investigate mysterious document appearing to be draft opinion in favor of Gulf Power Co. Boyd destroys document, changes vote, and writes opinion against the company. Edwin L. Mason, counsel for other utilities, gives Dekle another copy of the document.

August 1973: *Tampa Tribune* reports anonymous, unsubstantiated charges that Supreme Court bribed in racetrack case, ignites media interest in court. Tip from JQC chair Richard T. Earle Jr. prompts *St. Petersburg Times* article on McCain and Nell.

September 1973: Miami Circuit Judge Jack Turner asks Supreme Court to halt JQC investigation on terms that could protect Supreme Court justices.

October 1973: Boyd circulates opinion against Gulf Power. Dekle uses Mason's document to draft a proposed "dissent."

November 1973: Press reveals secret JQC investigation of Dekle. Mason visits Dekle regarding *Gulf Power*. Dekle dictates memo asking McCain to support "dissent" and mentions Mason's lobbying.

December 1973: Schwartz and law clerk David LaCroix recognize "dissent" as document Boyd destroyed, copy Dekle's memo that reveals Mason's lobbying. Chief justice tells Dekle to rewrite "dissent." *St. Petersburg Times* reports evidence of improper conduct. Arthur J. England Jr., opposing counsel in *Gulf Power*, demands explanation from Mason, files formal grievance with Florida Bar.

January 1974: Supreme Court adopts revised Dekle opinion 4-1 for *Gulf Power.* JQC tries Dekle in secret on Fitzpatrick allegation.

February 1974: Carlton retires. Ben F. Overton appointed to court. JQC finds Dekle unethical in Fitzpatrick case, but cannot agree on discipline. Court rules for Turner that judges are immune for misconduct more than two years preceding current terms.

April 1974: Education Commissioner Floyd T. Christian is indicted, and he resigns. Grand jury pursues and eventually indicts Treasurer Thomas O'Malley and former state senator George Hollahan.

June 1974: *Times* reports JQC investigating a document that Boyd destroyed.

July 1974: Chief Justice Adkins halts grand jury probe of political corruption until after the November election; court sustains order 4-3; Adkins withdraws it under intense criticism.

August 1974: Court orders election for seat of retiring justice Richard Ervin. JQC initiates formal proceedings *in camera* against Boyd and Dekle regarding *Gulf Power.*

September 1974: *Miami Herald* names Mason as source of mysterious document, reveals Boyd hospitalization and intrigue within court. Boyd reelected. England elected Ervin's successor. Adkins reelected without opposition. Overton wins full term.

November 1974: Voters ratify constitutional amendment erasing Turner precedent, allowing any evidence of a judge's "present unfitness." First DCA voids Christian, O'Malley, Hollahan indictments on technicality. JQC tries Boyd in public, Dekle in secret, reopens Fitzpatrick case, and urges court to remove Dekle and Boyd.

February 1975: Special panels cite absence of "corrupt motive," refuse to remove Boyd, Dekle in *Gulf Power* cases, and dismiss Fitzpatrick allegation. House Speaker Donald Tucker orders impeachment inquiry of Boyd, Dekle, and McCain. Supreme Court affirms First DCA decision voiding Christian, O'Malley, and Hollahan indictments.

March 1975: Dekle resigns during House impeachment investigation.

April 1975: House committee votes to impeach McCain; he resigns.

May 1975: Committee votes against impeaching Boyd. Askew appoints Alan C. Sundberg to succeed Dekle.

August 1975: Askew appoints Joseph W. Hatchett, first African American Florida justice, to succeed McCain.

January 1976: Supreme Court orders Mason suspended from Bar for a year.

March 1976: Supreme Court lifts stay and authorizes disbarment proceedings against McCain.

November 1976: Voters approve constitutional amendments for merit retention of appellate judges and overturning "corrupt motive" requirement for removal. Fred Karl elected to succeed Roberts. Hatchett and Sundberg win full terms in last contested Supreme Court campaigns.

June 1978: Supreme Court disbars McCain.

November 1980: Voters ratify constitutional amendment restricting Supreme Court jurisdiction.

September 1982: McCain accused of conspiring to smuggle marijuana.

January 1983: McCain forfeits bond and becomes a fugitive.

November 1986: McCain, never captured, dies of cancer.

Preface and Acknowledgments

Although the events in this book transpired in the 1970s, the issues are as current and compelling as tomorrow's headlines. They are as timely as the latest attempts to conceal offenses against the public trust or to punish journalists and other citizens who venture to speak the truth.

Thomas Jefferson famously wrote that "the tree of liberty must be refreshed from time to time with the blood of patriots and tyrants." As history has shown, however, it is sunshine that serves as the most essential nutrient of democracy. The saga of the Florida Supreme Court in the early 1970s is a case study. Several justices were callously indifferent to cardinal principles of judicial ethics, but the only consciences capable of being shocked into action were those of the court's young clerks. Were it not for their courage and their faith in a free press, nothing would have changed. In all likelihood, Florida's judges of last resort would still be elected like common politicians, with justice for sale at auction in each increasingly expensive campaign.

At this writing, Florida is in clear and present danger of forgetting this history and of consequently being condemned to repeat it. I hope that this book will help avert that result.

For the inspiration, I am especially in debt to David LaCroix, who persuaded me that the time had come to tell the story. He and Roger A. Schwartz were the young law clerks who risked their careers to reform the Supreme Court. Sharyn Smith did not work for the court, but she was instrumental in helping them fulfill their duty to the people of Florida. There is another former public servant who deserves to be mentioned by name but who still commands the anonymity that I promised more than thirty years ago; such a pledge is to a journalist as the sanctity of the confessional is to a priest.

As governor, Reubin Askew was instrumental in putting the bad examples to good use. He is the father of merit selection and merit retention in the Florida judiciary, and he gave several vital interviews for this book. I am also in debt to Justice Harry Anstead; former justices Rosemary Barkett, Arthur J. England Jr., Joseph W. Hatchett, Fred Karl, and Gerald Kogan; Judge Charles Kahn of the First District of Appeal; Judges (and former law clerks) Larry Sartin and C. McFerrin Smith III; Judge Walt Logan; Sid White, retired clerk of the Supreme Court; William J. Rish, Talbot D'Alemberte, and Marc Glick, in regard to the House impeachment investigation; attorneys W. Dexter Douglass, Richard R. Swann, and Wilbur Brewton; former representative Marshall S. Harris; journalists Duane Bradford, Virginia Ellis, and Clarence Jones; and to Richard McFarlain, Mark Hulsey, Burton Young, Marshall Criser, Herman Russomanno, and Steve Metz of the Florida Bar. I acknowledge the late Richard T. Earle Jr. as a source and am grateful to Richard T. Earle III for invaluable insights. My wife, Ivy, read the text patiently and made cogent suggestions. To Susan Albury, my project editor, and Elaine Otto, an infinitely patient copyeditor, and to all the others who have given generously of their time and advice, "many thanks."

This book deals with a discrete episode and its consequences. It does not purport to be a comprehensive study of the Florida Supreme Court, a function that is being performed magisterially by Professors Walter Manley II and Canter A. Brown. The second volume of that enterprise, *The Supreme Court of Florida, 1917–1972*, sponsored by the Florida Supreme Court Historical Society and published in December 2006 by the University Press of Florida, was graciously made available to me in draft form and was enormously helpful to this work.

⇥ 1 ⇤

Seventeen Equal Pieces

Nobody recalls whether there was a document shredder at the Florida Supreme Court in the summer of 1973, but in any event Justice Joseph A. Boyd Jr. would not have let himself be seen using it. He intended for nobody but his law clerk, twenty-four-year-old Roger A. Schwartz, to observe what was about to happen to the fourteen sheets of legal-sized paper Boyd held in his hands. Leading Schwartz into the second-floor men's room that was marked "Justices"—in contrast to the other facility labeled "Women"— Boyd ripped the document into strips he would describe later as "seventeen equal parts" and flushed them down a commode. Asked why he disposed of it in such an unconventional way, Boyd said that he used to be an investigator, "and I found that this was the most complete way to get rid of something." Years later, Schwartz said of the incident, "I was naïve. I remember thinking, 'Why would you do this?'"[1]

What Boyd shredded and flushed was evidence of an improper attempt to influence the court's forthcoming decision in the most important case on its docket. The litigation had the potential to decide whether the stockholders of Florida's regulated electric, telephone, and natural gas utilities would absorb the millions of dollars imposed by the state's new corporate income tax or whether the costs could be padded into their customers' monthly bills. Boyd's low-tech document shredding initiated a cascade of scandal that eventually cost two other justices their offices and nearly took his, overhauled the court's character and reputation, severely restricted the court's discretionary jurisdiction, and put an end to political election of Florida's entire appellate bench.

The issue in the case, *Gulf Power v. Bevis*, was whether to allow the electric power, telephone, and natural gas companies to add the tax to the cost base on which rates were calculated in the same fashion as fuel, salaries, and other operating expenses. After ruling for the utilities, the Florida Public Service Commission (PSC) had reversed itself in response to petitions filed by Governor Reubin Askew and Attorney General Robert Shevin. Askew's attorney was Arthur J. England Jr., a Miami tax lawyer who for a time had been his consumer counsel and had helped draft the tax legislation. The PSC, composed at the time of three elected commissioners, doubtlessly felt intense public and political pressure. The corporate tax had been Askew's signature issue in the 1970 campaign that vaulted the dark-horse state senator from Pensacola into the governor's office over three better known Democratic primary opponents and the combative incumbent Republican, Claude R. Kirk Jr. Askew had assured the public that corporations rather than consumers would bear the freight of this tax. Now that promise was on the line.[2]

In January 1972, Gulf Power Corporation, the Southern Company subsidiary serving Pensacola and much of the Florida Panhandle, petitioned the Supreme Court to hear an appeal. Tampa Electric Corporation and Florida Power Corporation, two of the three other large Florida electric utilities, asked to be heard as friends of the court. So did St. Joseph Telephone and Telegraph Company and Gulf Telephone Company. The ruling under appeal did not apply to them, but the precedent would. Although St. Joseph and Gulf were two of the smallest Florida utilities, St. Joseph's involvement was a potential lightning rod for public and media attention. Had they thought twice about it, the Florida justices should have been keenly sensitive to any impropriety in the case. St. Joseph belonged to a statewide financial empire ruled by the financier Edward Ball in his capacity as managing trustee of the estate of his late brother-in-law, Alfred I. duPont. The estate—Ball's fiefdom—also comprised the thirty-one Florida National banks, at one time the state's largest financial group; the Florida East Coast Railroad; and the St. Joe Paper Company, owner of more than a million acres of Florida forest land. Two decades earlier, Ball had declared the estate's intention to "rehabilitate, develop and virtually control the State of Florida and become the financial bulwark of the South." For a time, he had indeed controlled Florida, orchestrating the repeal of a state-imposed tax levy on real and personal property and the enactment of a regressive sales tax. Although his power was waning by 1973—among other things, the legislature refused to enact a branch-banking bill in time to help him avert divestiture of the banks as ordered by Congress—Ball still had profound influence at the Supreme Court through his friend B. K. Roberts, the senior and dominant justice.[3]

Bonny Kaslo Roberts had been so poor while attending the University of Florida that from time to time a pup tent had to serve as his living quarters. Thereafter, he had practiced law with enough skill and luck to make him wealthy. One close friend was Fuller Warren, the newly elected governor who appointed him to a vacancy on the Supreme Court in 1949. Another was Ball, who had befriended him while Roberts was a Coast Guard officer at Jacksonville during World War II. As his personal attorney, Roberts had won Ball a long-delayed divorce that cost him only a minor fraction of his wealth. Rumors persisted that Roberts remained Ball's personal lawyer after ascending to the court despite a constitutional provision that justices "shall devote full time to their judicial duties" and "shall not engage in the practice of law."[4] Roberts, who had retired to private practice by the time Ball died, complained bitterly to the lawyers for Ball's personal estate that he should have been appointed instead of them because, in the words of a witness, "he said that he had been Mr. Ball's private lawyer the whole time he was on the court."[5] In 1971, Roberts attempted to recruit C. McFerrin Smith III, a research aide at the court, to be Ball's personal attorney of record. Smith said Roberts told him, "I have been telling my good friend Ed Ball for 15 years that he needs a personal attorney, someone to go around with him and give him his legal advice personally, and I'd like you to take that job." Smith said Roberts "kind of leaned on me to take it." Smith demurred and eventually became a circuit court judge.[6]

Roberts rarely voted on cases of interest to Ball or one of his corporations, but his influence was assumed in most of them. Although Ball's telephone company was a minor player in that litigation, the duPont connection should have alerted every justice to be exceptionally scrupulous in how he approached it. In particular, none should have discussed the case in private with Edwin L. Mason, St. Joseph's attorney, let alone have used a document supplied by him outside the record to draft a proposed opinion for the court. It was that document which Boyd ultimately destroyed.

The court in those days assigned most cases to rotating panels of five justices, adding a sixth or seventh only when necessary for the four-vote majority required by the constitution. By random selection, Boyd was assigned to summarize the Gulf Power case before oral argument. That meant he would be the first to write an opinion, even if it was intended as a dissent. In that case, as it happened, all five justices agreed during a closed conference following the May 22 argument to decide the case in favor of Gulf Power.[7] Under oath, Boyd and Mason told dramatically different accounts of what happened next. It was impossible for both to be true.

Boyd's version: With the decision pending, Mason—a former colleague of his on the Metropolitan Dade County Commission and a former member of the Florida Public Service Commission—telephoned to ask about the procedure for filing a supplemental brief. It was long after the filing deadline. Boyd told him to check the rules and file a petition with the court. In the same conversation, they talked about playing golf, as they had "a few times" before. Boyd told Mason, "Don't bring it [the petition] over to me." After the golfing date, they returned to Boyd's home. Boyd went to his garden to gather vegetables to give to Mason. Boyd may have had the Gulf Power file at home with him, but he was not sure. Within a day or two after Mason's visit, back in his office, Boyd found an unfamiliar document in the file. He had no idea at that moment how it came to be there.[8] That was his story, and he stuck to it.

Mason's version: He had learned through "common gossip" at the PSC that the justices had voted in favor of the utilities. He and Boyd—whom he had once urged to be a candidate to succeed him at the Public Service Commission—talked about the case while they were playing golf. It sounded to Mason as if Boyd was finding it difficult to write the opinion. "I don't know if he brought it up or I did. We discussed this Gulf Power case, the complexity of it, how the governor had been involved. . . . We talked about the points, the issues. . . . I don't know whether he asked or I offered. . . . I do have the distinct recollection it was understood I would put together an outline, a memorandum, call it what you want, that would assist in articulating the position the court had agreed to take." He drafted the document with the help of Lewis Petteway, a lawyer who had been a high-ranking staff counsel for the PSC, and delivered it in person to Boyd at Boyd's home either just before or after a subsequent golfing engagement. Boyd never suggested that the transaction was improper; had he done so, Mason said, "I would not have pursued this any further."[9]

Mason's document was not a trivial impropriety. It was, in the subsequent words of a Florida Bar referee, "so fundamentally wrong that there is scant precedent." Bar rules adopted by the Supreme Court prohibited lawyers from discussing cases with judges *ex parte,* that is, without the knowledge of the other side. Canon 3 of the Code of Judicial Conduct, similarly adopted by the court itself, admonished every judge to "accord to every person who is legally interested in a proceeding, or his lawyer, full right to be heard according to law, and except as authorized by law, neither initiate nor consider *ex parte* or other communications concerning a pending or impending proceeding." Although it was acceptable practice for trial judges to instruct lawyers to draft proposed decisions, it required notice to both sides and opportunity for the losing party to object to specific provisions. Appeals courts, beyond helping themselves to verbiage from briefs already in the record, were not supposed to seek or accept *ex parte* draftsmanship.[10]

The awareness of impropriety evidently overcame Boyd at some point, perhaps at the moment when Schwartz, who was familiar with the Gulf Power file, first saw Mason's document and exclaimed, "What the hell is this?"[11] Schwartz had already attempted to persuade Boyd to change his position and write a short opinion upholding the PSC. His reluctance to overturn the PSC meant that if Boyd could not convince him otherwise, he would either have to hire a new clerk, borrow someone else's clerk, or write the opinion himself. As Boyd did not write many opinions for himself, he would have been susceptible to an offer of help from another source such as Mason.[12]

It was later in June or July, Schwartz subsequently testified, that Boyd called him into his office "and he handed me a fourteen . . . legal page white memorandum, and he said that . . . he thought somebody had dropped this off at his house. He didn't know quite what it was, and he wanted me to do two things with it. He wanted me to check it out and see if it was part of the file, if it represented any brief in the file, and he also wanted to check it out and see if it was legal and direct."[13]

Schwartz quickly determined three things: Nothing resembling it had been filed with the clerk of the court, it was better researched and better written than any of the briefs on record, and "it was written from the utilities' point of view."[14] That conflicted with Schwartz's personal bias against the utilities' side of the argument, and he spent a week in the basement of the Supreme Court library looking for conflicting utility law and precedents. "The thought that some . . . *ex parte* communication had come into the court on behalf of the power company angered me, and I was determined to be able to prove to the judge that this was also, beyond being *ex parte,* was legally wrong. So I spent about a week in the library checking it out . . . checking all the cases cited by it. It was very extensive, very well written. . . . And after a week of hot July days in the sub-basement of the library, I came to the conclusion it was legally correct, perfectly accurate."[15]

Ever since the 1920s, utility companies had been allowed to pass taxes through to their customers even if the laws imposing the taxes said otherwise. Schwartz reported that to Boyd, advising, "I think you have to go that way."[16] He could see, however, that Boyd was "very nervous" about having the mysterious document in his possession. Even if it were legally correct, Boyd said, it would be "judicial suicide" to use it in an opinion. Nonetheless, the justice allowed Schwartz to start work on an opinion corresponding to the points that the document made. Schwartz thought he had quoted nothing directly. But when he gave it to Boyd, the justice rejected it as "too close to that" and instructed him to "write it up differently." Schwartz, with the memorandum in mind though not in hand, wrote something "half the length" and in his view not as good, but Boyd rejected it again for fear that "somebody might think we were influenced" by the mysterious document. When the justice suggested that they write an opinion upholding the PSC instead, Schwartz complained that Boyd was allowing himself to be influenced in the wrong direction "just because someone might accuse you."[17] The outcome, at Boyd's insistence, was a one-paragraph opinion taking note of a second PSC decision that said in effect that it was premature to calculate the impact of the tax on consumer rates. The court, Boyd held, should simply defer the case arising from the PSC's first decision.[18] Colleagues who had expected Boyd to write an opinion reversing the PSC were in for a surprise.

Soon afterward, Boyd told Schwartz he wanted to be rid of the mysterious document. They went to the men's room where Boyd, wearing his suit jacket, tore Mason's product into strips and flushed it. Schwartz felt a twinge of regret; he regarded the document as virtually poetic compared with the pedestrian briefs that were in the official record—it had, after all, overcome *his* view of the issues—and he had no proof of its unethical origin. Boyd left that day for a vacation in Europe.[19]

But if Boyd thought that would be the end of it, he was wrong. Schwartz had shown Mason's document to another research assistant, David LaCroix. Worse for everyone, another justice had a copy.

⊣ 2 ⊢

Justice Dekle's "Dissent"

That week, possibly the same day Boyd went on vacation, Mason paid a call to Justice Hal P. Dekle's chambers at the Supreme Court.[1] By his own account, Dekle sensed nothing improper and made no objection when Mason began to talk about the Gulf Power case. As Dekle recalled the conversation under questioning before the Judicial Qualifications Commission, Mason said to him, "Well, I want to know when we can expect something in the Gulf Power case. Time is slipping by, and we're just curious." But that was not all. "Well, I prepared a memorandum for Justice Boyd," Mason added. "If your thinking turns out to be along that line, I would like to leave a copy with you." Dekle said, "I remember that phrase because I thought to myself, 'This is a nice way to put it. He is not lobbying me, really, he is just leaving me a copy if he is lucky enough for me to be with him, which I think is a nice way for an attorney to do.'"[2]

Dekle was trying to rationalize what was incontestably wrong. He should not have allowed Mason to allude to how he hoped the court would decide, let alone accept any document, without the knowledge of lawyers for the governor and attorney general who were defending the Public Service Commission decision that Mason wanted to overturn. Dekle maintained later that he had assumed it was a copy of something properly filed in the official record, but he did not claim to have asked anyone whether it was. Instead, he put the manila envelope on his desk and forgot about it. That same week, the court

issued a revised Code of Judicial Conduct that had been heavily debated
—and, according to rumor, resisted—because it called on judges to forego
directors' fees and most other traditional sources of their outside income. Of
potential significance to the Gulf Power case, the code also reincorporated
the existing strictures against *ex parte* conduct. The issue of ethics should have
been on everyone's mind that week. But if it was on Boyd's—however belat-
edly—when he destroyed the Mason document, it was not on Dekle's.[3]

The court was in recess in August, and it was October 19 when Boyd actually sent the case file out of his office to circulate among the other justices
who had heard the arguments. It arrived in Dekle's chambers that day and was
not what he expected. Recognizing that Boyd had changed his mind, Dekle
remembered the Mason document, found it on his desk, read it for the first
time, and concluded that it was a "memorandum of law." He turned it over to
his research assistant, Jack Shaw, with a note calling attention to a "memorandum here that he (Shaw) may . . . find useful." Shaw and Dekle finished their
draft, a "dissent" destined to become the majority opinion, on November 27.
Three days later, Mason paid him another visit. He was impatient for a decision. Dekle did what he could to hurry the case along.[4]

Dekle's indifference to the ethical consequences was astounding, given
that he was already in trouble. He knew of possible charges before the Judicial
Qualifications Commission (JQC), an agency established six years earlier
as an alternative to impeachment by the House and trial before the Senate,
concerning an attempt to influence the decisions of a circuit judge presiding
over litigation at Panama City (see chapter 5). The JQC had issued a notice of
investigation to Dekle on May 3, before his first encounter with Mason, and
had sent him a notice of formal investigation on October 31, a month before
Mason's second visit.[5] Nonetheless, as soon as Mason left on November 30,
Dekle went to Justice David McCain's office, the next stop on the case file's
circulation list. Finding that McCain was not in, he left a message with Mc-
Cain's secretary, Barbara Williams. As she reported in writing to McCain:

> Judge Dekle asked me to write you this note: "HPD says that he
> thought you were with him on his 'dissent'; that Ed Mason spoke to
> him on it but missed seeing you."

That note, easily the most fateful document in the Supreme Court's history,
went into the file on McCain's desk along with Boyd's and Dekle's draft

MEMORANDUM

TO: McCain, J.   DATE: November 30, 1973

FROM: SUBJECT:
      Barbara   Gulf Power Co
                                    Bevis

Judge Dekle asked me to write you this note:

"HPD says that he thought you were with him on his
'dissent'; that Ed Mason spoke to him on it but
missed seeing you."

B.

The memorandum that exposed unethical lobbying at the Florida Supreme Court.

opinions. The quotation marks around the word *dissent*, a sarcasm implying that Dekle's draft would be the majority opinion, were specifically dictated by him.[6]

A few days later, at the clerk's office, Schwartz found Dekle's "dissent" in the case file; it had not yet returned to Boyd's office. There was a cover note in Dekle's handwriting to the effect that Boyd had avoided the issue. On reading the dissent itself, Schwartz thought it was "essentially the same memorandum that we had received, almost word for word." To Dekle's misfortune, Elizabeth Potts, the secretary for Boyd and Schwartz, was filling in for McCain's secretary that week. The note that Williams had dictated was on her desk. Schwartz knew a smoking gun when he saw it. He copied it with no objection from Potts and reported to Boyd everything he had found. At that point, he said, the justice remarked, "This pretty well cinches who dropped this off to me." But even as he acknowledged Mason's probable authorship of the document that he had destroyed, Boyd still insisted that he had not solicited it.[7]

Soon afterward, Schwartz asked David LaCroix, Chief Justice Vassar Carlton's research assistant, to read Dekle's "dissent." LaCroix recognized it as the anonymous document that Schwartz had shown him months earlier. "It looked exactly the same with just a cover sheet attached to it," LaCroix said.

The case was ready for the chief justice's attention by that time; he would be the last justice to see it before publication. LaCroix told Carlton that he suspected the opinion "was not written by Dekle, and that I thought it had been written by somebody off the court, and was given to Judge Boyd and Judge Dekle by somebody involved in the case." Carlton went straight to Dekle's office. When he returned, he told LaCroix that he had instructed Dekle to rewrite the "dissent" in his own words.[8] But Carlton's concern over the impropriety extended only to sanitizing the court's work product. He took no action to report the misconduct to the Florida Bar or the JQC or to preserve Dekle's draft as potential evidence. Carlton would testify later that the *ex parte* issue did not concern him. "There is an old saying that you don't care who carries the lantern as long as it shows light on the subject. . . . I wasn't particularly disturbed," he said.[9] Subsequent investigations found no trace of the Xerox copy Mason had left with Dekle or of the draft in Dekle's name that had struck LaCroix as "exactly the same." What might have been a manageable matter of an ethical misstep with no lasting impact on the law had taken on the ponderous weight of a cover-up.

It did not remain covered up for very long. Schwartz, LaCroix, and several other research assistants, young lawyers in their first jobs, saw the Gulf Power situation as part of a general attitude of indifference and irresponsibility at Florida's highest court. They were astounded at the extent to which the justices deferred important decisions to them. They talked about it frequently, not keeping the matter to themselves. Their outside confidante was Sharyn Smith, an assistant attorney general who had attended the University of Miami law school with Schwartz and had casually dated him there. In Tallahassee, she said,

> All of my closest friends were clerks on the Supreme Court . . . and we had a dinner group that we used to go to each other's houses and cook dinner. I was the only nonjudicial person there, so I would sit back and listen . . . and I remember one night . . . some of the clerks started arguing about how they were going to write the Uniform Commercial Code case, which involved millions and millions of dollars, and I'm sitting there kind of amazed and thinking, "What is wrong with this picture? I've got law clerks who have been out of law school maybe a year . . . and they're deciding these things, not the judges." And eventually I think the clerks got concerned about it.

The realization that justices were tolerating Mason's lobbying shocked the clerks into action despite their fear that "all hell was going to break loose" if they exposed it. Lacking faith in the JQC or any other official channel, they accepted Smith's suggestion to leak to the press a copy of the memorandum that Dekle had dictated to McCain's secretary. The press, Smith said, was "the one group that we know cannot be bought, that cannot be pressured, that cannot be intimidated." I was the reporter they chose to receive the document. It would have been easier and certainly safer to have mailed it anonymously, but as Smith explained to me many years later, "We thought it would have more credibility" if it were delivered to a journalist by someone he knew.[10]

Smith's instrumental role in exposing the misconduct is told here for the first time. The messenger, however, still invokes the confidentiality promised on the day in December 1973 when the copy was brought to me at the *St. Petersburg Times* Capital Bureau, situated at the time in the subbasement of the old state capitol building. The messenger was a lawyer, subject to discipline by the Supreme Court. It had the power to disbar any of the lawyers who contributed to its embarrassment. Indeed, it did threaten to disbar Schwartz over another document leak that he could not deny.

"We all used to get together," the messenger told me retrospectively, "and Roger would just tell these stories about the idiots he worked for, the justices—not all of them—and it just got to be almost like a standing joke, well, what did they do *this* month?" Schwartz was particularly upset about Mason's *ex parte* document. "We had a talk. I told him that in my opinion you could be trusted and if he was concerned about the direction of the court I would find an opportunity to get with you and get an assurance from you, and that's the way it would be done. Ultimately, he gave me the memo."[11]

The cloak-and-dagger delivery was contrived to protect Schwartz. Although he swiftly became the court's prime suspect, wrathful justices—who went so far as to enlist the local state attorney in a fruitless inquiry—could not come up with firm evidence against him. "They could never prove I did, and I could never prove I didn't," Schwartz said years later.[12]

The messenger brought me only Dekle's memorandum to McCain, *prima facie* evidence of an ethical violation, but said nothing—and perhaps knew nothing—of how Dekle prepared the "dissent" to which the memo referred. At the messenger's urging, some six months later, Schwartz eventually disclosed to the *St. Petersburg Times* how he and Boyd had disposed of Mason's document.[13]

In December 1973, the morning after I received the Dekle memorandum, I was on my way to the Supreme Court building, a block from the Capitol, to ask questions about it. I met Askew, who was walking to work from the executive mansion ten blocks away. As a lawyer, the governor instantly recognized the significance to the pending case in which he was a party. "It looks like we're being *ex parted,*" he said. The *Times* published the story on December 15 under a banner front-page headline. The opening paragraph read: "A Florida Supreme Court memorandum has disclosed that Justice Hal P. Dekle privately discussed a pending utility-tax case with an attorney for two companies participating in the suit." It reported Dekle's explanation in an interview that Mason was interested only in when the court might rule on the case. "He wanted it out, and I don't blame him," Dekle said. Dekle insisted they had not talked about the merits of the case. He did not disclose the conversation in his office in July or the memorandum that Mason had left with him on that occasion. Carlton, sitting in on the *Times* interview, maintained that it would have been proper for Mason or any attorney to inquire of the chief justice or, in his absence, the next senior justice on the premises, as to the status of a case. That would be their cover story for Mason's attempt to see McCain. Carlton, meanwhile, said he considered it "really disturbing" that an internal memorandum had been leaked to the press. "We've put new locks on, and we may have to close that door at the end of the hall," Dekle said.

The court was outraged over the leak and the *Times* inquiry and considered itself in crisis. The justices summoned their research aides and secretaries to a meeting with the justices where the single topic was security. Dekle was irate, McCain even more so, threatening physical violence against any aide responsible for leaking the document. As B. K. Roberts subsequently testified, "All of his Irish temper came out and he exploded and he explained it to them, that he wasn't going to have anybody burglarizing his office, and what he was liable to do to them if they did. I can't say that I blame him." The clerks were astonished that none of the justices appeared to care about the ethics of *ex parte* lobbying or the fundamental impropriety of a litigant's counsel secretly coaching the court on how to write an opinion in his favor. At that point, however, only a few people—primarily Boyd, Dekle, Schwartz,

LaCroix, and Carlton—knew that Mason had done more than merely talk about the case.[14]

Meanwhile, a witch hunt was under way for whomever had leaked the Dekle-to-McCain memo to the *Times* and, as some supposed, to the Judicial Qualifications Commission. Boyd was as eager as any other pursuer, and his speculations were not far off the mark.[15] Carlton deputized Roberts and Justice James C. Adkins Jr. to find and plug the leak. The trail led directly to Schwartz and LaCroix. "I thought that the two research aides should be fired that day. I still think so," Roberts testified to the JQC eleven months later. "They both confessed to what I consider to be a heinous offense, and I thought they should be fired and disciplinary action taken against them by the Florida Bar." But Carlton, whose resignation was imminent, was unwilling to part with LaCroix, and Roberts conceded that one should not be fired without the other. Both left for other jobs soon after; neither was officially discharged. "Oddly enough, we haven't had any leaks in the court since we got rid of them. I think they were bad news," Roberts said.[16]

That was the apparent sum of Roberts's concern: a leak had offended the court. The aides inferred from what Roberts said at the meeting that loyalty to the court outweighed any duty to report improper conduct. Unbeknown to them, Roberts had long since privately confided to the governor that he had misgivings about most of his fellow justices and had urged Askew to arrange funding for the JQC, the agency responsible for monitoring judicial ethics in Florida. Whatever happened, however, was not to have his fingerprints on it; above all, the public was not to know. Thus, at almost the same time that Roberts was imploring the governor to clean up the court, he was in effect intimidating the court's staff against cooperating with anyone who might be trying to do precisely that.[17]

The ink was barely dry on the *Times* exposé when I received a telephone call at home from Harry Morrison, state attorney for the Second Judicial Circuit, whom I knew to be Roberts's cousin. He wanted to see me at his office "to find out how that memorandum got stolen from Justice Dekle's office." I replied that to my knowledge it was copied, not stolen, and from McCain's office rather than Dekle's, but that I was not going to come to Morrison's office or talk further to him without a subpoena in hand and a lawyer at my side. Morrison, whose detractors nicknamed him "Pussycat" for his reluctance to investigate possible political corruption, did not pursue the matter. Probably not by coincidence, Morrison's description of the leak as a criminal event corresponded with Roberts's verbiage; the phrase he used in subsequent testimony was the "burglarizing of Judge McCain's office." What I did not know was that Morrison had also subpoenaed Schwartz under the pretext of possibly charging someone with unauthorized use of a state copying machine, but had backed down when Attorney General Robert Shevin—who as counsel of record in *Gulf Power* had an official interest in the matter—let it be known that he would intervene in Schwartz's behalf.

Meanwhile, having learned from Elizabeth Potts and Barbara Williams that it was Boyd's aide who copied the memorandum he had dictated, Dekle confronted Boyd in a rage. "I invited him out of the office and said, 'I don't want to have anything to do with you,'" Dekle testified to the JQC.

When the rewritten *Gulf Power* opinion was finally issued on January 30, 1974, by a four-to-one vote, it was less than a complete triumph for the utilities. Although the court granted that the income tax should be treated as any other cost of business, it could not "result in a full, dollar for dollar increase in the rate." It would be controlled instead by the bottom line in utility regulation, the "fair rate of return," a fluctuating figure periodically adjusted by the Public Service Commission. This so-called sharing concept for applying the tax was confirmed by all seven justices in a second *Gulf Power* appeal on June 13, 1974. It was the case for which Boyd's solitary dissent had asserted the court should wait. Roberts said it was at his suggestion that Carlton assigned all seven justices to the second case. Mason's clients were not parties to the second round.[18]

The Judicial Qualifications Commission, already engaged in a secret (and fruitless) prosecution of Dekle in the Panama City incident, took note of the Mason intrigues but did not act immediately. England, the governor's counsel, reacted swiftly. He wrote to Mason on December 17 to rebut a suggestion by Mason in the *Times* article that England, too, had been probing into the status of the case. England said his inquiries had been directed solely to the office of the clerk and were proper. On December 28, he sent a more pointed letter to Mason asking him to explain the November 30 conversation with Dekle "and any other meeting." Alluding perhaps to what was still not public knowledge, he asked also whether Mason had "at any time furnished the Court or any justice with written material not on the record." If so, England demanded a copy. Mason replied on January 7, calling England's attention to Dekle's explanation in the newspaper article and remarking curtly, "Your present letter to me would indicate that you do not believe the Justice's explanation. Perhaps you should discuss the matter with him." England retorted on January 22: "I am distressed at your lack of sensitivity to the ethical considerations involved in such discussions. . . . Since you read the *Times* article, you must know that Justice Dekle's explanation does not fully comport with the language of the memorandum to Justice McCain." When Mason did not reply, England filed a complaint with the Florida Bar. In January 1975, the Bar formally charged Mason with unethical conduct. A year later, the Supreme Court—with circuit judges sitting in for five of the justices—suspended Mason's law practice for a year. But that gets ahead of the story.[19]

⊰ 3 ⊱

School for Scandal

The 1970s saw the flowering of a political renaissance that would be recalled wistfully as Florida's "Golden Age," a product of U.S. Supreme Court decisions requiring state legislatures to represent all citizens equally. Nowhere was the reform as dramatic as in Florida, where rural counties with merely 12 percent of the population had been empowered to elect a majority of the Senate and 18.8 percent could control the House.[1] The rulings swept away a ruling clique of rural senators famously known as the "Pork Chop Gang" and their counterparts in the House. The urban leaders who took their places carried out a comprehensive reform agenda that included a new constitution, executive reorganization, a modern judicial system, tax reform, environmental protection, and financial disclosure and other ethical strictures for public officials, all of which would have been inconceivable under the old guard. Askew, elected in 1970, would have a profoundly constructive impact on the judiciary in general and on the Florida Supreme Court in particular.

In the first half of that decade, however, the court was a scandal in progress. So was the elected state cabinet: three of its six members would face criminal charges. In two of the cabinet cases, the Supreme Court went to extremes to hamper the investigations. The court's laissez-faire attitude toward corruption in other branches reflected an internal culture in which some justices were heedless of their own conduct. Once the legislature took note of it, there were two constitutional amendments and the impeachment investigation that eventually forced Dekle and McCain to resign. At one point or another, five of the seven justices were in some sort of difficulty: Adkins, Carlton, Boyd, Dekle, and McCain.

The common denominator was politics. Of the five, only McCain owed his seat to appointment rather than election, but every unethical act subsequently charged to him was rooted in either an unsuccessful candidacy for the court or his 1972 campaign to keep his appointed seat.

James C. Adkins Jr., a self-described "hard-nosed, conservative" circuit court judge from Gainesville, defeated McCain, the Republican nominee, in the same 1968 elections that also put Boyd and Carlton on the court. Attracted in part by the higher salary, Adkins filed for the seat without confidence that he could win. But the tough judge from North Florida won name recognition statewide when he denied bond to two local civil rights activists who had been charged with contempt for criticizing a grand jury and his house was firebombed (with minor damage) in what some said was retaliation. It was a banner year for "law and order" candidates such as Adkins appeared to be, and he easily dispatched Woodie A. Liles, an appeals court judge from a more urban constituency, with 63 percent of the Democratic primary vote. Liles led only in Hillsborough, his home, and three smaller counties.[2] McCain, a judge in another appellate district, was a much stronger opponent in the general election, but Richard Nixon's Republican coattails were not quite long enough, and Adkins won with 53 percent. The nineteen counties that McCain carried were all heavily Republican in voting habits if not in registration, and the results were similar in the two other Supreme Court races that November.[3]

Adkins, who had been the Supreme Court's only research assistant in his first job out of law school, was a published expert on criminal law and an unquestionably competent judge. He ought to have had an unblemished tenure on the state's highest court. But he brought to Tallahassee a failing marriage, his fifth, and a vulnerability to alcohol that prompted numerous reports to the Judicial Qualifications Commission.[4] In 1972, Adkins was obviously drunk at a singularly unfortunate time and place: the morning investiture ceremony in St. Petersburg of Paul Roney, a federal appeals court judge from that city. The audience included St. Petersburg attorney Richard T. Earle Jr., vice chairman of the Judicial Qualifications Commission. The JQC soon convened secretly in Tallahassee, where Roberts and other colleagues pleaded on Adkins's behalf. The panel gave Adkins an inventive choice: sign an undated letter of resignation to be presented to the governor if he ever drank again, or face a trial and removal from the court. Adkins signed. After Adkins's death in 1994, Earle said, "As far as I know, he never had another drink." Although it took three years for the story of the star-chamber probation to leak to the press, it was an open secret in court circles, where it was assumed that Roberts's intercession had left Adkins heavily in his debt.[5]

Carlton, too, owed a personal debt to Roberts. Roberts had written the July 1958 Supreme Court opinion that granted a divorce to Carlton, a circuit court judge at Titusville, overturning an adverse decision by another trial judge. Roberts wrote that the "unrefuted evidence" of Mary Carlton's nagging "was ample to show that the wife's conduct constituted extreme mental cruelty... entitling him to a divorce." In so saying, the four justices in the majority abandoned a rule of restraint that most appeals courts strictly observe; they substituted their analysis of the evidence for that of the trial judge who had personally heard it. Justice Stephen O'Connell, the dissenter, objected that there was "sufficient evidence in the record... to support the chancellor's decree."[6]

Carlton had enjoyed his twenty-eight years as a humanistic and popular trial judge much more than he would the cloistered and semi-academic existence of an appellate court. The Supreme Court, then as now, chose a new chief justice every two years, with the post almost always going to the most senior justice who had yet to hold it. Carlton's turn, which Roberts nearly took for himself, coincided with the breaking news of the Mason scandal and the fatal illness of Carlton's second wife, Grace, whose death from leukemia on January 17, 1973, left him all but unable to function.[7] So far as the law clerks could tell, Carlton delegated virtually all his opinion writing as well as administrative decisions affecting the entire court system to one of his research assistants, William Falck. "He never wrote, as far as I know, any opinion while he was at the Supreme Court," one of them testified. "Justice Carlton's major time was spent in sitting in his office, smoking a cigar, and I do not mean that in a derogatory fashion. I was very fond of Justice Carlton. I think he felt he was inadequate to the job for some reason unknown to all of us, because I thought he was quite an intelligent man."[8]

Carlton also loved to gamble, a habit of keen interest to various authorities in light of the court's frequent intervention in the bitterly contested racing dates of Dade County's horse and dog tracks. Tipped off by a confidential source, investigative reporter Clarence Jones of the Miami television station WPLG followed Carlton on what appeared to be a subsidized junket to Las Vegas. "We didn't hide them [the cameras], and the photographer got this marvelous shot of me standing right behind Carlton as he threw the dice, a great big cigar in his mouth," Jones recalled. Jones's source had claimed that Carlton's expenses were being paid by a dog track that had a case before the court; Carlton said that he had reimbursed whoever advanced them. Under Florida law at the time, a subsidized junket would not necessarily have been illegal, and Carlton would not have been required to report it. Carlton was also a regular patron of the dog track near Tallahassee, where his research assistant observed that he was a shrewd and successful bettor.[9]

When he announced his resignation in January 1974, to coincide with his marriage to a third wife half his age, Carlton said he was weary of office, would take home more retirement pay than his net salary after deductions, and was not quitting because of any investigation by the JQC. Earle, who had become the JQC chairman, issued a statement that he asked the newspapers to print in full. It concluded:

> I know of no reasons for his resignation other than those stated by him therein. There is no investigation by the Florida Judicial Qualifications Commission of Mr. Justice Carlton either pending or contemplated. I can tell you this because after tendering his resignation, the chief justice called me and waived the confidentiality rule.[10]

Years later, Earle said that he had not been asked the right question, which would have been, "*Had* you been investigating Justice Carlton?" The remark implied that Carlton had negotiated his resignation with the JQC.[11]

After Carlton's retirement, Justice Richard Ervin told a curious story to Sharyn Smith, the assistant attorney general who was also a confidante of Schwartz and LaCroix. Ervin was, in her words, "sort of persona non grata" with the other justices, at least partly because of his frequent liberal dissents. As he was rarely invited to lunch with his colleagues, he often had lunch with Smith. Ervin scrupulously avoided any discussion of pending cases, but one day when Carlton's name came up, he mentioned a pari-mutuel appeal in which he and Carlton had been on opposite sides. Smith recalled, "Ervin said he and Carlton had been a regular golf pair for years. When that racing date case came around . . . Carlton came to see him and said, 'I thought you were with me on this,' and he said no, and Carlton walked out and never played golf with him again." Ervin "looked at me and said, 'Do you think that's strange?'"[12]

The court's shifting posture on racing date cases seemed strange to many Floridians and fed a generalized suspicion among the news media. The intrigue began with a split 1971 decision declaring unconstitutional a law that the court had upheld in 1948 perpetually entitling the Hialeah track to the most profitable of Miami's three winter horse racing schedules. The 1947 law stated that the track producing the largest sum of state racing tax in the previous season—a description tailored to Hialeah—would have the choice dates in each ensuing year. In 1971, Roberts wrote an opinion on behalf of himself, Ervin, McCain, and Dekle that said changed circumstances, notably improved facilities at competing Gulfstream Park, made a case for restoring the state racing commission's discretion to allocate the dates. Writing in dissent for himself, Carlton, and Adkins, Boyd retorted, "If the law was constitutional in 1948, it still is. . . . If a change in the law is required, the legislature should change it."[13] A month later, however, the racing authorities used their newfound discretion to award Hialeah the choice dates yet again. This time, the court voted 6-1 that the Board of Business Regulation should have read the first decision as a mandate in Gulfstream's favor. "To preserve the separate and equal branches of the government," Boyd objected in a solitary dissent, "each branch must avoid encroachment into the other's sphere of activity."[14] As it turned out, the encroachment was only beginning.

The Board of Business Regulation awarded Gulfstream the choice dates for 1972, on the premise that the first season, which yielded $400,000 less for the state than Hialeah's better schedule the year before, was not sufficient to prove its potential. Lo and behold, the Supreme Court reversed the board yet again, this time in Hialeah's favor, contending unanimously that it had never intended to allow the board much discretion at all:

> [T]he changing, altering and varying of the racing periods from year to year, solely as the Board may see fit, is unsound and unwise. Such changing, altering, and varying creates a condition of uncertainty which retards the natural expansion and development of this business and influences the financial stability of the State and the counties.[15]

Such language would commonly be found in the legislature's findings of fact in support of a House or Senate bill. As the rationale for a *judicial* decision, it was distinctively activist. However, it was the last of its kind. In 1973 and 1975, the court refused to consider appeals of the agency's decisions to rotate the prize dates. There was nothing in the record as to whether the bad publicity and unrelated JQC investigations had contributed to the court's reluctance.[16]

Ervin's relations with Roberts, the only justice senior to him, were strained on occasion, too. Arriving at Ervin's office for another lunch date, Smith found him hiding from Roberts, who wanted to see him for a reason Ervin did not share. On hearing Ervin's secretary tell Roberts that she did not know whether Ervin was in his office, Smith told me, "He was afraid he [Roberts] was going to walk in, so we actually hid under the desk. . . . We waited there about ten minutes. We didn't leave his office until we were absolutely convinced that B. K. was out of the hall, and then we snuck down the back stairs and went to lunch." Ervin never said why he wanted to avoid Roberts on that occasion.

Roberts was not only the senior justice but also the undisputed first among equals, a dominance he achieved after the death in 1955 of Glenn Terrell, who had served since 1923. Speaking on the record much later, Ervin remarked that during Roberts's last fifteen years, "because of seniority, changes in personnel of the court, his recognized judicial ability, personal magnetism and political influence, he was able to command a majority vote for his views in practically every case in which he participated."[17]

Despite the best efforts of several justices widely respected for their integrity, judicial restraint, and scholarship, the court's reputation had been questionable for a long time among those who most needed its help: Florida's African American citizens. In their eyes, it was "a bastion of privilege and white rule," Walter M. Manley II and Canter Brown Jr. write in their official history, *The Supreme Court of Florida, 1917–1972*. Apart from a 1936 decision holding racial zoning to be unconstitutional, the court predictably upheld segregation laws as well as questionable convictions of black men for rape.[18] During the 1930s, a series of dubious decisions set free a gang of Tampa policemen who were suspected of belonging to the Ku Klux Klan and were accused of flogging and murder.

In the same era, questionable invocations of the court's habeas corpus jurisdiction led to the acquittal of a politically prominent Tallahassee slot machine distributor who was the defendant in a seemingly open-and-shut murder case. Roberts, the future justice, was one of his attorneys. A decade later, there were controversial decisions to upset corruption cases against two sheriffs, one of whom, Jimmy Sullivan of Dade County, had been snared in the net of U.S. senator Estes Kefauver's organized crime investigation. Throughout, there was the specter of Edward Ball, whose business ties to Justices Alto Adams and Rivers Buford were controversial even before Roberts joined the court. Ball was instrumental in Adams's decision to run for governor in 1952 against his Fort Pierce townsman, Dan McCarty, whose reform agenda was anathema to Florida's most influential businessman. Ball's St. Joe Paper Company subsidized Adams by purchasing the justice's Tallahassee home for $60,000 while allowing Adams and his family to remain as tenants for little rent.[19]

Adams's subsequent resignation to make the race—he ran a distant third—enabled Fuller Warren to appoint a second crony to the court. He was John E. Mathews Sr. of Jacksonville, who had lost his Senate seat for supporting the sales tax that Warren desperately needed to balance the budget in 1949.[20]

Mathews was one of Florida's most outspoken white supremacists; in 1947 he had held the floor for two hours in a vain attempt to persuade the Florida Senate to defy the U.S. Supreme Court decision that put an end to the exclusion of blacks from Democratic Party primaries in the South.[21] His last campaign ad in 1950 proclaimed in large type, "In Dixieland I'll take my stand."[22] Sixteen months later, he was on the Florida Supreme Court. He died of an intestinal hemorrhage on April 30, 1955.[23]

However, Mathews was not the only bitter-end segregationist on the court. In an otherwise routine November 1954 school bond validation decision, the court denounced the U.S. Supreme Court's public school desegregation decision six months earlier. "In law I think the *Brown* decision was a great mistake," wrote the senior Florida justice, Terrell, who as a state senator in 1915 had attempted to pass a constitutional amendment to disenfranchise blacks permanently.[24] Heedless of unfavorable national publicity, the court conspicuously defied a series of U.S. Supreme Court decisions favoring the admission of Virgil Hawkins, a black man, to the University of Florida law school.[25] The strategy was to pay lip service to the higher court's mandates but at the same time stall Hawkins indefinitely by one pretext or another.

A majority decision written by Roberts appointed a special master to take public testimony as to when—i.e., whether—Hawkins could be admitted without disrupting the university. Terrell wrote separately and at length to extol segregation:

> It is and has always been the unvarying law of the animal kingdom. The dove and the quail, the turkey and the turkey buzzard, the chicken and the guinea, it matters not where they are found, are segregated; place the horse, the cow, the sheep, the goat and the pig in the same pasture and they instinctively segregate; the fish in the sea segregate into "schools" of their kind; when the goose and duck arise from the Canadian marshes and take off for the Gulf of Mexico and other points in the south, they are always found segregated; and when God created man, he allotted each race to his own continent according to color, Europe to the white man, Asia to the yellow man, Africa to the black man, and America to the red man, but we are now advised that God's plan was in error and must be reversed.[26]

"It was thus in 1955 that massive resistance made its debut," recalled one of Hawkins's attorneys, Constance Baker Motley, a future federal judge.[27] Although Virginia subsequently declared a policy of "massive resistance" to integration of its public schools, it desegregated its colleges and universities years before Florida did.

In 1957, responding at leisure to a U.S. Supreme Court opinion unanimously admonishing Florida that "there is no reason for delay," the Florida court interpreted the master's report to conclude that integration would "seriously impair" student and state support for the university. "We cannot assume that the Supreme Court intended to deprive the highest court of an independent sovereign state of . . . the right to exercise a sound judicial discretion as to the date of the issuance of its process in order to prevent a serious public mischief," Roberts wrote. The 5-2 decision left little doubt that Florida would defy the U.S. Supreme Court forever.[28]

Terrell's separate concurring opinion invited lasting notoriety as "some of the most racist ideas ever written in a judicial opinion."[29] Segregation, Terrell wrote, "is as old as the hills. The Egyptians practiced it on the Israelites; the Greeks did likewise for the barbarians; the Romans segregated the Syrians; the Chinese segregated all foreigners; segregation is said to have produced the caste system in India, and Hitler practiced it in his Germany, but no one ever discovered that it was a violation of due process until recently." In dissent, Justices Elwyn Thomas and E. Harris Drew remarked that Florida had a "plain duty" to obey the U.S. Supreme Court's mandate, especially if their colleagues wanted their own orders to be respected.[30]

In frustration, the U.S. Supreme Court referred Hawkins to a federal district court, which eventually (but reluctantly) ordered the desegregation of the Florida law school. Hawkins, however, never saw that promised land; the state insisted as a condition of the deal that he withdraw his own application.

In 1965, Roberts persuaded the legislature to establish a law school at Florida State University, a decision that entailed closing the law school that had been hastily set up at Florida A&M University, less than two miles away, in a vain attempt to persuade Hawkins and the U.S. Supreme Court to accept a segregated legal education.[31]

Despite the state's original intent, FAMU alumni had taken pride in their law school, were offended that it was closed to the advantage of predominantly white Florida State, and particularly resented the FSU law school building being named after Roberts. Roberts's attitude was revealed by a casual remark to Eleanor Hunter, an African American assistant to another justice and a graduate of the FSU law school, at a reception celebrating her passing the bar examination. Roberts told her that she should thank him for getting rid of the FAMU school "so you don't have that on your diploma instead of FSU."[32]

Although the court's segregationist roots hardly needed nurturing by public opinion, the requirement that justices seek reelection at six-year intervals unquestionably contributed to the court's defiance of the U.S. Supreme Court. The U.S. Supreme Court order that the Florida court flatly disobeyed electrified the 1956 political campaign in which Gov. LeRoy Collins, a moderate, was seeking renomination against three extreme segregationists. Sumter Lowry, a retired National Guard general who talked about nothing but segregation, fell just 14,232 votes short of forcing Collins into a runoff.[33] In that climate, justices contemplating their next campaigns might plausibly have been fearful of doing the right thing. Yet Drew was unopposed in 1958, his next time on the ballot, despite his having dissented in Hawkins's favor. Roberts was unopposed, too.[34]

That was how Supreme Court elections usually went. From 1932 to 1976, the last year of competitive contests, sitting justices were unopposed in forty-one candidacies and challenged only eleven times. Six justices served without ever being opposed. The only justice to lose his seat during that era was Wade Hopping, who had been appointed just three months earlier. There had been a close shave for Drew soon after his appointment in 1952. Otherwise, the only elections that mattered were for the seats of retiring justices. In all but one of those open-seat races between 1926 and 1976, the winning candidates were those whose names came first on the ballots thanks to a law stipulating alphabetical order. The voters' inclination to pick the first names they saw clearly worked to the advantage of Adkins, Boyd, and Carlton in the 1968 primaries.[35]

Boyd, a member of the elected Metropolitan Dade County Commission, had considered running for the Public Service Commission before opting for one of the Supreme Court seats that Elwyn Thomas and Millard Caldwell were vacating. Although Boyd had no judicial experience, he won the decisive Democratic runoff over Richard Cooper, a well-regarded circuit judge at Orlando, on the strength of his 67,000-vote margin in Dade.[36]

Long after he had won the seat, Boyd's political instincts were on display wherever he went. He worked the aisles aboard airplanes and the crowds at public events, invariably offering his hand to everyone—including people he had met before—and saying, "Hi, I'm Joe Boyd." A colleague once described him as "unnaturally attracted to registered voters." Always sensitive to the accusation that he was unqualified, Boyd once playfully chided *Miami Herald* reporter David Von Drehle for writing that he had not been a judge before he was elected to the Supreme Court. "That's not true," he said with a wink. "I was a judge of the Miss Hialeah pageant."[37]

The voters rarely had any objective guidance to vote for or against a Supreme Court candidate. Appellate court races typically went begging for publicity, there being little that any of the candidates could say without taking positions on legal issues they might have to decide. In 1968, however, Carlton made a brief splash by filing a lawsuit that accused Dekle of spending money on a fund-raising letter before formally declaring his candidacy. Nothing came of it.[38]

Republicans were running for the court for the first time that year, inspired by the 1966 election of Florida's first Republican governor since Reconstruction, Claude R. Kirk Jr. His success owed mostly to conservative Democratic resentment that incumbent Democrat Haydon Burns of Jacksonville had lost the primary to a Miami liberal, but Kirk chose to regard it as a mandate for Republicanism. Anyone seeking a judicial appointment from him generally had to be a registered Republican or agree to become one. Alto Adams, the former justice, did so in 1967 when Justice Stephen O'Connell's resignation to become president of the University of Florida gave Kirk his first opening on the Supreme Court. Rumor held that Adams was interested only in qualifying for retirement and was keeping the seat warm for Wade Hopping, a rising star on the staff of the Florida Bar whom Kirk had "borrowed," supposedly for only sixty days, at the start of his term. More than a year later, Hopping was still with Kirk when O'Connell left, but he was two months shy of the ten years of Florida Bar membership required of a justice. Whether the placeholder rumor was accurate or not—Hopping said he never knew—Adams seemed to confirm it by giving up the seat after only eleven months. Kirk then appointed Hopping to it, but it was just three months before the election in which he would have to defend it. Carlton had already disposed of Dekle in the Democratic primary.

"I kind of knew from the start that we wouldn't win," Hopping told me. Kirk's political strategist told him that no Republican could be elected to the court that year and the prediction proved true. But Hopping made Carlton work for his 56 percent victory. "We were running in races at which we all met at civic clubs and bar associations," Hopping said. "Every time we were together and Carlton's wife was along, she went crazy over the cost of the campaign. She would say something like, 'You're costing us a hundred thousand dollars to run this campaign.'"[39]

> There is no certain harm in turning a politician into a judge. He may be or become a good judge. The curse of the elective system is the converse, that it turns almost every judge into a politician.
>
> —Henry T. Lummus, *The Trial Judge,* 1937

⊰ 4 ⊱

David McCain, Eagle Scout

David McCain had been an Eagle Scout and the valedictorian of the Vero Beach High School class of 1949. His photograph remains in the Hall of Fame at the University of Florida, where he was chosen for Blue Key, a prestigious leadership society. He served honorably as an air force legal officer and built a thriving law practice at Fort Pierce, where he was also city attorney. He counted Alto Adams, the former justice, as a family friend and patron. He was physically fit, happily married, and the father of five children. He was active in the YMCA, the Jaycees, the American Legion, and the United Fund. Everything about him, apart from losing a legislative race in 1962, seemed to augur success. He was respected for his intelligence. B. K. Roberts once remarked that David L. McCain could analyze and dissect a case faster than anyone else on the Florida Supreme Court. Even so, he became the only Florida justice ever to resign in the face of certain impeachment, the only one expelled from the practice of law for misusing his judicial office. When he died in 1986, eleven years after his resignation, he was a fugitive from justice, a bail-jumper on the run from a federal indictment in a marijuana-smuggling conspiracy. Some attributed his fall to the bottle, others to ambition, and his family contended that he had been grievously mistreated by the press. The depth of the tragedy in hindsight was that so much was obvious but so little if anything was done to turn him around.[1]

A "DemoKirk" in the 1966 election and a convert to the Republican Party soon afterward, McCain came to Kirk's attention much as Wade Hopping had. The new governor, a skillful pitchman who had helped to build a thriving Florida insurance company, had no experience in government. He recruited volunteer legal help to analyze the bills cascading from the Democrat-controlled legislature under short deadlines to sign or veto them. Adams, not yet back on the court, bore a hand; for alternating weeks, so did McCain and a partner. One of those bills added judgeships to the Fourth District Court of Appeal, temporarily housed at Vero Beach. McCain seemed to Kirk to be a natural choice for one of them.[2] The appointment was his to make; no nomination process or Senate confirmation was required, and McCain took his seat in August 1967.

He had been there only a few months when the retirements of Justices Elwyn Thomas and Millard Caldwell created two open seats on the Supreme Court. McCain decided rashly to run. He won the Republican primary with nearly three times as many votes as his opponent, Miami attorney Ellis Rubin. But what Kirk's strategist had warned Hopping proved true for McCain as well: no Republican was going to be elected to the court in 1968. Although McCain tried, Adkins had nailed down the law-and-order vote.[3] So conservative was the tenor of that campaign that the *St. Petersburg Times,* a liberal newspaper that did not think much of Kirk, recommended McCain over Adkins. "He has made fewer headlines than Judge Adkins," the October 22 editorial said, "but he has revealed much more balance, and mature judicial temperament."

The seeds of McCain's destruction were planted in that campaign. It left him deeply obligated—or so he seemed to think—to Joseph D. Farish Jr., an accomplished West Palm Beach plaintiffs' attorney who supported his candidacy. McCain's career came to grief in large part over his indifference to the appearance that he was favoring clients of the Farish firm, including a highly publicized Palm Beach socialite whose case rewrote American libel law. Although there was never any evidence that Farish sought favors from McCain, the justice scarcely bothered to conceal an inordinate interest in his cases. McCain's campaign manager, David Smith, in 1968 a partner with McCain's brother Willie in a Ft. Lauderdale highway supply distributorship, fell out bitterly with the McCains after the election and began denouncing them to anyone who would listen, including a grand jury. The criminal investigation turned up dry.[4]

Testifying in public at McCain's impeachment hearing in 1975, Smith charged that McCain sought campaign contributions for the 1968 campaign from two of Farish's wealthy clients who had cases in which McCain eventually participated, accepted unreported contributions in the form of 168,000 brochures that were disguised on a paint company's books as "paint can labels," failed to report the value of an airplane lent to him by a phosphate company, and accepted a "stack" of large-denomination currency from two criminal lawyers whose client subsequently figured in McCain's disbarment.[5] None of these charges was ever tested in court. Among other reasons, the statute of limitations on crimes had elapsed before Smith made them public.

The Farish clients whom Smith said McCain solicited for contributions were what the media calls "hot copy." One was Nancy Wakeman, a Palm Beach heiress (to the John Deere fortune) who was accused and later convicted of aggravated assault for shooting her husband. The other was Mary Alice Firestone, another Palm Beach socialite who was suing *Time* for misreporting the terms of her divorce from her husband, tire heir Russell Firestone.

According to Smith, McCain took him one night to Farish's office for what McCain said would be a meeting with Mrs. Wakeman. Smith said that he did not witness the meeting but that McCain told him afterward, "That was a very interesting conversation we had with Mrs. Wakeman and she is going to be good for a substantial contribution." Wakeman herself eventually testified that she made a $1,000 contribution, but she never produced a cancelled check.[6]

Smith, who served in the Florida House of Representatives from 1970 to 1972, said that McCain complained that Mrs. Firestone's alleged contribution (none was reported) was not large, and that "if her old man would just let loose of some of that dough, it would be a substantial contribution to the campaign." Referring to a lawyer who had sent only $25, McCain remarked— according to Smith—that "this guy better not have a case before the appellate bench because he's lost it."[7]

It is important to emphasize that no testimony ever asserted that Farish asked for favors from McCain. Farish filed a $10 million defamation suit against Mrs. Wakeman over her testimony to the House committee, but in 1980 the Fourth District Court of Appeal upheld a trial judge's decision to dismiss the case on the grounds that legislative proceedings are "absolutely privileged." The Supreme Court rejected Farish's appeal without comment. So what Wakeman said was never put to an adversarial test.[8]

McCain wrote at least two opinions against Farish early in 1968. One case, decided 3-0, involved a landlord's claim for rent. There was nothing out of the ordinary about it.[9] The second, resulting from an automobile accident, was notable for a dissent that was three times as long as McCain's majority opinion, which allowed an injured couple to sue a driver for damages after rejecting a judgment against the defendant's employer.[10]

Farish had better luck after the election in the Firestone and Wakeman cases. Wakeman was on probation following a jury verdict that found her guilty of aggravated assault but recommended mercy. She was cut and bleeding when police arrived at their mansion after the shooting, likely signs of spousal abuse. Appealing the conviction, Farish won a unanimous Fourth District decision written by McCain that Wakeman deserved a new trial because her signed confession, which police obtained while she was waiting for her lawyer, should not have been admitted into evidence. It was a reasonable application of the U.S. Supreme Court's *Miranda* doctrine. But Wakeman would rather not be tried again. Since her husband would not testify, the only remaining evidence was that he had told the police in her presence that she had shot him and that she had not denied it. McCain's initial decision had pronounced the defense objection to that testimony to be "without merit." On rehearing, McCain was persuaded that too much time might have elapsed between the shooting and the husband's statement. Even so, there was precedent for allowing the hearsay evidence because it had been said in the defendant's presence. McCain disposed of that problem by holding that "the defendant's battered condition coupled with her state of intoxication refute any presumption that she had such full control of her faculties as to hear and understand the charge of her complicity." The vote was 2-1 this time. The state appealed, but by that time McCain had been promoted to the Supreme Court, and his new colleagues dismissed the petition without comment.[11]

Elected judges commonly depend on campaign contributions from lawyers who have had or will have cases before them. This is one of the Republic's apparently insoluble weaknesses. But if McCain had in fact solicited money from a criminal defendant, as both Wakeman and Smith swore under oath, he was risking a JQC investigation by sitting on her case.

McCain's critics also inferred bias from his participation in Mary Alice

Firestone's case against *Time*. It was an eight-year saga that resulted in Florida and U.S. Supreme Court decisions materially narrowing the latitude the news media thought it had won in an earlier series of landmark cases based on the successful appeal of an Alabama libel suit by the *New York Times*. In those cases, the U.S. Supreme Court held that not just public officials but also public *figures*—for example, a famous football coach and a politically active general—could not sue for libel or slander simply because what was said of them might have been untrue. They also had to show "malice," such as a deliberate or reckless disregard for the facts.[12] The *Firestone v. Time* cases eroded those precedents by holdings that Mrs. Firestone was not a "public figure" despite an intensely publicized divorce trial during which she gave news conferences.[13] The final U.S. Supreme Court decision in the Firestone case, wrote the *New York Times* on March 3, 1976, narrowed the definition of public figure "in a way that appears to exclude types of persons who formerly would have been assumed to be public people."[14]

Time had indeed gotten the story wrong when it reported, in a one-paragraph item on December 15, 1967, that a judge had granted Russell Firestone a divorce on "grounds of extreme cruelty and adultery." Although the judge alluded to allegations that each spouse had engaged in extramarital conduct sufficient to "make Dr. Freud's hair curl," the judge did *not* find Mrs. Firestone guilty of adultery. Had he done so, Florida law at the time would not have allowed the alimony he granted her.[15]

Farish appealed the divorce on behalf of Mrs. Firestone, who wanted alimony and child support without a divorce, but the Fourth District sustained the trial court ruling in a split decision. McCain dissented, saying that the husband's "hands are far from clean, and . . . he is not entitled to the aid of a court of equity." McCain acknowledged that a trial judge's interpretation of the evidence was "entitled to great weight" and should "not lightly . . . be overturned where there is conflicting testimony at trial." Nonetheless, he wanted to overturn it.[16] He delayed writing his dissent for more than a year after his promotion to the Supreme Court, where it appeared that he lobbied B. K. Roberts on Mrs. Firestone's behalf when she appealed the Fourth District's decision to Tallahassee. The high court sustained the divorce but ordered the trial judge to award Mrs. Firestone more money. Farish had a new co-counsel for that appeal: Fuller Warren, the former governor who had appointed Roberts to the court.[17]

When McCain's district court first ruled on the libel suit in January 1970, Farish was appealing a trial judge's decision to dismiss it on the basis of affidavits from *Time* staffers that they had done their best to check out the story after it broke perilously close to deadline. The district court opinion, which another judge wrote and McCain supported, ordered the trial court to give Mrs. Firestone a hearing on the question of malice to allow testimony as to whether *Time*'s reporters had been diligent or recklessly negligent. "The summary judgment procedure is not a trial by affidavits," the opinion said. "Ample opportunity should be granted to the opposing party to justify his opposition." The ruling also allowed Farish to submit an affidavit that made him a witness against *Time* and necessitated having other lawyers pursue the case. So far, the proceedings were not remarkable.[17] That changed when the Supreme Court later allowed McCain to participate in two threshold decisions—a deciding vote on one occasion—on whether she was entitled to Supreme Court reviews in her case against *Time* and to cast an ultimately decisive vote on the merits later on. It was the court's unwritten but acknowledged policy that justices should not sit on cases that they had judged from a lower bench. But McCain was exempted when Mrs. Firestone's case against *Time* might depend on his vote.[18]

By then, the case had an intricate history. Following the original district court decision, a jury awarded Mrs. Firestone $100,000, but the Fourth District—minus McCain—set it aside in October 1971 under the so-called *New York Times* doctrine. "The divorce of Mary Alice Firestone was an event of great public interest," said the Fourth District's three-judge opinion. "It is even possible plaintiff was a public figure, but we need not go that far to substantiate our result." There had been no proof that *Time* was negligent, let alone intentionally false or reckless, the court said; the divorce decree itself was "ambiguous" and would "lead a reasonable person to conclude adultery had been committed."[19] Mrs. Firestone appealed to the Florida Supreme Court, which ruled in 1972 that a divorce trial, no matter how notorious, did not necessarily entail a privileged public interest. McCain took part in the 5-0 decision to hear the case—his vote on that occasion was not decisive—but did not participate when the court ruled that Mrs. Firestone was not a public figure and sent the case back to the Fourth District to consider other possible points in *Time*'s defense.[20] The Supreme Court's decision irked the district court, which in ruling a second time in *Time*'s favor a year later (its third action in the case) protested sharply that it had already considered the issues that the Supreme Court assumed that it had overlooked:

> We deliberately did not discuss each of the points in detail because of the volume that would result and the basic fact that time and resource limitations preclude written opinions on each and every point presented in every brief. No court rule, statute, or court opinion requires such treatment to our knowledge. Of course, had we known at the time that our Point III opinion would not survive, we would have chosen another point to discuss in depth as a basis for reversal.[21]

This outburst gave voice to the resentment felt by most district appellate judges over the Supreme Court's disdain for staying in the place supposedly assigned it by the 1955 amendment that established the district courts. They were intended to have the last word in most cases, or so it was thought. But a Supreme Court faction led by Roberts had aggressively asserted a broader jurisdiction in a series of cases, and by 1973 that had become an underlying issue in the *Time*/Firestone saga. The jurisdictional struggle is the subject of chapter 17.

When Mrs. Firestone's attorneys appealed to Tallahassee for the second time, three of the justices wanted to let the district court's decision stand and objected to taking jurisdiction. Without McCain, that meant a 3-3 tie. Chief Justice Vassar Carlton waived the court's policy to allow McCain to break the tie in her favor. Confirming this later, Adkins, the new chief justice, conceded that it "might be somewhat of an impropriety" to let a justice participate in a case that he had heard at a lower level, "but it is not grounds for recusal." It was better to do it that way, he said, than to call in a judge from another court to break the tie. "That was not a final determination of the case.... Actually, all that is is, shall we hear it or not hear it?" Adkins said.[22]

That was, of course, a hugely important question of far more significance than Adkins implied. The issue was whether Mrs. Firestone would have another legal round to which the Florida Constitution did not entitle her. Had a judge substituting for McCain voted against hearing the case, she would have lost the suit and *Time* would have won. There would have been no precedent to the effect that celebrity socialites who give press conferences are not public figures.

It was foolhardy for the court to let McCain have any say in the Firestone-*Time* dispute. It was fairly well known by then that the Judicial Qualifications Commission had become interested in his fascination with Farish's cases. By the time the court ruled on the substance of Mrs. Firestone's second appeal in December 1974, McCain had once again taken himself off the case. He insisted, however, that it would have been ethical for him to remain on the panel. "I just got sick and tired of you writing about me and Joe Farish," he said. "So I didn't think I should sit on it."[23]

In reversing the district court yet again, the Supreme Court let off steam over the bad press it had been suffering. The *per curiam* opinion of Adkins, Roberts, Boyd, and Dekle, most likely written (but unsigned) by Adkins, held *Time's* reporting to be "clear and convincing evidence of the negligence in certain segments of the news media in gathering the news." That was the court striking back at the journalists whom it blamed for the Gulf Power exposés, which had just resulted in JQC recommendations for the removal of Dekle and Boyd, and other critical coverage. Ervin and Justice Ben Overton, Carlton's replacement, dissented in the final Firestone case. Overton wrote briefly that "in my opinion, there is no conflict jurisdiction" and that the district court had correctly applied the law in *Time's* behalf. For the vote to be split as it was meant that one of the justices who voted for Mrs. Firestone on the core issue had objected earlier to hearing the appeal, but it was never made clear which justice that was.[24]

McCain's interest in Farish's cases had long since become a matter of concern to other judges as well as to opposing lawyers. In July 1970, when McCain was still on the Fourth District bench, he asked colleague William C. Owen to sit in his place on some cases scheduled in October so that he could take a vacation. Such requests were common among judges, and Owen agreed. McCain, however, had said also that he would repay the favor by sitting in for Owen on cases the court was scheduled to hear just a few days later. When he got to thinking about that, Owen "felt it somewhat unusual that he should designate the date upon which he would sit in my place, particularly upon such short notice." Within a day or so, Owen found out that the Farish firm was scheduled to argue one of those cases, and he called off the exchange. "The other judges of the court were then aware of the fact that there was some talk among the lawyers of a feeling that Judge McCain was quite friendly to the Farish law firm and while we were unaware of any wrongdoing on the part of Judge McCain, we were concerned over the fact that there even existed any suspicion of wrongdoing," Owen wrote in answer to an inquiry from the Judicial Qualifications Commission four years later.[25]

Another curious McCain decision from the same period, in a case involving Farish's firm but not Farish himself, reversed a trial judge's ruling of justifiable self-defense in a lawsuit against a convenience store clerk who had shot a drunken, belligerent customer. Although the customer had threatened to kill the clerk and was starting to climb over the counter when he was shot, McCain's split decision ordered the lower court to award damages to the drunk. "The majority of this court has simply retried the issue . . . on the basis of a cold written record and substituted its judgment for that of the trial judge," the dissenting judge objected.[26]

Despite considerable gossip, the JQC was slow to begin a serious investigation of McCain's suspected partiality toward a particular law firm. By then, it was aware of a much more serious case against him: an attempt to fix a criminal appeal involving McCain supporters from the 1972 campaign. The JQC was also embroiled in the Gulf Power controversy and an older, still-secret case against Dekle. By then, too, the Supreme Court had also ruled on a Miami judicial scandal in a way that might bar the JQC from even investigating what Owen was saying about McCain.

McCain's Supreme Court tenure was controversial from its beginning. It was an open secret that the Florida Bar had tried to persuade the governor not to appoint him. Early in his administration, Kirk had agreed to let the Bar evaluate his proposed judicial appointments, so long as it was done confidentially. The arrangement owed in part to his cordial relations with Chesterfield Smith, a former president of the Bar and chair of the Florida Constitution Revision Commission when Kirk took office in 1967, and also to Kirk's appreciation for Hopping's services. Kirk wanted a new constitution as much as Smith did, and the agreement to let the Bar investigate Kirk's judicial appointments was an apparent byproduct of their frequent conversations. Similar in purpose though not form to an established working relationship between the White House and the American Bar Association, it did not last nearly as long. It fell apart over McCain's appointment to the Supreme Court.[27]

Justice Campbell Thornal's death created a vacancy for McCain the day after Askew's victory in the 1970 general election made Kirk a lame duck. There were rumors of politically connected people who might get the appointment, among them G. Harrold Carswell, a failed U.S. Supreme Court nominee who had lost a U.S. Senate race despite (or perhaps because of) Kirk's backing. But Kirk did not appear to seriously consider anyone but McCain for the appointment. Hopping, the previous appointee who had been unseated by Carlton, did not seek it; he felt the court "was a phase of my life that had closed," and he was busy in private practice.[28]

Within days of Thornal's death, Kirk forwarded McCain's name to Florida Bar president Burton Young. The McCain choice, unknown to the public or the Bar at large under the confidentiality agreement with Kirk, horrified Young's president-elect, John McCarty of Fort Pierce. "McCarty thought he was a crook ... an absolute moral degenerate," Young recalled.

McCarty knew McCain from having practiced law in the same town, but there was also an old enmity between the McCarty family and McCain's patron Alto Adams, who had run for governor against McCarty's brother Dan in 1952. The ferocity of McCarty's dislike for Adams and McCain struck Young as "obsessive," reminiscent of some of history's legendary feuds, and he took care to appoint an unbiased screening committee. But the committee still found McCain unqualified to be a Supreme Court justice.[29]

No copy is known to exist of the written report that Young presented to Kirk in person. As Young remembers it, "It was replete with suggestions, not only legal improprieties committed by Judge McCain, but of his *suspected* criminal activities and enterprises in which McCain *may* have been involved ... taking money, selling decisions, things like that." Kirk flipped to the last page, which summarized the recommendation, and became "livid with rage," accusing Young, who was a Democrat, of trying to block McCain for partisan reasons. At Young's insistence, Kirk then scanned the entire report and told Young that he would appoint McCain regardless of what it said. As the Bar president left Kirk's office, he saw with dismay who was waiting to see Kirk next: Alto Adams. Kirk announced the McCain appointment almost immediately. McCain, the governor said, had proved himself to be a good judge during his three years on the district court. Revealing a political motive, Kirk also remarked that McCain would "make a good statewide candidate, and that is important. He will make a good race." Kirk appointed his own legal assistant, Gerald Mager, to replace McCain at the Fourth District.[30]

Young considered making the Bar report public but did not do so, in part because nothing in the Bar's screening agreement with Kirk obligated the governor to respect the Bar's advice. To show his displeasure, however, Young boycotted McCain's investiture. But as it turned out, Kirk broke the agreement himself by not consulting the Bar concerning appointments to eleven circuit judgeships. The Bar's disapproval of McCain was common knowledge by then, and Young confirmed it by publicly accusing Kirk of a "kick in the teeth to the competent and efficient administration of justice."[31]

McCain had been on the Supreme Court less than two weeks when he joined a majority opinion in a 5-2 decision holding that the constitution empowered Kirk rather than his successor to fill new circuit judgeships authorized by population increases in the 1970 census. The suit, brought by the legislature's Democratic presiding officers, was successful in another respect: the court barred the Kirk administration from issuing new liquor licenses in response to the census. McCain dissented to that part, arguing that Kirk's administration, not Askew's, was entitled to dispense the licenses. Askew and the legislators would have much preferred to prevail over the judgeships. To Askew, who did not drink alcoholic beverages, winning the issue of the liquor licenses "was the last thing I wanted."[32]

It had occurred to McCain's law school classmates at the University of Florida that he drank more than they did, not reserving the indulgence for weekends. By the time of his appointment to the Supreme Court, he had developed an alcoholic dependency sufficiently severe as to contribute to his wife's decision to divorce him in 1968. The wife he took to Tallahassee was his second, a former college sweetheart, Helen Champion. McCain's alcoholism apparently escaped the Bar committee's notice, but it was soon obvious to his new colleagues at the Supreme Court and beyond. At his first meeting of the Tallahassee Bar Association, where he was invited to address the capital city's lawyers, McCain was so intoxicated "he could hardly stand up" and was barely coherent.[33] To share an elevator with McCain in the morning, Ben Overton said, was "like you were in a bar that had just opened up," full of stale alcohol smells. B. K. Roberts confided to Askew that McCain was a "falling down drunk."[34] Most mornings, though, Mc-Cain was not to be found at the court. Unless oral arguments were scheduled, he preferred to work at home, where his alcoholism would be of con-

Governor Reubin Askew (1971–79), who initiated merit selection of judicial appointees and appointed three reform-minded justices to the Supreme Court. *Courtesy of the Florida State Archives.*

cern only to his family. Occasionally, he would bring in draft opinions that the law clerks considered bizarre. One of them was a solitary dissent to a decision invalidating the Pinellas legislative delegation's attempt to require the St. Petersburg Housing Authority to conduct a referendum before undertaking any construction project. As five other justices saw it, it was an open-and-shut case—the evidence was uncontested—of the legislators failing to advertise the proposed legislation as required by the constitution. In not quite so few words, McCain maintained that the constitution did not matter. "My dissent," he wrote

> is not necessarily a difference of principle, but only the expression that every person must be free to be left to logical combat. At any call, every man should stand by the standard of law and resist any invasion of public order as a matter of his committed personal concern over our country and state. . . . In every case there are certain facts "apparently" distinct by themselves—never confounded by gifts or thefts. Nevertheless, they are open to analysis, observation, induction and deduction, and subject to the enduring test of "principle." This case obviously should be put to the test. Thereby the advantage of experience and the results and reasons of human actions can be weighed and balanced on the scales of justice.[35]

Whatever had fueled McCain's baffling rhetoric, it was an inauspicious case in which to display it. The Housing Authority's attorney was Richard T. Earle Jr., vice chairman of the Judicial Qualifications Commission. But even though McCain's drinking problem was so obvious that Roberts had reported it to the governor, there was never any public indication of the JQC attempting to take McCain's drinking in hand as it had done for Adkins.

As it turned out, McCain was the last Florida justice to owe his appointment to political cronyism. In one of his first actions as governor, Askew voluntarily gave up the governor's power to appoint whomever he pleased to vacancies on the bench. By executive order, he established a merit-selection process in which appointed judicial nominating commissions would select the candidates for him to consider. As the governor appointed only three members of each nine-member commission—the Florida Bar appointed another three and the first six then chose the last three—he could have only limited influence on the choice of nominees. Askew saw to writing merit selection into the constitution in 1972. "It was the most unselfish thing any governor ever did," said Richard McFarlain, assistant executive director of the Florida Bar at the time.[36]

⊰ 5 ⊱

What's a Politician to Do?

Hal P. Dekle's second Supreme Court campaign, for the seat of retiring
justice E. Harris Drew, was successful. The alphabet was his advantage in 1970, not his handicap, as Dekle's name preceded Leo Foster's on
every Democratic primary ballot. Foster also lacked the name recognition
that had helped Vassar Carlton, kin to a former governor and a well-known
former state senator, defeat Dekle in the 1968 primary. "I never knew a man
could have so many cousins," Hopping had said of Carlton.[1] Although Foster
was a law partner of another former governor (and former justice), Millard
Caldwell of Tallahassee, few Democratic primary voters knew of the connection and fewer cared. Dekle, a circuit judge at Miami who had been reelected
without opposition since Gov. LeRoy Collins appointed him in 1958, won the
primary with nearly 65 percent of the vote. The Republicans, mindful of what
had happened to Hopping and McCain in 1968, did not have a candidate and
thus had no influence in the selection. Dekle, 53, a fourth-generation Floridian from Marianna in the North Florida Panhandle, was highly regarded by
the Dade County Bar, there were no whispers of favoritism, and his decisions
had stood up well on appeal.[2] The only blemish on his record was Carlton's
complaint that Dekle had advertised his 1968 campaign before the legal date
for qualifying. If the truth could be told, it was the rare candidate who did *not*
offend against that archaic law, which the Supreme Court in 1977 declared
unconstitutional as a "limitation on the quantity of political speech."[3]

Dekle's 1970 relatively easy campaign victory cost him a frightful price in the form of a favor he thought he owed one of his supporters. In December, before Dekle left for Tallahassee, a campaign volunteer he might never have met sought his help concerning a complicated real estate lawsuit pending at Panama City. The man's name was Sam Jackowitz. He was a real estate broker living in North Miami Beach, and he was worried that he and his two partners from South Florida could not get a fair trial against a hometown litigant in a section of the state nicknamed "South Alabama." He had not contributed money to Dekle's campaign, but he had made telephone calls for him as a favor to a mutual friend who was a Dade County court bailiff. Now Jackowitz deserved a favor in return; such was the fundamental premise of Dade County politics. The bailiff arranged for Jackowitz and his Miami attorney to meet with Dekle over lunch. Jackowitz brought his copy of a real estate sales contract that Owen Wood Development Co. Inc. was suing to set aside. Jackowitz and his partners had filed a counterclaim for breach of contract and damages. Dekle read the documents.

As a Supreme Court justice-elect, Dekle should have been loath to familiarize himself, let alone get involved, in a lawsuit that conceivably could materialize on his desk some day. As he tried to explain later to the Judicial Qualifications Commission, "As with so many supporters, I don't know what a politician is supposed to do, he feels a gratitude and he's trying to stay within all bounds of proprieties, and I looked at it and attempted not to practice law. I said, 'Yes, you appear to have a contract.'" Dekle also recommended a prominent Panama City lawyer, former state representative Julian Bennett, whom Jackowitz retained.

The conversation was on Dekle's mind when he drove to Panama City on behalf of the Supreme Court eight months later to administer the oath of office to a new circuit judge. Another judge in that circuit, W. L. Fitzpatrick, had the Owen Wood case on his docket. Dekle took him aside to talk about it. As Fitzpatrick testified later, "The door was closed and Judge Dekle indicated very strongly to me that the defendants should prevail, that it was important to he and his friends, as I recall the words—I can't remember the exact words—that they prevail."[4]

Fitzpatrick was shocked and embarrassed that a Supreme Court justice would try to influence him; unsure how to react, he delayed his ruling. The case was still pending a year later when Fitzpatrick wrote to each Supreme Court justice to oppose a rule they had adopted. Dekle telephoned Fitzpatrick to acknowledge the letter and to remind him of their conversation about Jackowitz. That was too much for Fitzpatrick, and he took himself off the case. Officially, he explained only that matters *dehors* (outside) the record had come to his attention, necessitating his recusal. When he privately told the other local judges the full story, none of them wanted the case either. A visiting judge from Tampa took it on without inquiring into the reason. (He eventually ruled for Jackowitz, as Fitzpatrick said he would have.) Fitzpatrick also needed to tell Bennett and Owen Wood's lead counsel, W. Dexter Douglass of Tallahassee, why he was handing the case off to another judge. Douglass remembers Fitzpatrick being "absolutely incensed." So, apparently, was Bennett, who told Jackowitz to get himself another lawyer. Dekle, still heedless of the possible consequences, apparently advised Jackowitz on that step, too. The new attorney sent Dekle a blind copy of the initial correspondence with his new client.[5]

Fitzpatrick had hoped at the time that his recusal would be the end of it. "I didn't want a justice to think that I could be told how to decide a case in circuit court," he said. "What I had in mind was that Judge Dekle would get the message . . . and not contact me anymore in connection with any pending matter." But too many people knew the story for it to stay a secret. Among those who soon heard it was John S. Rawls, a judge of the First District Court of Appeal and a member of the Judicial Qualifications Commission. When Rawls inquired, Fitzpatrick confirmed the rumor. He said he did not want to file a complaint against Dekle but would testify if subpoenaed.[6]

When JQC chairman Thomas H. Barkdull Jr., a judge of the Third District Court of Appeal, called to inquire further, Fitzpatrick's written reply urged the commission to treat Dekle lightly. The incident had been "particularly embarrassing to me," he said, because he had introduced Dekle to "various friends" before the election and had voted for him himself. But he didn't want to embarrass Dekle by pursuing a complaint. "I feel when the Commission discusses the matter with him he will probably realize the position he might put a Circuit Judge in by discussing matters under consideration and refrain from doing this anymore. I certainly hope so," he wrote.[7]

The JQC on occasion would counsel a judge in an avuncular fashion without filing formal papers. Dekle was not to get off that easily. On May 3, 1973, the panel sent him a formal notice of investigation. Dekle replied that he had not realized Fitzpatrick was considering a decision when he spoke to him. "I am extremely sorry that he took umbrage at my conversation and most certainly regret that he says he was caused embarrassment by it. I did not notice any," Dekle wrote. "I assure the commission that I shall certainly desist from such comment in any future instance and I am sorry if I were in any violation." Despite the outwardly abject tone, the word *if* implied that Dekle needed a stronger lesson.[8] It was only two months later that he accepted Mason's *ex parte* memorandum in the Gulf Power case.

At the time, the JQC was one of the most obscure state agencies. So far as the public could tell, it had handled just one case since its creation in 1967, and that case was not particularly to its credit. Two tedious and unsuccessful impeachment proceedings in 1957 and 1963 had persuaded the legislature of the need for some less cumbersome way to discipline or remove judges. A constitutional amendment ratified in 1966 established the JQC with power to investigate all circuit judges, judges of the district courts of appeal, and Supreme Court justices. The decision whether to remove or discipline a judge for misconduct or retire one for disability was vested in the Supreme Court, on recommendation of the JQC.[9] Florida became only the second state to adopt this method, following California's example.[10]

Several problems appeared almost immediately. The constitution left it to the Supreme Court and later to the JQC itself to determine how much would be secret. The result was that hardly anything was open until a 1972 amendment required the proceedings to be made public once the JQC called for the removal of a judge. Second, any action by the JQC required the vote of at least six of its nine members, four of whom were judges elected by their peers. As would happen in Dekle's case, a minority could pigeonhole a misconduct charge and the public might never know. A third oversight was that the process did not apply to scores of county judges or judges of specialized courts established over the years by constitutional amendments tailored to the specific requests of individual counties.

The first case that came out of this—or at least the first that the public knew about—punished a judge not for abusing the public but for criticizing other judges. The defendant was Judge Richard Kelly of the Sixth Circuit —Pinellas and Pasco counties—a conspicuously eccentric figure whose 1963 impeachment trial had inspired establishment of the JQC. Kelly had gotten off on the wrong foot with Pasco County lawyers by narrowly defeating O. L. Dayton Jr., a beloved Democratic incumbent, in 1960. Some of them interpreted his idiosyncrasies—such as a lecture from the bench over the proper use of paper clips—as harassment.[11] Three years later, they persuaded the Florida House of Representatives to impeach Kelly over what the charges described as a "continuous course of conduct calculated to intimidate and embarrass" lawyers and others with business before the courts. After twelve days of trial, the Senate voted 23-20 to dismiss the case.[12] Kelly was reelected in 1966, and his Sixth Circuit colleagues gave him a turn as presiding judge in 1968 only to demote him a month later amidst turmoil over his orders and policies. Kelly complained in the press and filed a petition with the clerk that sharply criticized court administration and demanded reforms. When the JQC filed charges against him for that, Kelly made history by invoking his right under the rules to open the trial to the public.[13]

After failing to establish that Kelly was mentally ill, the JQC was left with no evidence except the petition he had filed with the clerk. Even so, it recommended that the Supreme Court reprimand him. In arguing the case before the Supreme Court, the JQC's prosecutors went beyond the formal recommendation and suggested that the court kick Kelly off the bench. The result by a 4-3 decision was a public reprimand to Kelly for offending his fellow judges. "The office of the Clerk of the Circuit Court is not a receptacle for the *ex parte* grievance of a politician, particularly when the object is to seek revenge by embarrassing public officials," Adkins wrote for himself, Thornal, Carlton, and Boyd. The punishment, he insisted, had nothing to do with freedom of speech, but only whether Kelly's "motive or method does violence to the Canons of Judicial Ethics." In words it would soon have to eat, the court also said that the normal rules against retrying old issues (in legal terms, *res judicata* and double jeopardy) did not protect an accused judge. The JQC, it said, "may at any time consider any acts of misconduct which reflect adversely upon the general character and fitness necessary to the proper duties of judicial office. The accumulation of minor incidents may only justify a reprimand at this time, but, if continued, may result in unbecoming conduct sufficient to warrant removal from office." The record of this case, the court said, could be used against Kelly if he got into trouble again. In other words, Kelly had better watch his mouth.

The majority opinion provoked a passionate dissent by Ervin, supported by two circuit judges sitting in for Roberts and for Drew, who had presided over Kelly's senate impeachment trial. Fundamentally, Ervin wrote, Kelly had as much right as any other citizen to speak his mind. Kelly's reprimand could have "tragic implications," Ervin warned. "The people of Florida will suffer if their judges must restrict their public statements to uncritical banalities in order to avoid the threat of similar sanctions." In a passage that was eerily prophetic, Ervin chided Kelly's colleagues and the JQC: "I do not believe his fellow judges should have been so sensitive to the attendant publicity since news reporting in areas of public interest is a fact of life. The commission should realize also no cloak of immunity can shroud the judiciary from the interventions of the press."[14]

With that, the JQC went underground again—so far as the public could see—until the court was asked to bar it from investigating a Miami judge, Jack M. Turner, who had been acquitted of criminal charges in an alleged bribery conspiracy.[15] By then, the news media had revealed the existence of a still-secret case against Dekle. Moreover, on September 19, 1973, the *St. Petersburg Times* had exposed McCain's attempt to fix a criminal case at the Second District Court of Appeal and had reported that the JQC was also investigating McCain's rumored favoritism toward Joseph Farish. The *Times* implied that the court would use Turner's case to insulate some of its own justices from exposure and discipline. Three weeks later, on October 7, the *Times* reported without naming sources that the JQC was looking into Fitzpatrick's recusal in the Owen Wood case. The JQC's interest, the newspaper said, was whether a Supreme Court justice was responsible. Finally, on October 31, the newspaper identified Dekle as the justice and suggested that his participation in the Turner case was improper because it could result in stifling the JQC's probe of him. Among other things, Turner's lawyers wanted the court to rule that the JQC was powerless to probe anything that took place before it was reorganized on January 1, 1973.

Obedient to the secrecy rule, Earle refused to comment for the record "one way or the other." Dekle virtually confirmed the story, however, by citing the confidentiality rule as a reason why he could not comment either. Nothing in the rule would have prohibited a judge from declaring truthfully that he was *not* under investigation. So, by citing the rule, Dekle tacitly acknowledged that he was. Moreover, the rule specifically allowed the subject of an investigation to waive confidentiality, which Dekle would not do. He insisted, however, that "there has been no wrongdoing . . . no big deal involved." Dekle said he was "not concerned in the least with having done anything out of line in any way other than my own interest in seeing justice done in any case."[16]

The timing of events was stunning. Dekle not only knew by November 1973, the month in which he wrote his *Gulf Power* "dissent," that he was under investigation by the JQC, but he knew that the public and the press were aware of it, too. Yet he apparently did not think twice about using the *ex parte* document Mason had given him or about creating a record of Mason's lobbying in the note he dictated to McCain.

Unlike Kelly, Dekle did not exercise his right to a public trial when the JQC heard the Fitzpatrick matter at Tallahassee in January 1974. As a result, even his own attorney was denied access to the transcript. Its belated release revealed that Dekle had pleaded with the JQC to treat the incident as if it had been an accident. Describing the reception at the Panama City investiture, Dekle testified:

And it came to mind, "Here's this judge, now, Dekle, that you've assured this foreigner down from Miami Beach coming up here he's going . . . to get a fair trial in front of this fellow," and just in my gregarious way I thought to myself, "I'll just tell him so." It was just a social affair to me and I thought I should tell Judge Fitzpatrick something that would be helpful in the interest of justice to put this fellow [Jackowitz] at ease. . . . And as well as I can remember I said, "Fitz, I want to mention something to you if you don't mind." I wouldn't have gone any further if he had stopped me. . . . All I remember is ever saying . . . that "I've got a supporter down in Miami . . . who's got a case coming up before you in your busy docket and probably you don't even know it. I says the name is probably strange to you, his name is Jackowitz, and I just want to bring that to your attention and hope you'll remember it because this fellow is nervous as a cat about coming up here into your North Florida area and is scared whether he'll get a fair trial, and I think it's important that he be put at ease." Maybe I used a phrase that he has a chance to prevail or something, but my point was I was anxious that he be assured that he had an opportunity to be fairly heard where he was afraid he was not going to get a fair trial, and this was my only purpose.[17]

Dekle testified that he could remember nothing about the telephone call that provoked Fitzpatrick to recuse himself other than possibly asking Fitzpatrick what had happened in the lawsuit. When he heard that he was being investigated, Dekle said, "That was like a bullet through my heart," and he wept.

"I'll tell you," he said, "I was so new, just getting up here, I was really more of a circuit judge than a Supreme Court justice and maybe I still think that way more because that was my greater background and I saw no offense, no impropriety. . . . I didn't know anybody would be so sensitive about a little matter . . . and [I] guess [I] don't know Fitz that well. . . . I'm basically a friendly type person . . . and I think that's the way I get in trouble sometime anyway by being overfriendly, trying to be sure justice is done." Fitzpatrick conceded to the JQC that during the meeting in his office he had said nothing to stop Dekle from talking about the case. He said he was too surprised, too shocked, to speak up. "Maybe I'm oversensitive . . . but I've always been a little supersensitive where the matters of the bench are concerned. . . . What I should have done was told Hal, 'Now be quiet, don't say anything about that case, get on out of here,' it would have been finished and I'm satisfied he would have done that," Fitzpatrick said.[18]

A 1972 constitutional amendment had enlarged the JQC to thirteen members, including six judges, without changing the requirement that two-thirds of them agree on any action. That meant nine votes were essential; any combination of five would constitute a veto. The new chairman, Richard T. Earle Jr., later implied to a legislative committee that at least some of the judges on the JQC had been voting as a bloc to suppress cases against their brethren.[19]

At a secret JQC meeting at Tampa on February 22, 1974, at least nine members voted to find Dekle guilty of conduct unbecoming the judiciary. In successive motions, six members voted to recommend Dekle's removal from the bench, but seven voted no; seven voted to recommend a public reprimand, but six voted no; seven voted to recommend a private reprimand, but six voted no, and four voted to dismiss the case, but seven voted no. They had a verdict but no sentence and could do or say nothing more. It was never revealed to the public how the individual members had voted, but the result was that the JQC was unable either to discipline Dekle or to dispose of the case.[20] It might have been in limbo forever had the law clerks not leaked

Dekle's memorandum to McCain to the *Times*, which provoked the JQC to investigate both Dekle and Boyd and to reopen the Fitzpatrick case against Dekle.

When that happened, the Supreme Court case file referred to the Fitzpatrick affair as "Inquiry Concerning a Judge No. 73-6." It meant that the JQC had opened at least five cases before Dekle's in 1973. They are still secret more than three decades later.[21]

⊰ 6 ⊱

Shadows of Treason

The Florida Judicial Qualifications Commission was facing the fight of its life when Richard Tilghman Earle Jr. became its third chairman early in 1974. Before then, it had been visible to the public only in the controversial capacity of censor to the iconoclastic circuit court judge Richard Kelly. Under Earle, it engaged the Florida Supreme Court in the judicial equivalent of mortal combat, building the cases that led directly to Dekle's resignation and indirectly to McCain's, and to two constitutional amendments strengthening its jurisdiction over wayward judges. Unlike today, the JQC had no staff, no office of its own, and no appropriation before Gov. Reubin Askew, at Chief Justice B. K. Roberts's suggestion, arranged for a modest transfer of funds from other agencies. It depended upon attorney volunteers to investigate and prosecute complaints against judges. If a volunteer was preoccupied with billable clients, there was little that the chairman could do but try to be patient. The secrecy rule kept Earle from acknowledging the existence of investigations that were already well known to the judiciary and the press, and it was impossible to explain why no progress seemed to be taking place. But he could hint. More than one speculative news story was based on his stock answer: "Any time anybody brings something to our attention, we will investigate it."[1]

This chapter, however, is about the secret Earle did not keep. Had he chosen silence, it is possible that none of the Supreme Court's scandals would have come to light.

The first thing a visitor would notice in Earle's St. Petersburg law office was the framed caricature proudly displayed on one wall. Drawn obviously by an amateur, but a fairly talented one, it depicted a short, stout, scowling man holding a hangman's noose. It had been slipped under his hotel room door during a meeting of the Florida Bar's Board of Governors, where Earle had earned a fearsome reputation for insisting on strict discipline of unethical lawyers. Richard T. McFarlain, the Bar's assistant executive director at the time, fondly recalled how Earle did it:

> He was very much a leader. One of his great speeches was about a young lawyer who had embezzled his trust account or some egregious thing like that, and they were about to turn him loose because he was young. And Earle made a speech about how you start giving up on the young, the next thing you know you'll be giving up on the old, and pretty soon there won't be anybody but you and me. And he carried the day.[2]

Earle, son of a lawyer and grandson of a Maryland judge, "was probably one of the most honorable men that ever practiced law," remarked former Pinellas–Pasco state attorney James T. Russell, on hearing of Earle's death. "Everything he did, he did from that standpoint. Honor above everything else."[3] Mark Hulsey, a fellow member of the JQC, remarked that Earle "wasn't afraid of the devil."[4] When the St. Petersburg Bar Association offered Earle a dues waiver on the occasion of his fiftieth anniversary as a member, he declined for fear that it might make him less likely to speak his mind on policy disputes.[5]

Earle, who was fifty-seven years old on becoming chairman, had lived in Florida since he was nine, and his plainspoken manner could lull an opponent into dismissing him as just another "country lawyer." His lifestyle implied as much: to the end of his days, he refused to air-condition his home. But he had been classically educated at St. John's College, Annapolis, and his law degree was from Harvard.

Earle was as fearless as he was brilliant. The engine fell out of his Porsche as he was driving to work one morning during a time when the JQC was investigating reports of corruption in the judiciary at Miami. When his mechanic told him that someone had removed bolts from the motor mounts, Earle took it as a warning if not an actual attempt on his life, but he said nothing to the police or to the press. "I don't think he wanted to give them the satisfaction," his son Richard said.[6]

Although the cartoon was intended to be unflattering—otherwise the artist would have signed it—Earle took it as a compliment. He brought the same zeal to the Judicial Qualifications Commission as one of the Bar's first appointees in 1967. Six years later, he was the vice chairman. Despite a secrecy regime imposed first by the Supreme Court and then by the JQC itself, the media understood that Earle was impatient with the panel's torpid pace and the timidity of some fellow members. He eventually hinted to a legislative committee that some judges on the JQC were bloc-voting to protect colleagues.[7]

Earle was the logical person for me to see in the wake of a competing newspaper's report that the JQC was investigating alleged bribery on the part of four justices in connection with Miami racing date cases. Most capital journalists considered the story questionable for several reasons—not the least of which was the fact that the accuser was anonymous. Still, my editors at the *St. Petersburg Times* thought that where there was smoke there might be fire, especially since the court was already widely regarded as "political," which was not a compliment. They told me to start digging.

Nothing would ever come of the "unsubstantiated, anonymous, bald-faced accusation," as Askew's general counsel, Edgar M. Dunn Jr., described it to the *Tampa Tribune*. The source for the story was a mimeographed document, devoid of verifiable details, that had been sent to several newspapers months earlier. The newspaper that finally dared to publish it did so on the basis that the JQC was said to be investigating it. The *Tribune* articles also noted, however, that the Florida Department of Law Enforcement had already discredited some of the elements of the memorandum before referring it to the JQC. Askew said in a statement that the referral was a routine procedure that "should not be construed to mean that the charges are to be given credibility or that I, in any way, subscribe to their truth and reliability."[8]

Privately, however, there were substantial reasons for Askew to be concerned about the racing date cases, even if there was no truth to the specific anonymous memorandum. A Miami pari-mutuel executive had predicted accurately to him that the Supreme Court would overturn dates set by Askew's regulatory boards. "What bothered me was the guy told me in so many words he had the votes," Askew recalled. Roberts had confided to him that he worried "that some of the justices might have been tipping their hands" to the outcomes of decisions that were still being written. The racing executive had either made a lucky guess or, more likely, received inside information. Nor was that the only case in which someone in the industry predicted precisely the outcome of a racing date appeal.[9]

At the time, Earle was concerned about something more worrisome than loose-lipped justices. There was nothing he could tell me about racing dates. But, he said, if a reporter were to telephone Judges Joseph McNulty and Robert Mann of the Second District Court of Appeal, they might say something newsworthy about a Supreme Court justice who had tried to influence a pending decision of the lower court.

They would indeed. It took two telephone calls because McNulty hated to see the press air judicial linen. But he finally confirmed the incident that would doom McCain's career. McNulty described a telephone call from McCain while he and Mann were considering *Nell v. State*, an appeal by Richard Nell, president of Local 675 of the International Union of Operating Engineers in Ft. Lauderdale, and two of his members, of their convictions and eighteen-month sentences for bribery. The charge was based on an envelope containing $1,000 in cash that was delivered to a Collier County commissioner as sheriff's deputies, tipped by the official, watched and taped the transaction. The purpose of the payment was to obtain a permit to dig a canal on land that the union owned. Unable to refute the evidence, the lawyers for Nell and his defendants argued that the money was not legally a bribe because the union did not need the county commission's permission to dig the canal.[10] The Second District was still pondering that argument when McCain called McNulty. As McNulty eventually testified in McCain's impeachment and disbarment hearings, McCain baldly asked him to throw the case in Nell's favor. "He said, 'Now, Joe, if it's a case that is close on the facts and can go either way, it would be appreciated, and if it is not close, clear on the law, so be it.'"[11]

When he confirmed this to me in 1973, however, McNulty was not completely candid as to just how brazen McCain had been. He minimized the significance, insisting that he did not consider it an attempt to influence his decision. "I shaded it a bit," he testified much later, because he doubted at the time that it was of "sufficient magnitude to constitute a full-blown JQC investigation." He did say in 1973 that McCain had mentioned that he was calling on behalf of "some friends" and that it was "the first such call I got in my life, in eighteen years on the bench." Although he conceded to me that the call had angered him, McNulty was much more offended than he would admit to a reporter at the time.[12] McNulty could not recall how the conversation began, "except he said, 'Joe, if I say anything improper, please stop me.'" Mann confirmed in a separate telephone interview that McNulty had told him about the call. "We're adults," Mann said. "We know the guy is not calling on behalf of the attorney general." Mann disclosed also that he had received a telephone call pertaining to the case from Gerald Mager, who had become a judge at the Fourth District Court of Appeal, which at the time was considering the union's appeal of a civil damage judgment. Unlike McCain, Mager did not imply how the Nell criminal appeal ought to be decided. He wanted simply to know when the Second District decision might be issued. When the story broke, Mager recused himself from the civil case.[13]

Mann and McNulty conceded that they had held the file a long time. They wanted to write a decision upholding the conviction "with some care" because they knew that Chief Justice William C. Pierce intended to dissent; Piece believed that the county commission was powerless to issue or deny the permit and intended to hold that there was no crime committed. Mann was aware also of certain troublesome Supreme Court precedents.[14] "In fairness to our Chief," Mann's opinion in *Nell v. State* read, "we must say that our Supreme Court has accepted weaker arguments than this as defenses to the charge of bribery." But regardless of whether the permit was necessary, Mann reasoned, "the activity of the defendants in giving money to accomplish their purpose constitutes the crime of bribery. . . . The key point is that whenever an act is within the apparent scope of duty of the person sought to be bribed . . . bribery occurs on the corrupt offer."

Mann and McNulty were not surprised when the Supreme Court overruled them and threw out the case against Nell and his codefendants. But they were astonished that McCain had voted on the case as part of the five-justice majority. McNulty promptly telephoned McCain, who explained that his vote did not matter because there were already four justices in favor of reversal when the case file arrived in his office. Nonetheless, Mann and McNulty agreed that Mann would notify JQC member John S. Rawls, a judge of the First District Court of Appeal, during a scheduled trip to Tallahassee. Only later did they learn that McCain had lied to McNulty; the vote stood at only 3-2 when the Nell file reached his desk on April 5, 1973, and his vote was decisive.[15]

McNulty and Mann had told me only what McCain did; they did not attempt to suggest a motive. Routine reporting filled in some of the blanks. Joseph A. Varon and Steadman Stahl Jr., the attorneys for Nell and his co-defendants, were the attorneys named by David Smith, McCain's repentant campaign supporter, as having given unreported cash contributions to Mc-Cain in 1968. A Dade County grand jury had looked into that without deciding whether it was true or not, remarking that "these allegations involve matters which occurred beyond the jurisdiction of this jury." A more significant—and uncontestable—fact was that McCain had asked for votes at the union hall and had met there privately with Nell during his 1972 reelection campaign. At the time, Nell had already been convicted and his conviction was on appeal to the Second District.[16]

Nell's union was also a target of the U.S. Justice Department's Organized Crime Strike Force at Miami, which would eventually send Nell to prison. The civil appeal pending before the Fourth District involved a $1.25 million verdict won by a worker who had been beaten by a union enforcer. There were dissident members trying to end Nell's long reign, and they were willing to talk to the press about McCain's private meeting with Nell and his remarks to the membership. (Merely being there was, under such circumstances, highly questionable conduct on the part of a Supreme Court justice.) "Judge Mc-Cain stated that he could not make any promises, but the local could rest assured that any appeal coming before his court would get special attention," one member said. "He said that we could count on fair treatment, but he could make no promises," said another. One of the dissidents, Ralph Frashier, eventually testified that he considered the speech so unethical that he reported it in a letter to Roberts, who was chief justice at the time. Roberts testified that he could not remember the letter but had heard about the speech and had questioned McCain about it.[17]

In an interview a year later, McCain tried to minimize the significance of his remarks. "I told them a few jokes, I got a few laughs, and I just told 'em my philosophy of law—to interpret it and not to make it. I told them the best thing to do if they wanted the law changed dramatically is to do it through the legislature, not the court." He said he did not recall mentioning "fair treatment" and would more likely have promised "equal" treatment. "I always say that to any group I've spoken to, that they could expect equal treatment," he said.[18]

Nell and his codefendants were free on bond while their attorneys appealed the Second District decision to Tallahassee. Before their file reached his desk, McCain executed a financial transaction that appeared significant and suspicious. In February 1973, he paid off the second mortgage on his home, an overdue balloon note, with $9,440 in cash consisting of $10 and $20 bills. Questioned two years later by reporters for the *Tampa Tribune* and Gannett newspapers who were pursuing a tip, McCain said the money represented accumulated cash gifts from William Champion, the father of his second wife, Helen, whom he had married in 1969. McCain said it was intended for his wife and their children and that he preferred to deal in cash rather than checks "so we wouldn't have to go through an audit" by the Internal Revenue Service. Champion was unavailable to confirm McCain's explanation; he had died in 1974.[19]

On April 2, 1973, two days before the Nell case came to McCain for what would be his decisive vote, he received a message from Nell at his office in the Supreme Court building. The messenger was Robert E. May, a twenty-five-year-old "public relations representative" for the union, who registered as its legislative lobbyist the same day. In sworn affidavits, May told the *St. Petersburg Times,* the JQC, and the chief counsel for a House impeachment committee that he gave McCain a pair of cuff links and a manila envelope from Nell that contained $10,000 in $20 bills. May said that Nell had ordered him not to open the envelope, which supposedly contained a "rare book," but that he had disobeyed and knew what was in the envelope, which he had resealed, before watching McCain dump the contents on his desk. At the time, May said, they discussed the bribery appeal and McCain told him to assure Nell that "everything's going to be all right, he will be all right. . . . I have taken care of everything." May claimed that he had telephoned Nell to try to beg off the assignment, only to be warned to carry it out or "you won't be around so long and neither will very few members of your family be around." He said Nell described the money as a "personal loan." But May also admitted in his affidavit that he had not told the same story when he appeared before a federal grand jury that was investigating Nell. "I was not asked specifically if

I had taken any money to Justice McCain," he said. Nor had he volunteered to say that he did.[20]

In interviews with the *St. Petersburg Times,* McCain admitted May's visit and to receiving the cuff links—although he said he got them weeks later than May said—but adamantly denied discussing Nell's appeal or receiving money from Nell through May. "I'm telling you he is a liar," McCain said. "Why would a man like Nell send a kid to do a man's job if he was going to bribe a judge?'" McCain did not threaten to sue the *Times* if we printed the story.[21]

Decades later, in the course of research for this book, an attorney in Tallahassee recounted an unsolicited telephone call from McCain in which the justice asked whether the lawyer had any "special interest" in a beverage law case awaiting decision. The lawyer did have an interest in the case, but he also had strong misgivings about McCain's motive for asking and ended the conversation as swiftly as he could.[22]

Amidst a series of articles on the Nell case, the *St. Petersburg Times* initially withheld what May's affidavit had said about the money out of concern that his account could not be substantiated. Editor Eugene Patterson ordered it into print in the aftermath of the *Tribune*-Gannett story that revealed how McCain had settled a second mortgage with cash. Although that transaction transpired a month before May's visit to McCain's office, it was curious conduct on the part of a lawyer or a judge. "There's your confirmation," Patterson said. His judgment was vindicated when McCain made no demand on the newspaper for retraction and did not try to have May prosecuted on a charge of swearing falsely to an affidavit. There was no response from Nell either.[23]

Three days after the delivery date that May alleged, the Nell file was in McCain's office for his signature on B. K. Roberts's majority opinion reversing the conviction. It was accompanied by Justice Joseph Boyd's dissent. McCain had not been assigned to the five-justice panel that heard oral arguments, but with the court split 3-2, it was necessary to bring in the other justices. McCain could have recused himself, leaving Carlton to provide the decisive vote to reverse the conviction, without having to explain anything to the court. Had he done that, McNulty and Mann would not have told the JQC about McCain's telephone call. Nor would they have encouraged McCain's former research assistant, Anne Marshall Parker, by then the Second District's new administrator, to tell the JQC what she knew about McCain. Earle would not have known about the telephone call and could not have informed me. There would have been no newspaper articles about McCain's implied promises at the union hall, his subsequent favors, or the inference of bribery. Robert May would have missed his fifteen minutes of fame.[24]

The Roberts opinion, supported also by Adkins and Dekle, embraced Pierce's Second District dissent that bribery occurs "only when the object sought to be accomplished comes within the scope of the official's public capacity or duty." It was irrelevant whether Nell thought he needed a permit. The record made it "apparent that no permit was required under the ordinance and no formal application for permit had been filed." Ergo, there was no bribery. Convictions reversed. Charges dismissed. "I must dissent," Boyd wrote for himself and Ervin:

> The record reveals that a controversy existed as to whether the defendants actually needed to secure a County Commission permit in order to dig the canal in question. The work was, in fact, stopped temporarily at the request of the Commission. Even if there was no lawful authority to permanently stop the project, if the Commission ordered the owners to abandon it, the owners would have suffered damages while establishing their rights in court. Faced with such a possibility, the owners apparently felt it was better to bribe than to fight. Thus, even assuming no permit was needed, there was still a clear violation of the Florida statutes on bribery. . . . It is the scurrilous peddling of one's influence as a public official which the law denounces. . . . The effective capacity of public officials is not limited to those areas prescribed by statute. Because of personal and political connections, public officials can persuade others vested with legal authority to grant favors to people which he [sic] could not personally grant though his own single vote or through the exercise of his official duties.[25]

Boyd's practical interpretation of the events reflected the fact that he was the only sitting justice with experience as a county commissioner. None but Boyd and Ervin, a former attorney general, had ever been elected to any office other than a court. They recognized what cloistered judges apparently could not see.

Although Boyd customarily left it to his clerks to draft his opinions, the Nell dissent was entirely his own.[26] If May told the truth about delivering a bribe to McCain, Boyd's eloquent penultimate paragraph in *Nell v. State* must have set McCain's ears to burning:

> The consent of the governed is essential to the very existence of government in this country. When the public loses confidence in public officials, respect for and allegiance to government diminishes. Because bribery erodes the foundations of government, it is one of the most despicable of all crimes. Those who pay or receive a price to influence the conduct of public officials place the personal enrichment of the participants above the public welfare, and walk in the shadows of treason.

The Nell decision of April 11, 1973, created a hugely inviting opportunity for influence-peddling. The legislature attempted to close it a year later. Legislators were aware by then of McCain's tampering with the lower court but not of any possibly corrupt motives. The resulting bribery statute in its present form (F.S. 838.015) provides for prosecution regardless of whether "the public servant ultimately sought to be unlawfully influenced was qualified to act in the desired way, that the public servant had assumed office, that the matter was properly pending before him or her or might by law properly be brought before him or her, that the public servant possessed jurisdiction over the matter, or that his or her official action was necessary to achieve the person's purpose."

Earle never discussed his reasons for telling me about McCain's telephone call to McNulty. But time and events suggest that he had tried unsuccessfully to motivate the JQC to pursue it. The secret investigation of Dekle's attempt to influence Fitzpatrick was moving sluggishly toward the closed hearing that would result in a paralyzed JQC. It may have been clear to Earle that too few of his fellow commissioners were as outraged by such conduct as he was and that only the press could arouse them.

The Supreme Court was about to make his job even more difficult, and it would take many more months and a constitutional amendment to overcome the obstacles that it created.

⇥ 7 ⇤

Circling the Wagons

Then as now, Miami was a good town in which to be a reporter, a cop, or a prosecutor. A net cast in any direction would haul up full, perhaps even including a squirming judge or two. In mid-1972, Sheriff E. Wilson Purdy and Miami police set up surveillance around the Market Truck Stop, a gasoline station situated at Dade County's wholesale produce market near the criminal courthouse. The focus of their public corruption investigation was seventy-two-year-old Frank Martin, a "pudgy, drawling political insider," as the *Miami Herald* described him, who used the Market Truck Stop's office telephone as his own. Martin was known as the "mayor of the market," a man whose favor any politician might seek. "A word from Frank Martin, it is said, will see a politician's campaign signs sprout on the hundreds of trucks that move daily in and out of the market area," United Press International reported. Governor Reubin Askew initially refused to authorize a wiretap when the Department of Law Enforcement approached him on behalf of the Dade authorities because he suspected the net was being spread too wide. About "half the people in Dade County" had patronized the market, he said. The governor had been there himself and counted Martin as a campaign supporter. But when the investigators narrowed the scope, Askew agreed to the wiretap, and the authorities obtained the necessary order from Chief Justice James C. Adkins Jr. The reasons why they did not want to approach the local judiciary became clear when two judges, Jack M. Turner and Murray Goodman, were charged with bribery conspiracies on the basis of intercepted conversations. So were Martin, Miami mayor David Kennedy, and three others. All told, 106 people, including Dade County state attorney Richard Gerstein and ten more judges, were notified that their conversations had been tapped. The special prosecutors Askew had appointed, state attorneys Stephen Boyles of Palatka and Jimmy Russell of St. Petersburg, intended to pursue election law violations after finishing the bribery cases.[1] But the anticorruption crusade began fizzling out with Turner's acquittal in August 1973. He was accused of bribery conspiracy for setting aside the eighteen-month prison sentence he had imposed on a marijuana dealer who had pleaded guilty. (The Third District Court of Appeal had restored the sentence on finding that Turner had no authority to let the defendant "whimsically" withdraw his guilty plea). Although it was undeniable that Turner had discussed the case with the defendant's mother, the jury was not persuaded that such curious wiretapped remarks between Martin and Kennedy as "It's three crates instead of one" and "Start the proceedings, the five baskets are agreed upon," were coded phrases for payoff money. There was nothing more concrete. Defense attorney Gerald Kogan—a future Supreme Court justice—conceded that Turner may have been doing a favor in reopening a conviction, but he argued compellingly that there was no evidence of a bribe. In the end, no one was convicted of anything.[2]

What remained of the "Market Connection" was blown away by a 4-2 Supreme Court ruling in December 1973 that forbade the use of the intercepted conversations in any prosecution other than for the twelve crimes—*not* including campaign law violations—specified in the wiretap law. It was analogous to holding that a police officer who properly apprehended a reckless driver could not charge him for untaxed liquor discovered in the car. Conveniently for some, it would also prohibit the JQC from using those wiretaps or any other conversations overheard during a different criminal investigation to support ethical misconduct charges against judges for discussing cases out of court.[3]

Roberts, Ervin, McCain, and Dekle formed the majority for the *per curiam* opinion. Adkins, who had authorized the wiretaps, did not participate. In a heated dissent, Boyd, backed by Vassar Carlton, contended that the court lacked constitutional jurisdiction to hear the case that "may well become a landmark decision." The majority, Boyd protested, "has failed to cite a *single* case where the use of preindictment motions to suppress has been allowed, as the majority has allowed in this case. Perhaps, this is because *there is absolutely no authority—federal or state—that has ever allowed such motions*" (emphasis in the original). Schwartz, who wrote the opinion for Boyd, said the words were chosen to signal to the public that "something terribly rotten was happening."[4] As it had implied in *Nell v. State*, the Florida Supreme Court was not shy about invoking fine distinctions to protect public officials. The Frank Cobo case—named for the Miami mayor's aide who sued to suppress the wiretap evidence—was not even the most remarkable in that line of decisions. Cobo's was still pending when word leaked to the press of another that the court could—and would—use to protect *itself* from the Judicial Qualifications Commission.

Although Turner had been acquitted of the criminal charges against him, he obviously had discussed at least one case in likely violation of the *ex parte* rule of the Code of Judicial Conduct. "A poor woman came to me and said that her son did not receive a full measure of justice," Turner explained after his indictment.[5] But when the JQC opened an inquiry, Turner petitioned the Supreme Court to stifle the probe. He contended that the JQC was powerless to investigate anything that took place before January 1, 1973, when it was enlarged by a constitutional amendment reorganizing the court system. Moreover, Turner argued that the commission could not touch him in any event because he had been a judge of the Dade Criminal Court of Record, which was not subject to the JQC's jurisdiction, before his election as a circuit judge in November 1972.

He had a point. The constitutional amendment had incorporated all such local judgeships into the circuit court system because they had been performing equivalent duties. No one had thought, however, to provide for disciplining them in matters that had not come to light before the transition. But what Turner was seeking from the court went far beyond even that. "If any judge did something two years ago, it's wiped out," one lawyer said of Turner's petition to the court. Among other things, Turner's case could cut short any JQC investigation of McCain's 1972 campaign and the meeting with Nell, the anonymous allegation regarding pari-mutuel decisions, and any other pre-1973 issue still undiscovered by the press. But despite all those implications, Carlton—chief justice at the time—intended to hold the hearing on Turner's petition in secret, just as the JQC investigation itself was supposed to be. By then, however, the *Miami Herald* had already reported Turner's secret petition, and the court had allowed reporters for other newspapers to read it.[6] At that point, the court conceded the uselessness of trying to keep it under wraps. Barely two weeks later, the *St. Petersburg Times* reported the possibility of a JQC investigation into the reasons for Fitzpatrick stepping out of the Jackowitz case. The story, citing unidentified sources, said he had done so because of a telephone call from a Supreme Court justice. The identity of the justice—Dekle—came out three weeks later, still officially unconfirmed, in a story that questioned whether Dekle as well as McCain might be protected by the forthcoming ruling on Turner's petition.[7] The eventual decision was no help to Dekle, who took no part in it, but it did temporarily protect McCain, who voted for it.

The attorney who took Turner's case to the Supreme Court was not the one who had successfully defended him against the criminal charge but another, Marion Sibley of Miami, who had been a political ally and confidante of B. K. Roberts since the 1940s.[8] The JQC, staring disaster in the face, was represented by four lawyers led by William Reece Smith Jr., immediate past president of the Florida Bar, whose presence underscored the significance of the case.

The court gave Turner less than he wanted but more than enough to protect him and McCain as well. It ruled 4-2 that the JQC could not investigate Turner for anything that occurred "during a prior term in a different office." It could not investigate *anything* that occurred more than two years before its new "origin" on January 1, 1973. Moreover, it would be allowed to investigate backward "for a reasonable time behind a present term of office" only in relation to a charge of misconduct occurring in a *present* term of office." There was enough whitewash in that decision to have repainted the entire Supreme Court building.

Roberts's majority opinion was contradictory to what the court had allowed in the Kelly case. Roberts tried to distinguish the situations by writing that Kelly's "was anchored to entirely different facts." As even Roberts had to concede, however, the decision would bar the JQC from investigating a judge for election law violations during his campaign to become a judge. The legislature, he wrote, "might want to provide some corrective remedy" in the form of a constitutional amendment.[9]

Unbeknown to the public, the court in 1972 had secretly forbidden the

Florida Bar to pursue an ethics case against a state attorney for a forgery allegation dating to his prior private law practice. The pretext was that because the constitution required him to be a Bar member to hold his job, any disbarment proceeding would usurp impeachment powers reserved to the legislature.[10] The protection for Turner was akin to that precedent.

Ervin, who had dissented passionately in Kelly's case, did so again in *Turner v. Earle*—this time in the JQC's behalf. He thought the section of the constitution establishing the JQC contained "no such impediments" as Roberts, Carlton, Adkins, and McCain had read into it. Judicial restraint, he wrote, should have compelled the court to wait to see what the JQC came up with against Turner before ruling that it could not charge him with anything. He implied that the majority had pulled the teeth of the recently amended Code of Judicial Conduct. The JQC, he wrote,

> has not been an instrument of oppression—it has not allowed itself to become a lever of any special group or interest to threaten the independence of Florida judges. The fear that "silk stocking" elements of the Bar and Bench through the medium of the Commission would ride herd upon highly independent judges has not materialized, with the one possible exception of Judge Kelly's case. . . . [I]t has the duty to take into account any serious and obvious misconduct of a judge that reasonably has a pertinent bearing upon his present fitness as a judge.

In Ervin's view, judges had a higher calling than other politicians and should be held to higher standards. The creation of the JQC was intended to do that, and "it should not be emasculated by narrow, restrictive precedents which are not expressly written into it." Boyd, agreeing with Ervin and also dissenting separately, wrote in *Turner v. Earle* that in creating the JQC the people of Florida intended to enforce "the highest ethical standards." The majority opinion, he said, "is not in the spirit of the people's intent. Those who cannot stand the bright light of public scrutiny should not hold judicial office." Within the year, that bright light would shine directly on him.

For the time being, however, the JQC was largely blocked from pursuing McCain even as more allegations of favoritism were coming to its attention. It was three months after the Turner ruling that Barkdull sounded out Owen about the time when McCain had asked to sit in his place at the Fourth District Court of Appeal on a day when one of Farish's cases was scheduled.

Owen wrote to Barkdull that, although he would testify if asked, "I am wondering, however, what effect the Supreme Court's decision in the Turner case will have upon investigation of any of the above matters, all of which occurred prior to Justice McCain's present term in office."[11]

Richard Earle and the Florida Bar, meanwhile, successfully lobbied the legislature for a constitutional amendment to erase the Turner decision. Ratified by the voters in November 1974, it empowered the JQC to investigate and recommend the removal of a justice or judge "whose conduct during term of office or otherwise" occurring any time after November 1, 1966, when the JQC was first established, "demonstrates a present unfitness to hold office" or deserved a reprimand. As inclusive as that might seem, the court would find yet another way to protect judges from punishment for unethical conduct.

Turner remained on the Dade bench until he retired in January 1991. In 1990, he stipulated to a public reprimand recommended by the JQC. He violated the Code of Judicial Conduct by campaigning for a candidate other than himself: his son.[12]

⇥ 8 ⇤

A "Good Old Boy" Court

The mid-1970s were in some ways the best of times for the state of Florida. A progressive agenda prevailed in the legislature, the afterglow of a historic reapportionment ordered by the U.S. Supreme Court in 1966 and 1967. Governor Reubin Askew, resoundingly popular despite his endorsement of busing to purge the public schools of racial segregation, won reelection in 1974 by more than 60 percent over three Democratic primary rivals (including his own disgraced lieutenant governor, who had been caught using a public employee to run his private farm) and by a comparable margin over Republican nominee Jerry Thomas. It was a particularly good time to be selling or developing real estate. The "Big Bang" (as historian Gary Mormino described it) that had begun in the 1950s, when Florida's 78.7 percent population growth led the nation, was still clocking a phenomenal 43.6 percent two decades later. Florida boomed by nearly 3 million new residents in the 1970s, more than the entire population of Iowa.[1] Only a few people, Askew among them, foresaw or even cared that Florida's economy, infrastructure, and political institutions would be inadequate to the challenge.

It was a bad time, however, for the Florida Supreme Court, for the elected cabinet (three of whose six members would leave office during corruption investigations that would send two of them to prison), and for U.S. senator Edward J. Gurney (who had to abandon his reelection campaign to concentrate on his successful defense against a federal bribery indictment).[2] As if the Supreme Court did not have troubles enough of its own, with five justices in some degree of difficulty at one time or another, it also found the means—some said the gall—to obstruct two of the cabinet investigations and erase a kickback case against a former state senator. With Chief Justice Vassar Carlton's resignation, however, Askew began the rehabilitation of the court by appointing Circuit Judge Ben F. Overton of St. Petersburg to succeed him.

It was the first Supreme Court opening subject to the nominating commission process adopted by Askew in 1971 and written into the constitution a year later. Twenty-six lawyers and judges applied; the nominees were Overton, Alan C. Sundberg, also of St. Petersburg, and Mallory Horton, a former district court of appeals judge from Miami.[3] Among those the nominating commission passed over without even an interview was former governor LeRoy Collins. Collins was disappointed that Askew, whom he considered a protégé, had not intervened for him.[4] But Askew was determined to keep aloof from the nominating process "because I wanted the system to work," and he said he had not even known that Collins, whom he considered a role model, desired the appointment. He welcomed the opportunity to appoint Overton because "I knew that court was in disarray."[5]

The disarray was well known also to Dixie Beggs, a Pensacola attorney who chaired the nominating commission and was influential in Overton's selection. A year earlier, he had enlisted Overton, who was chairman of the Conference of Circuit Judges, to help the Florida Bar persuade a reluctant Supreme Court to approve a strengthened Code of Judicial Conduct. Among other things, it would require many judges to give up outside business interests. The court's price for adopting it was a surprise decision, without the benefit of briefs or oral argument, to overturn a statute that forbade pensioned judges from practicing law. Although the law was plainly arbitrary, the court should have given the attorney general or the legislature an opportunity to defend it.[6]

Overton, forty-seven years old when appointed in March 1974, was known as a stickler on ethics. His secretary told a reporter that he had kept track of personal calls on his office telephone and written periodic checks to reimburse Pinellas County at ten cents a call.[7] Overton's appointment "was the beginning of the honest Supreme Court," said Gerald Kogan, who was appointed to the court two years before Overton retired.[8] "When I appointed

Overton, I told him that was his job; the main task was to try to rebuild the court," Askew said.[9]

There were times when Overton worried over what he was seeing and hearing. When he was appointed, he said, "I thought I knew what was going on, but I did not, really." Both Richard Earle Jr. and Henry Baynard, a St. Petersburg lawyer who had been a state senator, warned him, "Don't get obligated to anybody." They had B. K. Roberts in mind. Ervin, who as attorney general had given Overton his first job after law school, welcomed him back to Tallahassee with the advice, "Just be careful." Taking to heart what he had heard, Overton declined Roberts's invitation to occupy a cottage behind the senior justice's home while his family prepared to move to Tallahassee after the school term. "I don't think B. K. believed to the day he died that I was living in a motor home in Bell's Trailer Park," Overton said.[10]

He walked into a perfect storm. The JQC was already moving against Dekle in the Fitzpatrick matter and, ever so slowly, against McCain in regard to the Nell case. Not quite three months later, I wrote in the *Times* about the document that Boyd had destroyed and disclosed that the JQC was investigating that, too. "The Judicial Qualifications Commission," the June 8 story said, "is investigating how the Supreme Court may have used a document so potentially embarrassing that one justice tore up his copy and flushed the pieces down a toilet." In August, the JQC began formal proceedings against Boyd and Dekle in regard to the *Gulf Power* incidents.

As I was preparing that report, based on interviews with Boyd and Roger Schwartz, the court formally charged Schwartz with contempt of court for leaking a different document to an outside source. He was in serious peril this time. The document was an oral argument summary, not part of the public record, that he had shown to a former law school classmate at dinner the night before the case was to be argued. Although not dispositive of the outcome, such a document could help an attorney organize his argument. His friend betrayed him to the Bar, which notified the court. Roberts, who had informed Askew but not the JQC about justices whom he suspected of leaking the outcome of pending cases, sought the ultimate penalty of disbarment for Schwartz. To his surprise and relief, Schwartz was let off with his apology and probation. Later, Ervin told Sharyn Smith that he had warned his colleagues that he would tell the public about their internal intrigues if they voted to disbar Schwartz. Schwartz, who had already begun working at the Civil Rights Division of the U.S. Justice Department in Washington, said that when he told his new supervisors of the trouble he was in, they replied, "In this division, it's a mark of honor to be held in contempt by the Florida Supreme Court." The court had been so eager to be rid of a suspected leak to the press that upon Schwartz's resignation effective March 31, they gave him all of March off with pay.[11]

Meanwhile, State Attorney Ed Austin of Jacksonville, whom Askew had assigned to Tallahassee as a special prosecutor at the request of the Joint Legislative Auditing Committee, obtained grand jury indictments charging nineteen counts of perjury, bribery, and unauthorized compensation against Education Commissioner Floyd T. Christian. The indictments alleged under-the-table payments of more than $70,000 for contracts involving a reading program and mobile classrooms that had been awarded to companies connected to one of Christian's friends from St. Petersburg. Among the evidence: Bahamian bank accounts in the name of "Zera R. Tom," a fictitious person named after Christian's children. Christian, who had already decided against seeking reelection, resigned his office as a House committee was about to initiate impeachment proceedings.

Austin and the grand jury were just beginning to investigate a kickback scheme and other allegations against Treasurer/Insurance Commissioner Tom O'Malley when Adkins, who had succeeded Carlton as chief justice, abruptly ordered the probe shut down until after the November election four months later. It was unfair, Adkins said, to investigate politicians during their campaigns. He had given no notice to Austin, Askew, Attorney General Robert Shevin, or to his own court before issuing the unprecedented order. No one had applied to him for such a decree—at least not on the record. There was nothing but Adkins's own whimsy to support his finding that "such investigations of public figures as have come to our attention could well have been managed and many completed prior to the closing of qualifying dates." His declaration that "such investigations are being held so as to coincide with the campaign season" was an undocumented, unsupportable, and—to many lawyers—unfair slur on one of Florida's most respected prosecutors. Moreover, it violated the spirit if not the letter of a law explicitly forbidding trial judges from limiting "an investigation of any matter into which the grand jury is by law entitled to inquire."[12]

Arthur England, who was preparing to run for the seat of retiring justice

Richard Ervin, attacked Adkins for having done "a most appalling thing
. . . with no hearings, briefs or opportunity for public input." Among those
taken by surprise was at least one other justice. "I had to call the court and say,
'What's going on?'" said Overton, who heard about Adkins's order from the
press while he was on the campaign trail to keep his seat.[13]

At Overton's request, the full court took up the issue at its conference the
following week and agreed to hold a hearing. The grand jury foreman, a spec-
tator at the hearing, protested to journalists that the grand jury had not been
unfair to anyone. But it seemed to the attorney general's staff as they argued
against the order that the outcome was already decided. As they feared, the
vote was 4-3 to uphold Adkins.[14] Chesterfield Smith, a Florida lawyer who
was American Bar Association president at the time, denounced the decision
as a "novel concept of law I've never heard of."[15]

Adkins withdrew the order, almost as abruptly as he had issued it, after it
had been in force for twelve days. Former state senator George L. Hollahan
Jr. of Miami, who had been defeated for renomination in 1972, had admitted

The court in 1973, before the storm. From left, Chief Justice Vassar Carlton, Justices
Hal P. Dekle, B. K. Roberts, David L. McCain, Joseph A. Boyd, Richard T. Ervin,
James C. Adkins. They are listening to Gov. Reubin Askew address the legislature on
organized crime and pornography. *Courtesy of the Florida State Archives.*

to the *Miami Herald* that Austin and the grand jury were also investigating him for kickbacks and that the statute of limitations would expire, preventing his prosecution, before the grand jury could resume work in November. Although Adkins maintained that the order did not apply in such a situation, Austin said he thought it did, and the grand jury, meeting despite the order, declared unanimously that it needed to proceed. Shevin, meanwhile, "was as mad as I've ever seen" over Adkins's decree and the court's vote to uphold it, recalled Sharyn Smith. To put public pressure on the court, Shevin announced an appeal to the U.S. Supreme Court and sent a deputy on a well-publicized mission to seek a stay from Justice Lewis Powell in Virginia. There was only a remote possibility that Powell or his colleagues would actually override the Florida court, but Powell did agree to see Shevin's deputy, if only as a courtesy. Whether by coincidence or not, Adkins withdrew the prohibition a short time later.[16]

In short order, Austin obtained grand jury indictments against Christian, O'Malley, and Hollahan, a former senate rules chairman who had publicly admitted taking "referral fees" from a lawyer to whom he sent lobbying clients. O'Malley, accused of taking kickbacks from former law partners to whom he had steered insurance companies subject to his regulation, was reelected despite the scandal. His Republican opponent, a stealth candidate who had won a surprising primary victory over a well-known legislator, admitted that he had solicited support from the Ku Klux Klan and insisted that he did not know the Klan was hostile to blacks, Jews, and Roman Catholics. Voters evidently agreed with the reluctant advice of the *St. Petersburg Times* to reelect O'Malley so that the governor could appoint a competent replacement in the likely event of O'Malley's impeachment. It played out that way. O'Malley resigned in a plea bargain with Austin after the House impeached him in 1975. Concurrently, a federal grand jury investigation into financial relations with bankers he regulated ended the career of a third cabinet member, Comptroller Fred O. Dickinson Jr., whose renomination campaign was wounded fatally by news coverage of his refusal to testify to the jury. Dickinson eventually pleaded guilty to a misdemeanor income tax violation for which he was fined $3,000.[17]

With the Watergate investigations that would bring down a president already dominating the news from Washington, Floridians had never seen a year of scandal like 1974. But that summer and fall, Adkins and his allied justices were hardly finished with hindering the prosecutions.

The next occasion arose from a pair of rulings by the First District Court of Appeal that overturned the Christian indictments (and in effect the O'Malley and Hollahan charges, too) by holding that Askew had improperly assigned Austin to act in Harry Morrison's place, that Austin's assistants from his own judicial circuit should not have questioned witnesses before a grand jury in a different circuit, and that only one prosecutor at a time could appear before a grand jury. Christian's attorneys won on every point they took to the court except for a claim that he was not subject to indictment while holding office.[18]

To reach those results, the district court relied on such exquisite grammatical distinctions as a finding that the word *assist* meant that a visiting state attorney could "aid or help the state attorney of the circuit to which assigned by working with him, not replacing him." The Joint Legislative Auditing Committee's staff director complained bitterly, "A year and a half's worth of work by two branches of government can be thrown out on the ground the word *or* is disjunctive."[19]

Askew rarely criticized a court. This time he did, in the angriest words Tallahassee reporters could remember hearing from him. The governor said he could not "imagine the legislature ever intended the law to be interpreted" as the First District had and that it was "completely unrealistic" to expect state attorneys to work without their own assistants.[20] The real issue, as he knew, was whether any governor would be able to root out official corruption in the jurisdictions of state attorneys who, like Tallahassee's, did not inspire his confidence. Harry Morrison, for example, had accepted explanations from Christian that Askew knew to be misleading. Morrison had also admitted to the *St. Petersburg Times* that he had mislaid a file sent him by another state attorney describing evidence of a scheme to bribe O'Malley. The First District's decisions, Askew said, "would appear to emasculate the ability of Florida's chief executive to effectively deal with criminal investigations, particularly those involving alleged corruption by public officials where the resident state attorney often is put in a very difficult position in having to prosecute constitutional officers with whom he must work on a daily basis."[21] The governor called the legislature into special session to rewrite the laws that the court had applied, but the Christian and O'Malley cases would have to be reconstructed from the beginning if the Supreme Court did not overrule the decisions. Moreover, the case against Hollahan would disappear on account of a two-year statute of limitations. There were suspicions that the appeals court had ruled as it did not so much for Christian's benefit but primarily to protect Hollahan, who had been one of very few South Florida politicians on good terms with the Senate's Pork Chop Gang. The First District Court was regarded in those days as the last stronghold of those deeply conservative rural forces that had controlled the legislature before 1967. Two of the three judges in the Christian appeal had been Pork Chop senators.

Although the constitution did not oblige the Supreme Court to hear Austin's appeal, it did so because the district court certified that the case involved a question of great public interest. On February 11, 1975, six days after the House speaker threatened impeachment proceedings against Dekle and Boyd, the Supreme Court dismissed all the charges against Christian. Although it overruled the district court on most points, it contrived a new technicality. Yes, the Supreme Court said, Austin could have used his assistants from Jacksonville—but only by having them sworn in again by a judge from the circuit including Tallahassee. Although no such ritual would be necessary under the new law enacted by the special session, the repair could not apply retroactively. Adkins, McCain, and two circuit judges sitting in for Dekle and Boyd formed the majority. Overton and retired justice E. Harris Drew dissented. Overton wrote:

> I strongly dissent from that portion of the majority opinion that holds the indictments in this cause must fall because of the failure of the assistant state attorneys to take a second oath of office applicable to the circuit of the grand jury without any showing of prejudice by the defendant.
>
> The majority opinion recognizes that it is clearly proper for an assistant to aid his own state attorney before a grand jury in his own circuit. This being so, what is the magic need to have a separate oath for the assistant to aid the same state attorney before a grand jury in another circuit?[22]

But that was the minority view, leaving nothing for Austin to do but close the Hollahan file and bring weaker charges against Christian. The perjury charge, the most serious, had been washed out forever; Christian would not repeat the mistake of trying to sway the grand jury in his favor. As for O'Malley, Austin had seen enough of the Tallahassee obstacle course. He agreed to a plea bargain involving O'Malley's resignation but no prison sentence and gave the file "with ribbons on it" to the Internal Revenue Service and U.S. Justice Department. "It was so much a better federal case than a state case, an income tax case on a platter," he said. After a conviction and drawn-out appeals, O'Malley eventually served two years. Christian pleaded no contest to three state felony charges, for which he was fined $43,273 and put on probation, and he served 135 days in a federal prison for income tax violations.

Years later, long since retired, Austin was philosophical about the saga. "I remember the feeling when you got in town on an executive assignment to a different circuit, you knew you were not going to be warmly welcomed by the local establishment," he said. "The Supreme Court at that time was what I would consider part of that establishment." It was not deliberate corruption on the court's part, he thought, but simply "a 'good old boy' thing."[23]

But by then, the "good old boy" days of the Supreme Court were numbered.

⊰ 9 ⊱

A Florida Watergate?

With ironic timing, the *Florida Bar Journal* that went into the mail on the same day as the hearing on Chief Justice James C. Adkins's grand jury suspension order reported an interview in which the chief justice spoke bitterly of criticism from lawyers and the press:

> We on the court realize that many of the Florida newspapers would like to have a Florida Watergate if they could. Lawyers aren't too popular anyway and I don't think the courts are too popular, particularly after our freedom of the press decision. Consequently, we have been subjected to criticism and accusations—unwarranted—and anything we do is magnified in the hopes that it will bring something down on the court.[1]

The reference to Watergate was to the obstruction of justice scandal that would compel President Richard M. Nixon's resignation a few weeks later. The "freedom of the press decision" was Orwellian doublespeak: Adkins had in mind the court's 6-1 decision the year before that severely limited press freedom in Florida. The ruling upheld an arcane state law requiring a newspaper to print uncut and unedited "any reply" submitted by a political candidate whom it attacked. Joseph Boyd, the dissenter, objected: "To the extent that government limits or adds to that which a publisher must distribute, freedom of speech and freedom of the press are thereby diminished."[2] The U.S. Supreme Court unanimously reversed the Florida court in June 1974, after the *Bar Journal* had interviewed Adkins but before the article was published. The Florida law, wrote Chief Justice Warren Burger, "fails to clear the barriers of the First Amendment because of its intrusion into the function of editors."[3]

At about the same time, Adkins sent a letter rebuking the Florida Bar for giving awards to two newspapers that had written critically of his court. The newspapers were the *St. Petersburg Times* and the *Tallahassee Democrat,* whose writer, Larry Nichols, had reported that the court had overlooked a new state law in ruling that men could not be rape victims. Adkins complained that the Bar should not have credited Nichols's article for the court reversing its own ruling. As for the other object of his wrath, "The unjust accusations of the *St. Petersburg Times* have not been substantiated and no justice of this court has been reprimanded for misconduct," he wrote, adding that "the Florida Bar should not invite adverse publicity by dangling an award as bait for some overzealous, irresponsible investigative reporter." The letter came to light six months later, after the Judicial Qualifications Commission had recommended that Dekle and Boyd be removed from office.[4]

When Adkins complained to the *Bar Journal* about media coverage of his court, worse was soon to come. On September 4, a front-page article in the *Miami Herald* and *Tallahassee Democrat* accused the court of covering up the receipt and use of Mason's memorandum in the Gulf Power case. The article conclusively identified Mason as the source. "There should have been an immediate investigation," Adkins conceded to the reporters. "The court never made any request that anybody look into it. . . . I think frankly the thing got out of hand at the very beginning." The article also revealed tension within the court, with Boyd complaining of hostility on the part of other justices who blamed him for the entire Mason episode. B. K. Roberts and Adkins, the newspapers said, were gossiping about Boyd's recent visit to the prestigious Ochsner Clinic in New Orleans—where Roberts had suggested he seek treatment—"in such a way as to hint that it was for either psychiatric care or a nervous breakdown." Moreover, the article speculated that the "court majority, led by Roberts and Adkins," was actively supporting Boyd's election opponent, Rivers Buford Jr., and Arthur J. England Jr.'s opponent, Sam Spector.

Boyd held a press conference just before the primary election to accuse Roberts of tricking him into going to the hospital. Roberts, he claimed, told his family that other justices would no longer sit with him unless he submitted to mental and physical examinations. Boyd attributed the hostility not to his complex role in the Mason affair but to his dissents regarding the Market Connection, O'Malley grand jury, and *Miami Herald* cases. "I dissented so many times apparently some people would like for me to leave the court," he said.[5]

Boyd's most recent dissent was in yet another politically charged case in which the majority frustrated Askew's plan to appoint Ervin's successor and ordered the seat put up for election. Roberts had been "grandfathered" when the constitution was amended in 1956 to require judges to retire at age seventy, but the privilege had never been extended to Ervin, necessitating his retirement by January 26, 1975. Ervin chose instead to resign effective January 6, the beginning date of three other Supreme Court terms. His purpose was to require an election for his seat instead of an appointment through the new merit-selection process. Although Ervin unquestionably had misgivings about who might succeed him, he strongly preferred an elected judiciary to a selection process influenced by lawyers. He feared that appointments would be controlled by silk-stocking Bar leaders who disdained liberal dissenters. "Mark my words," he told Sharyn Smith. "Someday we're going to have a bunch of bland people on the court, people who are afraid to take risks. . . . I couldn't get past that group. My brother wouldn't vote for me."[6]

Reubin Askew, supported by an attorney general's opinion, insisted that it was his duty to appoint Ervin's successor. A test case developed when Spector, a judge of the First District Court of Appeal, filed campaign papers and the secretary of state rejected them. Spector appealed directly to the Supreme Court for an order allowing him to run. It appeared to Askew and the attorney general that the situation was a set-up. The court would not decide the case before the deadline for candidates to qualify. Should it rule in Spector's favor without reopening the filing period, Spector would become Ervin's successor by default. Someone on the court, perhaps a clerk or Ervin himself, confided to the attorney general's office that such was the plan. Even from afar, at Miami, England needed no inside source to know how it would end. Anyone familiar with that court "could have predicted the outcome, too," he said.[7]

Spector was known to be close to Roberts. Earlier that year, in a decision typical of the First District's philosophy, Spector had written a controversial opinion that allowed Ed Ball to maintain a fence across a navigable river barring boaters from Wakulla Springs, a privately managed resort and tourist attraction near Tallahassee. Spector's two-paragraph opinion simply upheld the decision of a pro-Ball circuit judge and made no mention of a vast body of contradictory sovereignty land precedents.[8]

If there was a plan to anoint Spector as Ervin's successor, it was foiled when England submitted his own filing papers—like Spector's, they were refused—and intervened in Spector's suit. Unlike Spector, England argued in support of the governor and the attorney general that the vacancy mandated an appointment. But if there were to be an election, he asserted the right to run for it. The court seemed in no hurry to decide; it let more than a month elapse. This tended to confirm the rumors that it favored Spector. Given the difficulty in lining up support for any statewide race, the uncertainty would discourage other potential candidates. "I was anxiously counting the days," England recalled in our interview. "I remember saying, 'If I'm declared a candidate, how do I run, how do I raise money?'"

The court eventually ordered an election limited to two candidates, Spector and England. It gave no reasons; the written opinion would be issued long after the election. "Interim appointments need only be made when there is no earlier, reasonably intervening elective process available," Dekle wrote for himself, Adkins, Roberts, McCain, and a circuit judge sitting in for Ervin. Overton dissented without an opinion. Boyd wrote that he had "searched in vain" for anything in the constitution to support the majority interpretation. The outcome left unsettled whether the election winner would serve only the remaining four years of Ervin's term or six years of his own, and the majority refused England's postelection request to settle that question. He served for six years without challenge.[9]

It was the second nonpartisan judicial election—1972 was the first—under a law that Askew was delighted to sign, as it was identical to legislation of his that Kirk had vetoed in 1970.[10] Adkins was unopposed. Boyd won with 64 percent despite intense publicity over his role in *Gulf Power*. Overton had an even easier victory over Shelby Highsmith, a Miami lawyer, with 65 percent. In the race that was fought the hardest and was of most interest to the press, England scored a comfortable 58 percent over Spector. But it could have been much closer or even gone the other way had England lost the powerful condominium vote in Dade and Broward counties. He very nearly did.[11]

Large numbers of condominium voters usually voted as recommended by their association leaders. The most influential was the legendary Annie Ackerman, "queen of the condo commandos, a veritable vote machine and a force to be reckoned with in Democratic politics."[12] Ackerman and her committee invited England and Spector to a debate. Only England showed up, but just being there was not enough. As he recalled the events, "Annie called me about two weeks later and said, 'You know, Arthur, we really liked you and we liked what you had to say. But we're going to endorse Sam Spector.'" England was stunned. Why, he asked, when Spector had not cared enough for the endorsement to pay a visit? Ackerman said, "He's Jewish and you're not." England protested, "Annie, it's just the opposite." The normally astute condo commando had assumed incorrectly that Spector was Jewish and that Arthur England *Jr.* was not. Jewish tradition discourages naming an infant after any living person, but England was an exception. Informed of her error, Ackerman arranged for England to visit her board a second time to talk about personal information he had "neglected" to share on his first visit, "such as having been president of Temple Israel in Tallahassee." England carried Broward and Dade counties, where condominiums had the most influence, with 61.3 percent of the vote, slightly better than his statewide margin.[13]

It was a low-budget campaign, "run out of the recreation room in my house with my wife, my four kids mailing and stamping envelopes, with my secretary coming in at the end of the day," England told me. A licensed pilot, he rented an airplane and flew around the state to bar association meetings, newspaper editorial boards, and radio and television stations whose free interviews were the lifeblood of judicial campaigns. It was widely seen how great the stakes were, and England won all but a handful of the major newspaper endorsements. During the campaign, Askew confided to a reporter that he considered England's election as important as his own.

An open seat on the Florida Supreme Court was an uncommon opportunity, yet only two people sought to take advantage of it. A few months earlier, twenty-six lawyers and judges had applied to the nominating commission for the appointment to Vassar Carlton's vacancy. The difference owed only in part to a prevailing distaste for soliciting campaign contributions. The more significant reason was that lawyers typically feared to run and lose against justices before whom they would later take appeals. England, on the other hand, enjoyed a sense of immunity; he practiced federal tax law and did not depend for his livelihood on the good graces of any Florida state court. "I didn't have any particular concerns about my professional life in the event I ran against the Supreme Court's candidate and lost," he recalled.

Moreover, he would not run an Alphonse and Gaston campaign. Near the end, England accused Spector of violating both the election law and the Code of Judicial Conduct by attending a Republican club meeting where the party's candidate for governor was the featured speaker. England cited a decision of the Committee on Standards of Judicial Conduct, quoted in the July *Florida Bar Journal*, that admonished judges to avoid partisan meetings under all circumstances. Spector retorted that the committee was wrong and that England "shrieks the shrill sounds of the desperate." He denounced England as the "scrivener of Florida's income tax" and the candidate of the "McGovern wing" of Askew's staff.[14]

The difficulty of campaigning politically for what ought to be a nonpolitical office was evident to England during an event at Jacksonville that he attended with State Representative Bill Birchfield, a friend. Some "sour-looking fellow," England told me, wanted to know his position on capital punishment. England said he could not comment on any issue upon which he might have to rule.

> Birchfield heard what I said and he came over and put his arm around the guy and put on his best Mayo, Florida, accent and said, "Why are you asking him about that? Capital punishment is decided by the U.S. Supreme Court." This guy looked at Bill with a cold eye and said, "I'm damn sight glad to hear that, because I sure don't like the way he feels about it." After, Bill came over to me and said, "You don't have to come back to Jacksonville. We'll handle this from here."

To some surprise, England carried Jacksonville, the largest constituency in Spector's appellate district.[15]

⊰ 10 ⊱

Like Calling Walter Cronkite

B. K. Roberts was a grumpy witness on November 7, 1974, his dignity offended by a subpoena for a deposition in the Judicial Qualifications Commission's secret investigation of the Mason affair. He wanted the commissioners to know he would have appeared voluntarily. He suspected—citing the "rumor mill"—that he was being made a witness only so that "I might be disqualified in sitting on final judgment." If that was what someone wanted, it was necessary only to ask. Both sides needed his testimony, but it turned out to be Boyd's defense attorney whose subpoenas eventually sidelined both Roberts and Adkins from ruling on the fates of Boyd and Dekle. Of the remaining justices, only Ervin participated, but Roberts, Adkins, McCain, and Overton would select the judges to sit in their places. The apparently arbitrary manner of the selection and the decisions the substitutes reached would result in impeachment proceedings in the legislature, passage of yet another constitutional amendment, Dekle's resignation, McCain's resignation, and a virtual revolution at the court.[1]

Roberts testified to the JQC that he cloistered himself and his staff in the south wing of the Supreme Court building, where the only other chambers were Ervin's, and he was among the last people in Florida to know about the Mason intrigue or anything else transpiring on the far side of the rotunda. This was amusing to anyone familiar with his influence over the court. What concerned him most about the Mason matter, he said, was the leakage to the press. "I thought that the two research aides should be fired that day," he said. "I still think so. They both confessed to what I consider to be a heinous offense, and I thought they should be fired and disciplinary action taken against them by the Florida Bar."[2]

Roberts described to the JQC a chance meeting he had had with me while I was waiting to ask the judges who had been on the Gulf Power panel about the evidence of *ex parte* lobbying. His reaction:

> We were having a lot of problems with security in the building; in fact, I was learning things outside the building about what was going on in the court that I did not know inside the building, and there could be little doubt that what we had some unfaithful people in the building that were feeding confidential information to the outside world. So I became very interested in knowing who that might be and so I took some interest in it.[3]

Roberts testified that Vassar Carlton, the chief justice at the time, asked him and Adkins to find out who had leaked the Dekle-to-McCain document, that Roger Schwartz and David LaCroix confessed to copying it, and that he had tried to have them fired on the spot.

Boyd's attorney, W. Dexter Douglass, was intrigued by the emphasis. Was there, he asked, "no investigation concerning the substance of the memo conducted by you and Judge Adkins?" In other words, did it not concern them that someone might have been lobbying *ex parte*? "No, sir, that was not within our assignment," Roberts replied. "Our assignment was to try to determine who had committed the offense." The offense, as he saw it, was not Mason's lobbying. It was not Dekle's willingness to be lobbied. It was not even Boyd's destruction of potential evidence. It was, rather, the *lèse majesté* of the two young men who had bared the court's secrets to the people of Florida. In the same vein, Adkins testified that he had been unconcerned over Dekle's use of Mason's draft opinion because "it covered the same matters that was [*sic*] in the briefs and correctly stated the law."[4]

Roberts confirmed that he had cajoled Boyd to enter the Ochsner Clinic, but he said he did so only because Boyd's secretary, Elizabeth Potts, had confided that Boyd was "acting very strange," looked very pale and weak, and said things that Roberts understood to be "completely illogical." According to Roberts, Potts reported that she had found in Boyd's desk drawer eleven bottles of different pain pills prescribed by "several different doctors." Roberts did not describe the story the way the *Herald* had. In his telling of it, there was no coercion, and he had asked the head of the clinic to admit Boyd to the internal medicine department rather then to neurology because "there are very few secrets anymore and it would get out somewhere and hurt him in his campaign."[5]

Roberts also disclosed that in February he had tried to tempt Boyd to leave the court and run for secretary of state, an office where he "would be happier." Over lunch, he said, he told Boyd "that's the second place in the Cabinet, it's a place of distinction, the work is not hard and if you wanted to get into that job I think you would run away with it." By that time, Boyd was resented by most of the other justices because of the disclosure of Dekle's memorandum to McCain, which they attributed to Boyd's research aide, Schwartz.[6]

Potts confirmed separately in a deposition that she had seen Boyd gulping "handfuls of pills" and was concerned about his health. She said that Boyd told her that Dekle was going to shoot them all. "The aide writes all the opinions," she said. "I don't believe since I have been there he [Boyd] has written an opinion. He has dictated a few dissents to me."[7] By then the JQC had heard enough to order Boyd to submit to a mental and physical examination at the University of Florida's Shands Hospital. But if there were JQC members who hoped to retire him from office on account of a disability, they were disappointed. Having consulted a psychiatrist of his own choice at the University of Miami Medical School, Boyd returned with a report from Dr. James N. Sussex, who had concluded that although Boyd was "tense during the interview and revealing an undercurrent of depression," the justice showed "no signs whatsoever of any mental or emotional disorder." The doctor added that Boyd "is a highly scrupulous and meticulous, almost overly conscientious, person who, in spite of his long experience in the political arenas, is probably more vulnerable to criticism than he likes to believe." Confronted with Sussex's findings, the JQC dropped the disability charge on the eve of Boyd's trial.[8]

Having formally charged both Dekle and Boyd with conduct unbecoming a judge in regard to the Mason intrigue, the JQC also notified Dekle that it was reopening the Fitzpatrick affair. Dekle's attorney, Robert M. Ervin—a brother of Justice Ervin—complained to Richard Earle that the chairman had left him with the impression that the case was over. He wrote that he had been attempting for ten months to obtain a copy of the hearing transcript. Earle replied by explaining what had happened but without saying how individual JQC members had voted. John T. Wigginton, the JQC's general counsel, told Ervin that he could not inspect the official minute book because it "contains a multitude of information concerning and references to other investigations, which under our rules must be held confidential."[9]

So, ironically, Dekle had become a victim of the secrecy that he had assumed would protect him. Even so, he refused to open to the public the commission's proceedings in his case as Kelly had done and Boyd was about to do.

On November 5, voters ratified the constitutional amendment inspired by the whitewash decision in *Turner v. Earle,* to which Boyd had dissented. Now anything that a judge or justice might have done on the bench or in private life since 1966 could be considered by the Judicial Qualifications Commission as evidence of a "present unfitness to hold office."[10] Without that amendment, the new term Boyd would begin in January might have tolled an end to the JQC's investigation of his conduct in the Mason case. It had not occurred to Richard Earle or the legislators who sponsored his amendment that it might also be necessary to define "unfitness." The court would teach them that lesson soon enough.

Out of public sight, during a prehearing deposition, Dekle struggled to put the best possible face on the encounters with Mason. Dekle said Mason told him, "I prepared a memorandum for Justice Boyd. If your thinking turns out to be along that line, I would like to leave a copy with you." Dekle said he remembered the phrase, "because I thought to myself, this is a nice way to put it. He is not lobbying me, really, he is just leaving me a copy, if he is lucky enough for me to be with him, which I think is a nice way for an attorney to do." Mason *was* lobbying him, of course, and with those words Dekle confirmed that he had willingly received a document that could affect the outcome of a case without knowledge of the opposing side. He acknowledged that Carlton had instructed him to rewrite the draft opinion that his law clerk had prepared with the aid of Mason's document. "To me," he insisted, "there had been no impropriety." He complained that his redrafted opinion was not as good as the first.[11]

At a secret hearing in September, ten days before the JQC formally charged him, Boyd complained that "it is like World War II" and that people were trying to paint him as "the culprit in the Gulf Power matter." He rationalized that his initial discussion with Mason was justified. With the more senior justices out of the building for one reason or another, he was—or thought he was—acting chief justice when Mason called to ask about filling a supplemental brief. Boyd's account of what followed was dramatically and irreconcilably different from Mason's:

> At the end of the conversation, which I didn't tell him anything except to look up the rules and file the petition, which I would have told any lawyer in Florida, something was mentioned about we should play golf sometime. . . . We had played golf a few times, not nearly as many times as some of the newspapers would like to have you believe. . . . But there was one thing I did tell Mr. Mason and I am under oath and I want this emphasized. I said to him, "Don't bring over an order or a brief to me." That I said for sure. . . . The reason being I thought a matter as important as filing a brief after oral argument on a case involving countless millions of dollars ought to be handled at least by the chief justice or the full court. . . .
>
> Mr. Mason and I have played golf occasionally since he has been in Tallahassee and on the particular time in question, he came back by my house. . . . Mr. Mason drank a soft drink with me. I don't recall whether I went out to the vegetable garden to get vegetables or not, but I have a routine that I normally get the vegetables for just everybody that comes by. . . . It is nothing but an old tradition to get them vegetables. . . . .
>
> The next morning I picked up some files. . . . I had taken some files home from the court to work that night. . . . The Gulf Power file might have been with them or might not, I don't know. . . .
>
> Within a day or two after this visit with Mr. Mason, I noticed in the file the memorandum of law which I referred to in my previous affidavit. Now, if I had been trying to have any hanky-panky with the Gulf Power Company, those of you who know Roger Schwartz, with his talkative, constantly motivated attitude, would assume I would not be-ing [sic] calling in Roger Schwartz. It is like calling in Walter Cronkite and telling him about it, because Roger goes from one end of the building to the other telling everything he knows about everything and I am

under oath. . . . If I was doing something wrong, I wouldn't tell Roger Schwartz about it.[12]

Boyd confirmed to the JQC that he had instructed Schwartz to compare the document to the official file. It appeared to be "in the form of a proposed court opinion and this is what got me upset," he said. When Schwartz told him it was extraneous to the official record, "I felt suddenly that this is a matter of great importance . . . and I then swore him to secrecy, because I thought it was my duty as a state Supreme Court justice to look for and to prevent any type of impropriety within the court." He said he also told Schwartz to memorize the document "so if you ever see another copy of this thing, you can swear that it is an identical copy."[13]

But why had he destroyed it?

> I have told this story at least five thousand times, it seems, during the campaign. . . . Mr. Schwartz and I determined that if we kept in our possession this memorandum, then suddenly an opinion shows up down the hall, someone might then say, "Well, it came out of Joe Boyd's office."
>
> I used to be a confidential investigator and I have done a lot of law cases where there were people that could have been knocked off if my confidential notes had [not] been destroyed, so I learned early in my life that if you have something confidential and you don't need it anymore, destroy it, so in Mr. Schwartz's presence as a witness, I did indeed destroy the document.

But why had he not told the other justices? Anticipating the question, Boyd said it was "common knowledge that three or four of them" were under investigation by the JQC. Moreover, he had "reason through my research aide to think that certain justices were favorably inclined to go for Gulf Power." So, he said, "I just felt that the ends of justice could be better served if we would simply wait out time and I was, frankly, hoping that this thing would never come up again."[14]

When it did come up again, he said—when Schwartz told him about Dekle's "dissent"—he notified Roberts of the document he had found and destroyed and then told the *Times* because "we have eight million people in this here state and I think they are entitled to know what is going on in the Supreme Court." Of all the things he had ever done, including his service in the Marine Corps in World War II, "the single thing I am proudest of and least sorry for . . . is blowing the whistle in the Gulf Power case."

Because of that, he said, "I become persona non grata to most of my colleagues. I know now how Robinson Crusoe felt on that island." Moreover, he believed he was in "all kinds of trouble" with them because he had sided with the JQC in his dissent in *Turner v. Earle*. But now, he said, if the commission ruled against him, "I might as well start packing up, because I don't think I would last too long." Boyd did all but get on his knees to try to persuade the JQC to clear him. If he was allowed to remain on the court and take his turn as chief justice, he pleaded, he would do all he could to "give aid and assistance and cooperation to this fine commission."[15]

Under cross-examination, Boyd conceded that he was "convinced" that the document had come from Mason, but he insisted, "I simply did not have any memory of receiving it." Moreover, that might not have happened the day they played golf. It could have been smuggled into his office, an easy thing to do "when people find out what kind of medication I have in my desk drawers, and when I find little pieces of metal on the side of the telephone, which indicates to me my phone is bugged, when things disappear out of my file." And on second thought, the document might *not* have been inside the file when he first saw it. "It was probably on the outside of the file." When he was asked whether he had asked Mason for the document, Boyd swore that he had not.[16]

"So, at no time then do you feel that you instigated or suggested what might now be termed an impropriety?" asked James M. Talley, a newspaper publisher who was one of Askew's nonlawyer appointees on the JQC. "Absolutely. I tell you that I did not do that," Boyd replied. "It would be the most stupid thing any judge could do on that level."[17]

With his answers to subsequent questions, Boyd dug his own hole even deeper. Asked for his opinion of Mason's reputation for truthfulness and veracity, Boyd told the JQC, "I would say generally that Mr. Mason is a truthful man." It was possible, he added, that Mason "may have misunderstood" their conversation about a supplemental brief. Another JQC member asked whether they had discussed the case on the day that Boyd admitted they played golf. "I don't remember," Boyd replied. "I am not going to say he didn't. I don't remember what was said that day. I was not impressed by anything he was saying. If he was lobbying me, he was a very poor lobbyist." Boyd was asked why he had not reported the matter to the JQC himself once he realized that Dekle's opinion was similar to the document he had destroyed. Boyd said he had relied on Roberts's promise that he would "take it up with the court and there would be appropriate action."

Finally, Thomas M. Barkdull Jr., a First District Court of Appeal judge who had been on the JQC since its inception, reminded Boyd that he had recently voted on a revised Code of Judicial Conduct and that it required judges to report improprieties.

Boyd replied, "I was told by Justice Roberts that this would be taken care of——"

Barkdull interrupted. "That is not what the Canon says. Let me read it to you, Judge. 'A judge should take or initiate appropriate disciplinary measures against a judge or lawyer for unprofessional conduct of which the judge may become aware.'"[18]

Boyd said, "I think I initiated it by telling Judge Roberts and then I told the whole court about it and then I told Dyckman about it and that is like telling Walter Cronkite . . ."

Barkdull responded, "It would have been a lot better for us to hear it from somebody that knew the true facts of what happened than trying to read it in the newspaper."[19]

The sum of what Boyd had accomplished in an hour and forty minutes of testimony was to confirm that he had destroyed evidence of an improper attempt to influence the court, that he had defaulted on his duty to report it to the Florida Bar and the JQC, and that the principal outside witness against him, Mason, had a reputation for telling the truth.

Mason's account, as told in a subsequent deposition and on at least four witness stands, was that they had discussed the case during a golf game and it was made clear to Mason that Boyd would welcome advice in drafting the majority opinion. "I thought that it might be helpful if he had something along this line to assist him in articulating what the vote had been," he said. He described the time and care that went into the document, which he said he handed to Boyd in person at the justice's home before a second golf date, and about giving the second copy to Dekle.[20]

The commission formally charged Boyd and Dekle, in separate cases, with conduct unbecoming a judge in regard to *Gulf Power v. Bevis.*

Boyd invoked his right to a public trial before the JQC. In so doing, he said that the JQC had also charged him with having a disability. "I don't know whether it's fallen arches or my hair turning gray too soon," he said.

"They don't tell me whether it is emotional, physical, mental, moral, or some other thing." (In fact, Boyd had already been notified this would not be an issue in the forthcoming trial.) The charges overall were so vague, he said, that "if I were anything but a Supreme Court justice I would have filed a suit in the Supreme Court or the U.S. District Court to quash the whole thing. Personally, I'd like to see all eight million people in Florida show up at the hearing."[21]

Public Trial, Secret Trial

F ar short of attracting eight million people, Boyd's trial was not even the
biggest draw for Tallahassee's legal community that week. A command
appearance for most lawyers and judges was the rededication of the building
that housed the Florida State University College of Law, which the legislature
had renamed in honor of B. K. Roberts. "I told Justice Roberts I was sorry I
couldn't attend," Boyd remarked with transparent sarcasm. "I was occupied
elsewhere."[1]

Those who chose the Judicial Qualifications Commission proceeding over
the law school ceremony witnessed the most dramatic day of Boyd's three-day
trial on charges of violating the *ex parte* rule, destroying evidence, default-
ing on his duty to report Mason's "improper and unethical conduct" to the
Florida Bar, and failing to warn the JQC or the court itself of "judicial misconduct" by another justice. Boyd denied under oath that he had accepted or
sought the document from Mason or that he was even certain of Mason as
the source. That contradicted Mason's testimony on four significant points.
Mason swore that he had not telephoned Boyd to ask how to file a supplemental brief, that they discussed the case during a game of golf, that Boyd
agreed to his assistance, and that when he delivered the finished document
to Boyd, "I handed it to him, I identified what it was, and he accepted it."[2]

Mason, the leadoff witness, testified on the trial's first day that he and Boyd
discussed the case over golf after Mason had heard "common gossip" at the
Public Service Commission that the court had voted in his favor. "I'm sorry I

can't tell you how the discussion of this case came up," he said. "I don't know if he brought it up or I did. We discussed this Gulf Power case, the complexity of it, how the governor had been involved. . . . I don't know whether he asked or I offered. . . . I do have the distinct recollection it was understood I would put together an outline, a memorandum, call it what you want, that would assist in articulating the position the court had agreed to take." Had Boyd been a circuit or county court judge, he could properly have asked for a draft decision from an attorney for the prevailing party so long as the other side was aware of it and allowed to critique it. This was emphatically *not* the practice in Florida appellate courts, although Mason said it was commonplace at the Public Service Commission.

At the insistence of Boyd's attorney, Richard Earle reluctantly allowed Andrew G. Pattillo Jr., the JQC's prosecutor, to question Mason about his contacts with Dekle, whose secret trial was to follow Boyd's. Mason told of taking a copy of the Petteway document to Dekle because "he had asked certain penetrating questions from the bench, he had indicated a unique understanding." Mason said he "simply told him I had given a copy of this to Justice Boyd . . . and thought he might like to have a copy, and I left him a copy."[3]

Boyd, who had objected that the entire trial was unconstitutional and threatened to appeal all the way to the U.S. Supreme Court, said he was being made a "sacrificial lamb for the utility companies of this state." During Mason's testimony, the *St. Petersburg Times* reported, Boyd "sat tight-lipped, staring intently at his former friend and smiling sardonically once or twice." During his turn on the witness stand, Boyd admitted only one key element of the charges: that he had destroyed the document. "I personally tore it into seventeen equal parts and flushed it," he said. Schwartz confirmed the incident and said that Dekle's subsequent opinion resembled the document Boyd had destroyed "word for word."[4]

Boyd's secretary, Elizabeth Potts, testified that he "told me several times he had asked Mr. Mason for it and had received it either at his home or at the golf course." Boyd, she said, had cautioned her that her memory of the document consisting of five or six pages clashed with that of LaCroix and other witnesses who put it at thirteen or fourteen pages. In what she said she took to be a threat, she said Boyd told her, "You know, I represented some Mafia people . . . some of my very best clients were members of the Mafia." It was not the first time he had alluded to the Mafia, she said, "and I felt it was a very threatening statement." She also reiterated her previously secret testimony to the JQC that Boyd "kept telling me Judge Dekle was going to shoot me, going to shoot him, going to shoot the aide [Schwartz]." Potts, who had also testified that Schwartz referred to Boyd as "Justice Fundamental Dumbness," said she expected to be fired. "You should be," retorted Boyd's attorney, W. Dexter Douglass, who was overruled when he tried to question Potts about health and personal financial problems. During his turn on the stand, Boyd categorically denied telling Potts that he had asked Mason for the document or knew him to be the source. "The State of Florida furnished the best research assistance available," he said. "I don't need Ed Mason to write a court opinion for me.... Betty dreamed that story up.... Seriously, nobody in this room believes that if I made a solicitation I'd go and tell people about it. She's not reliable. She's had more personal problems than anybody I've ever known personally in fifty-eight years of my life."[5]

Boyd fired Potts four days after the testimony that he described as her "farewell address." He taped that confrontation and called in his new research aide to witness it. Potts took it philosophically, saying she would have quit sooner, but "I felt sorry for him and tried to protect him all these many months. That's a secretary's job."[6]

Closing testimony from B. K. Roberts and James Adkins confirmed what the newspaper exposés had insinuated. Alerted to a serious violation of the ethics that supposedly circumscribed the relationship of lawyers and judges, Florida's highest court was alarmed only that it had been disclosed to the public. Three other justices—Vassar Carlton, Roberts, and Adkins—were informed of what Mason, Boyd, and Dekle had done, but although they took steps to sanitize the *Gulf Power* decision, none undertook to alert the Bar or the JQC, despite their obligations under the Code of Judicial Conduct. Adkins, who had succeeded Carlton as chief justice on March 1, testified that he did nothing between December, when he had learned from Boyd about Dekle's use of the document, and a time subsequent to March 1 when he heard that an investigator for the JQC was on the case. At that time, he testified, he talked with Mason because it was "important to say we at least made some effort to clean our own house."

As Boyd's attorney saw it, the ethical indifference of the court was Boyd's best defense. If the JQC were to find him at fault, Douglass argued, "You would have to reprimand every member of the court and a lot of members of the Bar, because we all, about the same time, were aware of what did happen." To the JQC's prosecutor, a soft-spoken lawyer from Ocala, the trial was a landmark. The mere fact that it took place should restore confidence in the Bar that "the other fellow will have no other means" to win, Pattillo said.[7]

A cloud of concern over favoritism toward the "other fellow" had hovered over the court during several eras that most lawyers hoped had been consigned to history. In the 1930s, Justice Glenn Terrell taught a men's Bible class at an air-conditioned theater in Tallahassee, often attended by other justices and many local attorneys. Out-of-town lawyers, on the other hand, "came to look upon them far differently than did the justices involved," wrote Florida Supreme Court historians Walter Manley II and Canter Brown Jr.[8] There had been the widespread perception that Ed Ball enjoyed special access to the court through his friends Adams and Roberts. Now, however, there was more to it than generalized misgivings. There were proven offenses and cases coming to a judgment that could not be avoided or deferred.

The cases against Dekle, although still officially confidential, were the worst-kept secrets in anyone's memory. Most newspapers reported as fact that Dekle had a one-day trial—unlike Boyd's, it was a case "without factual issue," according to Pattillo—the day after Boyd's ended. The *Tampa Tribune* and Gannett newspapers divulged the fact that it was Dekle's second trial and that there had been no outcome to the first because a JQC minority had insisted on nothing more severe than a secret reprimand. Dekle refused to open the second trial to the public despite the urging of JQC members who considered the secrecy absurd in light of Boyd's public hearing, which had ended the day before. Earle had obtained an order from Adkins declaring part of the Supreme Court building entirely off limits to the public and press; for the order to remain in force the day after Boyd's trial ended was tantamount to a billboard declaring that Dekle's was under way. "If it's got to be confidential," Earle remarked, "it's going to be confidential." The area barred to the public was large enough to allow witnesses to come and go without being seen and identified by journalists staking out the premises.[9]

There would be no inconclusive verdicts this time. The JQC swiftly found Boyd and Dekle guilty of misconduct in the Gulf Power case and recommended that they forfeit their offices. Despite Robert Ervin's protest, the JQC reconsidered the stalemate in the Fitzpatrick case and recommended Dekle's ouster in that regard as well. That had the effect of opening the files on both confidential Dekle cases as required under the constitution. These were, however, recommendations only. The decisions in each case, according to the constitution, would be made by the Supreme Court—the same court that had been offended not by the ethical violations but by their disclosure to the public. Moreover, the architects of the Judicial Qualifications Commission had not thought to provide for the inevitable conflicts of interest in the event that any of the justices themselves were on trial. Universal legal principles resolved some (but not all) of those issues. Boyd and Dekle obviously could not judge their own cases. Neither could Roberts and Adkins, who had been witnesses. McCain recused himself as well, the court said, because he was as "familiar with the facts" as Roberts and Adkins. That left only Overton, who had not been on the court when the scandal brewed, and Ervin, who had not taken part in *Gulf Power* except to sign Boyd's dissent when it was mistakenly sent to him. At that, Ervin could participate in only the cases involving Gulf Power because his brother was Dekle's lawyer in the Fitzpatrick matter. But to considerable surprise—amounting to consternation on the part of Earle and his allies—Adkins announced that he, McCain, and Roberts would help select the visiting judges who would sit in judgment on their colleagues and, in effect, on the court itself.[10]

⇥ 12 ⇤

A Politician First . . . a Justice Second

Ben Overton, the new justice whom the governor intended to reform the Supreme Court, was sidelined for the historic cases that exposed the court's flaccid ethics. Not saying why, Dekle asked Overton to recuse himself. Not asking why, Overton complied. Overton assumed that Dekle doubted his impartiality and conceded that the Canons of Judicial Conduct entitled Dekle to exclude him. "There was plenty to do," Overton recalled, since Dekle and Boyd were abstaining from all other cases while theirs were pending.[1]

Of the five living former justices, only three were eligible to sit on the special panels. E. Harris Drew, who was sitting in for Boyd and Dekle on other cases and was renowned for his personal and professional ethics, declined to judge them. That left only Richard Ervin and Alto Adams, the justice who had been patronized by Edward Ball and who counted David McCain as a protégé. Active judges were available at all four district courts of appeal, but the court chose only Dewey Johnson, who had been a Pork Chop Senate president and had participated in the First District's controversial disposition of the first Floyd Christian indictments. Four circuit judges rounded out the panels for the *Gulf Power* cases, with a fifth replacing Ervin in the Fitzpatrick matter. Harvie S. DuVal of Miami, the replacement for another circuit judge who had fallen ill, was as noteworthy a choice as Adams and Johnson because of old political ties to B. K. Roberts. It would turn out a year later that DuVal's own ethics were questionable.[2]

The Judicial Qualifications Commission, meanwhile, asked Ervin to step aside altogether, which he refused to do. The JQC then filed a motion asking that its two cases against Dekle be treated as one. That would have disqualified Ervin due to his brother's representation in the Fitzpatrick case, but the special panel overruled the motion.[3]

The question of who should be judging whom became even more confused when Arthur England's term began on January 7. Although he was ineligible to judge the *Gulf Power* issues as a victim of the *ex parte* contacts, England could have served on the Fitzpatrick case panel. He did not, perhaps because the legal pleadings had already begun. Despite Boyd's dissent in *Turner v. Earle*, Douglass argued that Boyd's case should be dismissed on the premise that his new term erased any liability for conduct occurring previously. It was the first test of the constitutional amendment, inspired by the Turner case, which provided grounds for investigation of a judge's conduct "during term of office or otherwise" that demonstrates "a present unfitness to hold office." The special panel denied the motion without explanation on January 6 and set final arguments in all the cases for January 28. As those were pending, the Florida Bar's Board of Governors formally charged Mason with unethical conduct in *Gulf Power*, creating yet another case in which the court would eventually have to rule.[4]

In the opinion of some of the Bar's leaders, the Supreme Court had been systematically too lenient in lawyer discipline. They were beginning to complain to the press about it. A published survey showed that the court had reduced or ruled out the Bar's recommended penalties in nineteen of forty-one cases contested by accused lawyers over a two-year period. One involved a public official accused of forgery whom the Bar wanted publicly censured; the court approved only a private reprimand for "John Doe."[5] The attorneys for Dekle and Boyd invoked this history in motions before the special panels in which they argued that if the court disbarred lawyers only for serious crimes and flagrant corruption, a justice should not be expelled for anything less. There was no "clear and convincing" proof, they said, that Dekle had knowingly violated the judicial canons. Douglass, conceding in "hindsight" that Boyd should have reported Mason's document to the chief justice rather than destroy it, stressed that the JQC had found no "corrupt motive" for Boyd's conduct. A justice, he said, should be expelled only on the same grounds for which lawyers had been disbarred: "severe transgressions which either constituted acts of dishonesty being a felony, or a series of acts of dishonesty and moral turpitude which were the equivalent." In a 71-page brief, Dekle's counsel urged dismissal of the Fitzpatrick case on the premises that too much time had elapsed without judgment, that Dekle had intended no wrong, and that he and his family already had paid "an immeasurable price for said indiscretion by two years of personal agony and suffering."[6]

In the JQC's arguments and briefs, Pattillo contended that Boyd's destruction of the Mason document "admits of no question that his was a guilty mind" and that he should forfeit his office because "no other action will vindicate the honor of the judicial system of Florida or restore public confidence in the integrity of its highest court." As for Dekle, he said, the justice "can hardly complain that his name and reputation will suffer by his removal from the office which his own conduct has dishonored." To allow Dekle to remain would inform the public "that this court deems unimportant the claim of the people to an unbiased and utterly impartial judiciary."[7]

To underscore the significance of Mason's *ex parte* activity, Andrew Pattillo told the special panels that the Dekle opinion based on Mason's draft had influenced Adkins to change his vote. "No one questions the impropriety of an *ex parte* communication by one side to a lawsuit," Pattillo pleaded. "It is a standard so well recognized it stands beside the Ten Commandments and all other standards by which we live." To vindicate Dekle would "give to every unscrupulous lawyer the opportunity to impose his influence on a judge without giving the judge any responsibility to protect the judiciary," Pattillo urged in his final argument. But questions from the bench during an unprecedented six hours of oral argument hinted that Dekle and Boyd's jobs were not in jeopardy. Ervin remarked that Mason's memorandum "wasn't coupled with any corruptions like a bribe." Adams, presiding at the time, told both sides to submit comments on a recent New York decision that he said forbade the expulsion of a judge for an ethical violation unaccompanied by "corruption." In his view, "corruption" meant money or other valuables more tangible than the reputation of a court for fair dealing. The commission's argument that there should be a higher standard for judges than for other politicians was falling on minds that were already made up.[8]

Four days later, the panels dismissed the Fitzpatrick case against Dekle and ordered only reprimands for Boyd and Dekle in regard to *Gulf Power*. Dekle came within one vote of escaping even the reprimand. DuVal, Adams, and Johnson—a quintessential "old guard"—held that there was no "clear and convincing evidence . . . to find him guilty of a specific major act involving any degree of corruption or willful violation of the law sufficient to warrant discipline." Adams, Johnson, DuVal, and two circuit judges formed the bloc to dismiss the Fitzpatrick case, ruling that "once the Commission has taken all their evidence and formally voted according to their rules and regulations, that . . . should spell an end to the matter unless there is a reason shown why it should be deferred or further evidence is taken." The dissenters, who said the case ought to be decided on the merits, were Circuit Judges Ernest Mason of Pensacola and Parker Lee McDonald, a future Supreme Court justice, of Orlando.[9]

Ervin, McDonald, Mason, and Circuit Judge James T. Nelson of Daytona Beach reprimanded Dekle in the *Gulf Power* case. Among their conclusions:

> There is no evidence that Justice Dekle personally profited in any way in the matter or that he was bribed in any way to use the ex parte memorandum. It does not appear that the Mason memo changed his mind about the case or that it was materially different in content from the properly filed briefs of the power company. . . .
>
> We are unable from all the circumstances to infer that his action in connection with the memorandum reflects willful and deliberate corrupt misconduct. . . .
>
> We do agree that he was lax, obtuse and insensitive in either not recognizing the memo was improper when Mason gave it to him or was not intuitive or anticipatory enough then or later on to have had the memo checked out to determine if it was proper for him to use it. Despite his protestations, the very nature of the affair smacks of the appearance of evil damaging to the State's judiciary at its top echelon . . . .
>
> Except for the fact there is no clear showing of corrupt motive or deliberate or intentional wrong, we would agree with the Commission's recommendation of the extreme discipline of removal. However, in view of the rationale analogously embedded in attorney disbarment cases, we feel constrained to stay our hand in this inquiry under the particular circumstances . . . .
>
> We take notice that Justice Dekle has authored many important opinions for the Supreme Court. . . . His contributions to the body of

the law have been notable and outstanding. . . . His status as an outstanding jurist for several years past must be considered in the overall picture herein and taken into consideration. . . .

[W]e find Justice Dekle guilty of impropriety and laxness and we publicly reprimand him therefore. . . but find him not guilty of corrupt motive."[10]

There were few kind words, however, in the panel's scathing verdict on what it called Boyd's "bumblingly bizarre" conduct. Six judges—DuVal, Ervin, Johnson, McDonald, Mason, and Nelson—voted to reprimand him. The seventh, Adams, wanted him kicked off the court. The majority was reluctant to find that Boyd knowingly received the document from Mason because Killearn Country Club records verified that the two played golf only once, not twice. In that regard the JQC was unable to substantiate a key point in Mason's testimony. Adams, however, said he was persuaded that Boyd "solicited the document in question, showed every indication of using it until suspicion occurred, and then destroyed it." As far as Adams was concerned, Mason told the truth and Boyd lied. Moreover, a judge *should* be held to a higher ethical standard than a lawyer. "The client can choose his lawyer, but the judge is chosen for him," Adams wrote.

The majority opinion, issued *per curiam* so as to identify no author, was most likely Ervin's draftsmanship. It went to lengths to rationalize Boyd's conduct without excusing it. Boyd was afraid of any scandal because he intended to run for reelection, it said, and there was "some support of Boyd's fears of leaks and rumors in the Court." He had been ill, his father was dying, and the justice "was unquestionably under considerable mental worry and pressure." He was often a dissenter on the Court and imagined that it created enemies in the Court. "No doubt these were figments of his imagination but still his mental attitude may explain his rather bizarre behavior in destroying the memo," the opinion said.

A more rationally oriented individual probably would have taken another tact [*sic*] than did Justice Boyd in respect to the Mason memo. . . . Certainly his opinions in the power company case do not square with an inference that he intended to use or did use the ex parte memorandum to side with the power company. . . .

Although Boyd's "trap" play was bumblingly bizarre, it did lead to public exposure of the Mason memo via his confiding in Schwartz, who brought in LaCroix, who in turn informed Carlton of the "striking re-semblance" of the memo to the Dekle dissent and set the stage for the leak of the Dekle to McCain interoffice memo to the press and the resulting furor and this inquiry. Boyd's ploy set in motion a train of events that produces an inference inconsistent with clear and convincing proof of guilty intent.

In retrospect or hindsight, it may be concluded Justice Boyd used execrably bad judgment in not immediately reporting to the Chief Justice and other members of the Court the mysterious appearance in his office of the ex parte memo and in destroying it. It was his duty to divulge it, to disown it openly and forthrightly. It was his duty not to destroy the memo, since it constituted the best evidence of its existence and contents—and was the most significant piece of evidence he had denoting an act of impropriety. We cannot condone his failure, in these respects, however much we sympathize with him because of the pressures upon him and his fears at the time.[11]

The majority considered Boyd a "friendly, affable fellow" who "sought to please the public and impress others, who at the time had an "excitable personality indicating an intellectual incapacity to cope with the responsibilities of his office," and who had been trying to postpone the core issues in *Gulf Power* (that is, whether the public or the stockholders would pay the tax) until after the election. At that point, the opinion made a remarkable concession: "This tends to substantiate the fear expressed indirectly in the Commission's recommendations that some decisions are being reached by political, rather than purely legal considerations." In that regard, "Justice Boyd's conduct has caused concern that he is a politician first, and a justice second—rather than the other way around." The same could have been said of other justices involved in *Gulf Power*.

But the panel could find no "clear and convincing" proof that Boyd was dishonest, "corrupt or venal, or that he accepted any bribe." Nor was it "clear and convincing" that Boyd had planned to use the Mason document until something or someone frightened him out of it. Although judges should be held "to even stricter ethical standards" than lawyers, "they too should not be subject to the extreme discipline of removal except in instances where it is free from doubt that they intentionally committed serious and grievous wrongs of a clearly unredeeming nature."

Citing Boyd's dissent in *Turner*—"Those who cannot stand the bright light of public scrutiny should not hold judicial office"—the majority remarked, "Perhaps one's views on that may be dependent on whether he is shining the light or whether the light is shining on him. That light now shines on Justice Boyd." But to do more than reprimand him "would be too extreme"; it would "leave us with the unresolved but lurking suspicion that in view of the doubt as to his guilt of corrupt motive, we would possibly be making him a tragic martyr—a suspicion that would be difficult for us to live with in good conscience."[12]

Although they were now the first Florida judges ever officially reprimanded for unethical behavior—a stain that like every other appellate decree would be on record forever—Dekle and Boyd hailed the outcomes as victories for them. Compared to the alternative of removal, that was true. Neither appeared, however, to contemplate the potential political price.

"I feel vindicated," Dekle declared, describing himself as "perfectly happy" and confident of reelection the next year. "I anticipate trouble only with big paper editors like yours," he told this author, "and with over-eager prejudicial reporters." A day later, however, he conceded that he had committed a "procedural wrong" by accepting Mason's document. "I'm sorry for it. I took my beating—it was a good one. I think I'll be a better judge for it," he said. But in the same breath Dekle said he had been the victim of a "wicked vendetta" by the press and the commission and insinuated that someone, perhaps Governor Askew, was trying to pack the court. "When you see a packing of the cabinet, the next thing is a packing of the court," he said. To some, it sounded as if Dekle was faulting the governor for the ongoing corruption investigations that would be seriously impaired by the court's forthcoming decision in the Floyd Christian case. Dekle did admit to learning one other lesson: that all JQC proceedings should be open to the public once probable cause was found to proceed against a judge. "Nothing could be worse than what I've been through in a semi-private, semi-secret situation where I did not know whether I was coming or going," he said. Ervin and Adkins endorsed the change, which the JQC was already proposing to the legislature.

Boyd's remarks were uncharacteristically restrained. He would not say whether he thought the outcome was fair, but he was pleased that his panel refused to conclude that he had lied about asking or agreeing to receive the document from Mason. After thinking about it for another day, he said he was "totally unimpressed" by the reprimand.[13]

The decisions were not a total loss for Earle and the JQC. There were now precedents that an appellate judge must "disown" any *ex parte* communication "openly and forthrightly." A judge in a multi-judge court must report to his colleagues and "others in authority"—meaning the Bar and JQC—any improper attempt to influence him. Most important, a justice—and by extension any judge—could be reprimanded or removed for misconduct in a prior term. The *Turner* precedent was now only a footnote to history. But because the Fitzpatrick case had been dismissed, there was no lodestar on what to do about a judge—such as McCain—who tried to fix a case in an inferior court.

Earle and the JQC were far more concerned by the new requirement that only a "corrupt motive" could justify the removal of a judge. Earle may have had McCain in mind; the same edition of the *St. Petersburg Times* that reported the Boyd and Dekle outcomes disclosed the JQC's interest in what seemed to be favoritism on McCain's part. His research aide, Anne M. Parker, had told the JQC that McCain, at the Fourth District Court of Appeal, had assigned her to research grounds for appealing a case that was not before him. When it eventually came to him at the Supreme Court, the lawyers' petition, which he voted to grant, resembled her research. Two of the lawyers involved had purchased McCain's Fort Pierce home a few years earlier, and the third was Farish, his acknowledged campaign supporter. Although Parker subsequently could not be certain of the similarity in documents, McCain's premature interest was noteworthy because the case involved lawyers with whom he had done personal business. There was no suggestion, however, of the sort of "corrupt motive"—such as money under the table—that would have to be proved to expel a justice under the Dekle and Boyd precedents. Meeting behind closed doors four days after those decisions were issued, the JQC voted to petition for rehearing. "It's almost impossible to prove the motive of a judge," Earle told the press. "And a judge shouldn't conduct himself, in my view, in a manner unbecoming a judge in order to achieve a good objective. The objective really doesn't matter. It's the conduct. The end doesn't justify the means, let's put it that way."[14]

There would be no rehearing. The panels had foretold the outcome of any such request by allowing the JQC only six days to file it. Ervin, however, remarked to the press that the precedent was not as confining as it seemed. "Under the same circumstances, with this warning, it's possible that removal might ensue," he said.[15]

Earle was not mollified. Once again he would ask the legislature to amend the constitution, this time to remove the "corrupt motive" hurdle that the panels had erected. Because the 1974 amendment had also empowered the JQC to adopt its own rules, it promptly put in place new regulations calculated to facilitate faster action on complaints against judges. It would now be optional rather than mandatory to notify judges who had become the target of an investigation or to offer them the opportunity to make a statement before the filing of formal charges.[16]

But if Dekle and Boyd had won a victory, it was truly of Pyrrhic proportions. There was widespread outrage in the media and in the Bar, and one JQC member, James M. Talley of Brooksville, urged the legislature to begin impeachment proceedings.[17] On February 6, The Orlando Sentinel-Star, charging editorially that the JQC process had failed because of a "bad supreme court that treats the judiciary and the legal profession as a private club," called on the legislature to dust off the impeachment process. The Miami Herald echoed the impeachment theme that day in an editorial that said judges should not be allowed to judge their own conduct. The Tampa Tribune, concerned that impeachment had proved to be "exceedingly cumbersome" and political, agreed on February 6 that there should be some process independent of the supreme court when justices were accused. The most "execrably bad judgment," it said, was that of the judges who found Boyd and Dekle still fit to sit on the Supreme Court.

Within a day of the special panels' decisions, Speaker Donald L. Tucker of the Florida House of Representatives announced that he was considering impeachment proceedings. Tucker, a lawyer himself, was aware of intense protests over the light punishments and the implication that a judge could be forgiven almost any breach of ethics short of accepting a bribe. Tucker met privately with Earle that weekend; yet another provision of the 1974 amendment gave the speaker access to the JQC's normally secret files. Six days after the decisions were published, Tucker appointed a select committee to undertake what had never been attempted before: impeachment proceedings against justices of the Florida Supreme Court.[18]

The Bar, meanwhile, pursued its own case against Mason. In language reminiscent of Dekle's explanation of wanting to help a constituent, Mason tried pleadingly to rationalize his having crossed the line for Boyd. "Gentlemen, as practicing attorneys," he said in an emotional personal appeal to the Board of Governors, "I solicit your sympathetic understanding of the position I was in and how to refuse a Supreme Court judge who needed assistance in preparing a draft opinion. . . . I am not an unethical lawyer. I only ask that you believe there was in fact a total absence of intent to do wrong."[19]

Dekle and McCain were gone when the court a year later suspended Mason's license to practice law for a year and ordered him to pay the Bar $8,479 for the costs of prosecuting him. With all but two of the justices disqualified for cause, five chief circuit judges chosen by seniority sat in their places. The decision adopted Bar referee Eli Subin's findings of guilt and recommended discipline on two counts, those concerning the improper contacts and Mason's failure to reveal them when England wrote to him in response to the first *St. Petersburg Times* article. The court quoted with approval what Subin had written:

This case has been the focus of statewide attention which is entirely justified by a record replete with proof of a threat to the integrity of the judicial branch. Although that threat has passed without having inflicted lasting damage on substantive Florida jurisprudence, it has impaired the public confidence in the Bar and in constitutional processes.

[Mason] has admitted without reservation that he communicated privately [ex parte] with justices of the Supreme Court of Florida concerning a pending case in which he and his clients had an interest. He has admitted to more than mere communication. He admits, and the proof shows, that he attempted to influence the Court's decision in a manner contrary to the Florida Appellate Rules, contrary to the traditions of the Bar, and contrary to what is the commonly accepted notion of equal and untampered justice. In fact, the Respondent's conduct is the antitheses of an independent judiciary, which Chief Justice Charles Evans Hughes envisioned as "weighing evidence in scales with which prejudice has not tampered," a judiciary that is a symbol of firmness "in resisting both solicitation and clamor."

[Mason's] conduct was so fundamentally wrong that there is scant precedent. . . . . The gravity of the proven offenses, and the Respondent's refusal to admit the plain fact that he actively concealed his wrongdoing negate the timeworn clichés that "he has learned his lesson," or "that he is unlikely to do it again," or that "he has already suffered degradation and humiliation in public proceedings." These facts, his past good record, and prospects for the future serve only to avoid disbarment.[20]

In the process, two of the Bar's original four charges were set aside for insufficient evidence, one by the referee and the other by the court. Those charges had accused Mason of not telling the truth about his reasons for discussing *Gulf Power* with Boyd and for preparing the document. Dismissing them meant that the issue of Boyd's alleged complicity would remain unresolved forever.

↤ 13 ↦

Dekle Resigns

Lawyers who feared that the special panel decisions undermined judicial ethics were offended by Boyd's remark that he was "totally unimpressed" and by Dekle's claim that he was "vindicated." The justices seemed to be saying that they had learned nothing. Simultaneously, Speaker of the House Donald Tucker announced that he was considering impeachment proceedings against Boyd and Dekle and against McCain as well.[1]

The court had not anticipated the swiftness or intensity of the political reaction, which reflected considerable public outrage. The opinions had been in print only six days when Tucker appointed a select committee to consider impeaching the justices. That development followed a closed-door briefing at Miami with Thomas Barkdull, a senior member of the JQC. The 1974 constitutional amendment prompted by the Turner decision gave the House speaker and the governor access to the commission's otherwise secret files "for use in consideration of impeachment or suspension, respectively."[2]

Now it was apparent that Barkdull and Richard Earle were encouraging impeachment proceedings that would spare the JQC the time, the expense, and—in light of the Dekle-Boyd decisions—the futility of perfecting charges against McCain. "They feel they had their teeth pulled," said a source—most likely a member of the commission—quoted anonymously by the *St. Petersburg Times*. Moreover, Tucker said the potential case against McCain "seems to be, may well be, more serious" in that there were implications of criminal conduct and that he would request the commission's files for use by the committee. Earle said that he could not disclose whether the JQC actually had any files on McCain, but he emphasized that Tucker would get whatever the commission could lawfully give him.

Tucker appointed Representative William J. "Billy Joe" Rish, a third-term Florida House member from Port St. Joe, to chair the impeachment committee. Rish was also chair of the House Judiciary Committee, which would be responsible for initiating legislation inspired by the impeachment hearings. In 1970, Rish had defeated an incumbent, John Robert Middlemas, whom one of the local newspapers denounced as "Middlemas the liberal" because of his popularity with the South Florida media. Rish proved to his skeptics that the liberal-conservative issue was irrelevant to judicial integrity. The other Select Committee members were Representatives Alan S. Becker of Miami, Richard S. Hodes of Tampa, John R. Forbes and Eric Smith of Jacksonville, and Granville R. Crabtree of Sarasota. All but Hodes, a physician, were lawyers, and Crabtree was the only Republican.

Rish rejected the "corrupt motive" standard that the special panels had applied. "I don't think you have to find a payoff of money to find an impeachable offense," he said. He said the committee would also reopen the Fitzpatrick case, which was of particular importance to him because Fitzpatrick was a judge in his circuit. Rish said the committee was interested also in why the other justices did not report Mason to the Bar or Dekle and Boyd to the JQC.[3]

The board of directors of the Dade Bar Association, Florida's largest voluntary legal society, strongly advocated impeachment. The association elaborated in a letter to Rish that the conduct of Boyd and Dekle "has so seriously compromised the integrity of the Supreme Court of Florida that each of them should resign or be removed from office through impeachment proceedings." The letter charged that "fear of public scandal" motivated Boyd to destroy the Mason document and change his vote. It accused both Boyd and Dekle of engaging in a cover-up. One of the Dade Bar directors at the time was Janet Reno, the future attorney general of the United States in the Clinton administration.[4]

Not all the court's critics agreed. Andrew G. Pattillo Jr., the JQC's prosecutor, warned Rish that the proceedings against Dekle and Boyd should be called off. That the justices were merely reprimanded "does not suggest

Three justices under investigation. From left, Hal P. Dekle, David L. McCain, and Joseph A. Boyd listen to Gov. Reubin Askew address the 1975 opening session of the Legislature, which is considering whether to impeach them. *Courtesy of the* St. Petersburg Times.

to me that the system does not work, or that it ought to be circumvented or rejected in favor of the ponderous, expensive and seemingly impractical impeachment procedure in this instance," he wrote. The letter was conspicuously silent, however, with regard to McCain.[5]

Pattillo had a point. The "corrupt motive" precedent that worried the JQC more than the immediate future of either justice could and would be erased by yet another constitutional amendment. Passed by the 1975 legislature and ratified by the voters in 1976, it said in part that "Malafides, scienter or moral turpitude on the part of a justice or judge shall not be required for removal from office of a justice or judge whose conduct demonstrates a present unfitness to hold office." The amendment also wrote into the constitution the commission's new provision requiring proceedings to become public upon a finding of probable cause rather than only after a recommendation of removal. There would not likely be another void such as had swallowed the Fitzpatrick case. A third change inspired by the Mason affair provided for the automatic disqualification of all justices upon any of them becoming the subject of a disciplinary recommendation from the JQC. The seven most senior chief circuit judges would sit in their places. Seniority would also control which other chief judges would replace any who might be unavailable or disqualified for cause.[6] James Adkins endorsed that proposal in his "State of the Judiciary" address to the 1975 legislature, although the speech bristled with criticism of the press and the Bar regarding the events that illustrated the necessity. Adkins decried "an unrelenting barrage from the news media fusing an almost hysterical hatred of this court in the minds of some people" and complained that there had been no aid from "many who should have protected the institution of the Supreme Court."[7]

On rereading the Dekle and Boyd cases years later, Mark Hulsey, a former Florida Bar president and member of the JQC when it prosecuted Dekle and Boyd, said he thought reprimands would have sufficed in their cases. McCain's, he said, was different because he was "evil from the word go."[8] But in 1975, Boyd and Dekle were to be held accountable not only for what they had done but also for the unpopular special panel decisions in their cases.

As there had been no impeachment proceeding since Kelly's in 1963, few sitting legislators had applicable experience. However, Fred Karl, a former legislator from Daytona Beach whom Rish chose as the Select Committee's counsel, was a master of relevant procedure. As a state senator from 1968 through 1972, Karl became the upper chamber's expert on how to hold hearings for constitutional officers suspended by the governor. Karl was also the leading authority on the sufficiency of the evidence upon which the Senate could rely to remove or reinstate them. Having served earlier in the House, from 1957 through 1963, Karl was also familiar with the protocols of the lower chamber. His appointment signaled to any doubters that Tucker and Rish were serious about investigating the Supreme Court.

Because so much about their cases was already on the record, Dekle and McCain would be investigated first. But after venturing that he would release the JQC's McCain files to the press, Rish reconsidered out of concern that publication could compromise the JQC's ability to act against McCain should the impeachment probe falter. Even without the files, there was new information about Dekle and Boyd upon which the media could feast, including the deposition in which B. K. Roberts revealed his attempt to inveigle Boyd to run for secretary of state.

As the hearings were about to start, the court voted "in principle" to adopt a loyalty oath compelling its research assistants to respect the court's secrecy. "It sounds like something out of the Joe McCarthy era," Forbes complained. Roberts denied that it had any relation to the House investigation or that it would prevent the law clerks from reporting misconduct to the JQC or to the Bar. Committee members were skeptical, however, because of David LaCroix's testimony that when he had asked Roberts, "Is my loyalty to the court greater than my loyalty to my oath as an attorney?" Roberts replied that his duty would be fulfilled by reporting misconduct to the chief justice. With newfound prudence, the court abandoned the oath and left each justice responsible for the conduct of his own aides.[9]

Buoyed by Pattillo's letter, the lawyers for Boyd and Dekle argued unsuccessfully that impeachment would constitute double jeopardy for the justices. Inconveniently for their case, the constitution was clear on that point. It said that the removal power conferred to the JQC and Supreme Court "shall be both alternative and cumulative to the power of impeachment and to the power of suspension by the governor and removal by the senate."[10]

There were few surprises when the committee restaged Mason's and Boyd's dramatically conflicting testimony. Unexpectedly, however, Mason said that during his Public Service Commission membership from 1959 through 1968, "it came to my knowledge on more than one occasion" that the Supreme Court asked the commission's legal staff to help draft decisions in utility cases. The purpose, he said, was to ensure that the decisions were sound law—which was all he had in mind in offering to help Boyd. The committee did not follow that historical trail, perhaps because only one justice from that period was still on the court. That justice, of course, was B. K. Roberts.[11]

Mason, who testified without immunity, said he regretted his conduct. "In retrospect," he said, "a man would have to be a fool to engage in this again." He insisted that Boyd was a knowing accomplice. "I don't know whether he suggested or I suggested," he said, "but the understanding was I would put an outline together that would assist him, if he chose to use it, in articulating the vote the court had taken." One reason for giving a copy to Dekle, he said, was that they were friends. "The other factor was the questions he had asked at oral argument. They were questions that indicated an obvious comprehension of this whole matter . . . and because of that, I thought I could give it to him without him feeling there was any impropriety or without imposing on a friendship."[12]

Hoping to break Boyd's story and confirm Mason's, Karl and the committee tried to prove that the justice and the lawyer had played golf on two occasions. A serious problem for Karl was that Killearn Country Club sign-in sheets recorded only one such event. When Mason said it was possible that they neglected to sign in, or went to the driving range instead, or perhaps were rained out, Boyd's lawyer, W. Dexter Douglass, had heard enough. "Let's be precise," he insisted. Mason replied, "I'd like to be. I'm sorry. I cannot. I wish I could." If anything could discourage the committee from impeaching Boyd, it would be that ambiguity, which Douglass diligently exploited.[13]

McCain, in his only appearance before the committee—primarily as a witness in the *Gulf Power* controversy—got a taste of what was coming his way from Karl's question, "Have you asked that specific cases be sent to you?" McCain, his hands trembling throughout his testimony, replied, "Yes, I have." Karl abruptly changed the subject because Rish did not want anything to detract from the Boyd-Dekle issues. Fitzpatrick, meanwhile, testified in stronger terms than the JQC had heard, saying that Dekle told him forcefully over the telephone that it was "very important to me and my friends that Jackowitz prevail." Fitzpatrick said he should have stopped the first conservation, the one in his office, the year before. "I wish to high heaven I had," he said. Digging deeper than the JQC had, Rish also brought Jackowitz's first lawyer, Julian Bennett, to Tallahassee to testify that Dekle had interceded with him concerning the fee he charged Jackowitz.

That day, Dekle accused Douglass, who was also counsel for Jackowitz's opponents in the Panama City case, of instigating the Fitzpatrick investigation because of an opinion Dekle wrote that had cost him $10,000 in fees. "He said I cost him $10,000 and that he was going to take it out of my hide," Dekle said. Douglass retorted, "It cost me $12,000," and he denied that he had ever talked about Dekle "in public" or had anything to do with the JQC's investigation of Dekle.[14]

Committee members were intrigued by Vassar Carlton's testimony that he never thought of ordering an investigation of the *Gulf Power* case beyond the question of how the *St. Petersburg Times* acquired Dekle's memorandum to McCain. Acknowledging that "it may sound strange and it may seem funny,"

Carlton said that what Dekle had written with the aid of Mason's document "was a good opinion, it was the law, no one was hurt by the opinion itself." When Forbes, one of the more aggressive committee members, said he found that "hard to believe," Carlton replied, "I couldn't go on rumors and I didn't see any reason to start a lot of stuff on rumor alone. That's all I had—rumors. Frankly, I don't see any indiscretion about the way it was handled." He thought that the Mason document "was not nearly as important" as the media made it seem.[15]

To underscore the court's questionable ethics, Karl queried Barbara Williams, the secretary who had typed the explosive Dekle memorandum, regarding retired Justice E. Harris Drew, her employer before McCain. She told of an incident when a woman came to Drew's office and attempted to talk to him about a pending case. "It was explosive," Williams said. "He threw her out almost bodily. He grabbed his hat and went home. Later, he called to apologize to me for losing his temper." Karl said he wanted the committee to know "how it used to be."[16]

Meanwhile, the committee started looking for more evidence of favoritism than the JQC had found. Under pressure from members who thought he was trying to protect Boyd, Schwartz submitted a statement mentioning two instances in which Boyd had voted to accept appeals after discussing the cases (or so Schwartz thought) with the attorneys petitioning the court to hear them. The committee took testimony from one of the lawyers, but nothing came of it beyond his admission of having "told many people I'm friends with the justices." At another point, Boyd admitted that a lawyer involved in a case before the court had put eight $100 campaign contributions on his desk at the Supreme Court building. It was colorful commentary on the ethical perils of electing a judiciary.

The more consequential action the committee took that day was to vote to send letters asking all other Florida judges to state under oath whether any Supreme Court justice ever had tried to influence their decisions. As the examples involving McCain and Dekle in the Nell and Jackowitz cases were already well known, this pursuit meant either that the committee was on a fishing expedition or, more likely, had leads. "There are always statements from other people that there may be things out there," Rish said. "I hope we don't find any more, I'll tell you that for sure." In fact, Karl was pursuing certain rumors about Dekle. "I had people whispering, 'You don't know the half of it,'" Karl said many years later. It was never established, however, whether those rumors were true or false.[17]

Dekle's career imploded two days later. He spent nearly two hours trying to persuade the committee that Fitzpatrick had misunderstood him. He said he intended only to advise Fitzpatrick that Jackowitz was apprehensive about a trial in North Florida. Far from being unethical, it was "an opportunity, I thought, to strike a blow for justice." Contradicting Fitzpatrick's statement that he had said it was "very important" that Jackowitz "prevail," Dekle testified, "I might have said, 'Give him a chance to win.'" As for the telephone call a year later, Dekle said he was afraid that Fitzpatrick wouldn't remember that Jackowitz was "the nervous fellow." His only purpose, he pleaded, "was to try to put a litigant at ease in a strange environment." As to why he had ventured to say *anything* to a judge presiding over an active case, Dekle rationalized that he considered Fitzpatrick "a real cracker"—that is, a fellow Florida native—to whom "you could speak freely." (Although the word *cracker* now has a pejorative connotation, that was not so in Dekle's time.) The judge, he said, "was so super-sensitive, he must have gotten the notion I was challenging his integrity."

Dekle was making no progress with the committee, and the atmosphere turned from bad to worse when he implied that Fitzpatrick may have been unhappy with the Supreme Court for reversing him in a notorious Port St. Joe murder case. The 1971 decision in question ordered new trials for two black men, Freddie Pitts and Wilbert Lee, who were convicted again but subsequently pardoned by Gov. Reubin Askew and the cabinet. Rish, who admired Fitzpatrick, reacted to Dekle's insinuation with undisguised anger, "Do you really believe in your heart that's the reason Judge Fitzpatrick complained to the Judicial Qualifications Commission, because he was reversed in a case?" The prudent answer would have been "no," but Dekle said, "I hope not." As Rish knew, the Supreme Court had no choice in its unanimous 1971 decision because Attorney General Robert Shevin had conceded that the defendants were entitled to a new trial. It was implausible that Fitzpatrick would have resented the Supreme Court for accepting the attorney general's "confession of error."[18]

Dekle's ordeal before the committee was only minutes away from an abrupt, painfully embarrassing, and unexpected finale. Implying that there might be examples similar to Fitzpatrick's, Karl asked Dekle whether he had "any recollection of having contacted any circuit judge or any district court of appeal judge about a case then pending or about to come before them." Dekle started to reply that he had "done nothing improper, nothing intentionally improper . . . I just don't know," when Robert Ervin, his attorney, abruptly ordered him to say no more. Dekle obeyed. "I am unable to answer any open-ended questions, on advice of counsel," Dekle said. He said he would answer any specific question, but the committee had none. Karl contended that Dekle's "selective refusal" broke an agreement with the committee and that all of his prior testimony should be ignored. Dekle's face turned crimson as the committee debated Karl's objection, which Rish refused to put to a vote.[19]

Ervin's legal advice was sound and basic. Not knowing whether Karl already had other evidence against Dekle or whether something that Dekle had forgotten would be alleged by one or more of the nearly 500 judges receiving the commission's interrogatory, Ervin had to assume that the line of questioning was meant to trap Dekle into committing perjury. However, his refusal to answer left Dekle in a nearly hopeless predicament with the committee and the public. Although he had not invoked the Fifth Amendment, it would be a distinction without a difference to people unfamiliar with the law.

Dekle resigned four days later, effective April 30, saying that his departure would "best serve the public interest and my beloved bench and Bar." He said two years of investigations were jeopardizing his health and had already burdened him with more than $50,000 in legal fees and costs. "I commend the judicial and legislative processes in having discharged their responsibility effectively and with distinction," he wrote to the governor. "I harbor no rancor. I look to the future as God grants in his wisdom for me to see it." Rish praised Dekle's decision, saying he regarded him as "basically a good man that made some mistakes." The mistakes, Rish said, quoting from Dekle's letter, were "of his head, not his heart." The committee wrote an end to the Dekle investigation by voting to recall the questions it had sent to the trial and district court judges and reissue them with respect only to McCain and Boyd. "I feel strongly we've got too many other pieces of cane that need chewing," Rish said. "Nothing is to be gained by beating him [Dekle] on the head."[20]

Boyd and McCain had no intention of following Dekle's example. "I never retreat," said McCain. "I have no reason to resign," said Boyd, whose testimony to the committee the day before Dekle's had been even more unpleasant and embarrassing. Having endured more than two and a half hours of questioning about the contradictions between his story and the testimony of Mason and Potts, his former secretary, Boyd appeared to break under the strain. He portrayed himself as the victim of a plot orchestrated by "white hat" enemies, "some people who are extremely popular in Florida and strongly endorsed by the news media and who would like to have some new faces on the court." Boyd said also that he had "both the black-hat and white-hat boys after me." Boyd went on to accuse his former secretary of setting up his trip to the New Orleans clinic in a failed attempt to get him off the court for mental illness. "They couldn't get me for being crazy, so they were going to get me for being dishonest," he said. As the next day's *St. Petersburg Times* described the ordeal, "even committee members appeared uneasy and embarrassed by Boyd's vivid verbal images of persecution, the product largely of their own cross-examination," and they called an overnight halt to it. Boyd was calmer the next day, although he continued to insist that his hospitalization had been part of a plot to get him off the court. "It sounds more like something you'd learn in the Kremlin than in Tallahassee," he said.[21]

The hearings were declared in recess for at least a week so that Karl could undergo elective surgery for a sac on his esophagus, but there were complications that nearly killed him. He was in intensive care for ten days and in the hospital for forty-five. The investigation stalled, to Boyd's benefit, while Rish and his staff waited to hear whether Karl could return. After several weeks, former representative Talbot "Sandy" D'Alemberte, who had chaired the House Judiciary Committee for the 1972 court reform constitutional amendment, was recruited to take Karl's place. He was skeptical of the offer because he knew that Donald Tucker was a cousin of B. K. Roberts. "Tucker had to convince me that he was for real," D'Alemberte said. By then, however, the focus was on McCain, and the committee had no heart left for impeaching Boyd.[22]

There would be one last round of testimony potentially damaging to Boyd. The witness was William Falck, the former research aide who shouldered much of Carlton's work as the chief justice was preparing to retire in 1974. Falck described a series of conversations with Boyd early in 1974, when only the justices and staff knew about the document Boyd had destroyed and the JQC investigation had yet to begin. Saying that he was "intensely sympathetic" to Boyd and was only trying to help him get his story straight, Falck contended that Boyd admitted and later denied having reached an "understanding" that Mason would write something to help him. In their final conservation, he said, he told Boyd that to a prosecutor it would appear that Boyd knowingly accepted the document from Mason at his home, took it to the court, and had no second thoughts until Schwartz—as Falck said Boyd had described the incident—found the document in the file and said, "What the hell is this?" At that point, he said, he told Boyd, "You got caught with your pants down and you were not prepared at that point to admit to Mr. Schwartz that you had participated in picking up an *ex parte* memorandum. . . . As a sign of your outrage and indignation which was a charade, you then went through the business about tearing it up and flushing it the drain and subsequently laying labyrinthine plots to see if anybody else was involved, whatever."

When he had finished playing the role of a hypothetical prosecutor, Falck said, "Justice Boyd was as red as this very bright red folder. His lips were pursed and his hands were together. His head was tilted as he was looking at me and he glared at me for about forty-five seconds. . . . He said nothing and I sat there with the sudden sinking feeling that I had gone too far."[23]

Some committee members seemed to think so, too. Regardless of what they thought of Boyd's conduct, they were put off by the idea of a junior employee bluntly interrogating another elected official, and a Supreme Court justice at that. Although the committee now had two witnesses—Falck and Potts—to testify that Boyd had admitted Mason's version of how the document came to be, there was little interest in pursuing that issue. One obvious complication was Falck's acknowledgment that he had not offered his testimony to the JQC. He said he did not read newspaper accounts of the investigation after he left the court and was busy with new responsibilities, including an unsuccessful campaign for a seat in the legislature.[24]

Boyd's previous appearance before the committee had left some of its members with the uncomfortable feeling that they were harassing someone who was emotionally or mentally ill. By the time the committee reconvened on May 5 to decide on Boyd's fate, the atmosphere was anticlimactic. The McCain hearings—the subject of the next chapter—had elicited such damaging testimony that there would have been an overwhelming vote in the House in favor of the committee's recommendation to impeach McCain had he not resigned the day before it was scheduled.[25] A week later, the committee voted 4-1 against impeaching Boyd. The recommendation was contingent on his promise to undergo a psychiatric examination to be ordered by the JQC. Should the doctors diagnose a serious disability, the JQC could then recommend Boyd's involuntary retirement, to which the court would be virtually forced to agree. It would spare the legislature the time, expense, unpleasantness, and uncertainty of proceeding with impeachment.[26]

Becker, the representative who proposed that way out, said that he believed that Boyd "accepted the memorandum knowing in fact what it was and from whom it originated." But he said also that he was "not prepared, at this point, to find Justice Boyd willfully lied to this committee." Rish said he too believed Mason's version, not Boyd's, but thought that Boyd "told a version as it was true to him." If Mason was lying, Rish noted, "he was lying himself into a peck of trouble." It seemed to Crabtree, the only Republican and the only member who voted to impeach Boyd, that his colleagues were avoiding their duty. "If you believe that Justice Boyd believes he is telling the truth as it occurred, is he then able to distinguish between fact or fiction?" Crabtree argued. "If he cannot, can he be expected to be an effective member of our highest court?"

The absent committee member, Hodes, had collapsed aboard an airplane en route to Tallahassee and was hospitalized at Tampa with a virus and fatigue. He was thought to be leaning toward impeachment, so his attendance would have made the vote closer and perhaps even altered the outcome. Some Republican legislators were skeptical of the result because Boyd was a Democrat, but minority leader William James said that from what Crabtree had told him, the committee had performed well and "there's absolutely nothing partisan." Boyd said, "I'm glad it's over and I want to get back over there and do the job to which I was elected." He remarked, "I'm about as happy now as I was the day World War II was over."

Boyd's avoidance of impeachment coincided with the second of Askew's four appointments to the Supreme Court. The governor chose Alan C. Sundberg, the St. Petersburg attorney who had been a finalist with Overton, to replace Dekle. Sundberg, a forty-one-year-old graduate of Florida State University and the Harvard Law School, was a member of the Bar's Board of Governors. Repeat nominee Mallory Horton, sixty-one, and Stephen Grimes, forty-seven, a judge of the Second District Court of Appeal, were the nominating commission's other finalists. (Grimes would be appointed to the court in 1987.) It was no coincidence that Askew chose the youngest of the nominees. As one of the governor's aides remarked, he "wanted someone who will make a career of it." It was significant also that Sundberg, on behalf of the Bar, had helped Earle draft and promote the series of constitutional amendments strengthening the JQC's authority. Earle was delighted with Askew's choice, but there were rumblings in the legislature over two consecutive appointments from one county. There would soon be a third.[27]

Boyd was not crazy, except perhaps in the sense that a fox is said to be. The examination to which he agreed, conducted over four days at the University of Florida's Shands Hospital, reached much the same result as the four-hour interview he had undergone at the University of Miami. He passed splendidly, impressing the doctors not only with his mental competence but with his character as a "highly principled man." The report, signed by two psychiatrists and a psychologist, said they could find no evidence of a disability that would interfere seriously with his duties on the bench. They did discern "some minor personality problems which were interpreted within the context of current stresses, especially legal." The doctors observed:

> It is a credit to his moral and psychological strength that the stress of the past two years—whether self-induced or not—have not taken a greater toll.
>
> Being an honest, conscientious and hardworking individual, Judge Boyd tends to suppress many of his more negative feelings and he exerts an almost super-human control over his emotions. . . . Judge Boyd is a highly principled man and in his efforts to maintain the ideals which he has set for himself, he tends at times to become somewhat rigid and unrealistic in his self-expectations.

They recommended that Boyd take a vacation as soon as possible because "he could benefit from a much deserved rest and renewed dialogue with his inner, though distanced, feelings."[28]

The Boyd report leaked to a newspaper before the JQC could act on it. Some JQC members blamed Earle and wanted to unseat him as chairman, but they were satisfied with his promise to step aside at a more convenient time.

Boyd remained on the court. During his next (and last) candidacy for retention five years later, the press wrote relatively little about the Mason affair, and nearly 62 percent of the voters said "yes" to another term. That was from 9 to 10 percent lower than the favorable votes for five other justices on the ballot. Boyd lost only Collier County, a notably wealthy and conservative constituency.[29] He was passed over four times for chief justice, finally serving in the post from July 1, 1984, to June 30, 1986, the last opportunity before his mandatory retirement in January 1987. "The folks finally felt it was time for him to have a chance," said Chief Justice Parker Lee McDonald, who had been a member of the special panel that reprimanded Boyd. Adkins said he had voted for Boyd on all five occasions because "Any person who's a member of this court is qualified to be chief justice."

Five years after Boyd's retirement, the court unanimously disbarred Granville Crabtree over "complex" financial dealings. His attorney was Richard T. Earle Jr.[30]

Appearance of Impropriety

One of Sandy D'Alemberte's first steps as the House committee's new chief counsel was to determine what the Florida Department of Law Enforcement (FDLE) knew about McCain. He was surprised to find nothing in its files but newspaper clippings.[1] There was no sign of an independent investigation of McCain's interesting connections with a labor union—Nell's local—that was a target of the U.S. Justice Department's Miami-based Strike Force on Organized Crime. A noteworthy link between McCain and Nell was Samuel Altman, the member whom McCain acknowledged as a personal friend and his contact for the local's political support. When the FDLE did check, it turned out that Altman was a former prison guard who became a convict in 1959 for letting inmates out of the Lowell Correctional Institution to commit burglaries. Testimony would show that McCain pulled strings with the Parole Commission in 1972 to help Altman get his civil rights restored. At the time of the impeachment hearings, Altman, a licensed pilot, faced a marijuana smuggling charge in Highlands County.[2]

In contrast to the FDLE's files, those of the Judicial Qualifications Commission were helpful to D'Alemberte. The credit belonged largely to the JQC's new volunteer investigator, Gavin Letts, who worked feverishly to make up for the time the JQC had lost. Letts was a Scottish-born lawyer with an authentic brogue, impeccable manners, a keen mind, a Palm Beach society practice that honed his expertise in matrimonial law, and a commanding presence in anybody's company. To some, Letts resembled the fictional Major Charles Emerson Winchester III of the television program *M*A*S*H*—minus the character's arrogance. Letts was "a warm and gregarious man with a playful sense of humor," to whom "the only thing worse than being boring was being dishonest." It seemed almost incongruous for a man of his position and bearing to immerse himself in such a rude business as McCain's contacts with a tainted labor union. Letts did so because he was terribly proud to be a lawyer, idealized the judiciary, and assumed it to be his duty to his profession to help eradicate what he perceived as a stain on the integrity of the courts. (Letts later became a widely respected judge of the Fourth District Court of Appeal, where he was twice nominated for the Supreme Court before dying of cancer in 1993.) "I think we found each other, and damned if I know how," said Richard Earle. "I was amazed, I'll tell you that, but he was interested, and he wanted to help."[3] The final report of the Select Committee described the JQC files that Letts fleshed out as "invaluable in constructing the House's investigation."[4]

Letts spent an estimated 250 hours pursuing rumors and leads. He had Robert E. May's affidavit in hand not long after I did.[5] May had agreed to be an on-the-record source on the condition that the newspaper stake him to a bus ticket out of Florida. The policy of the *St. Petersburg Times,* like that of most American newspapers, is to pay for articles only to the people who write them. In this case, the editors agreed to an exception for May on the premise that he would be in danger when the story broke. Knowing that there would surely be a subpoena for his affidavit from the JQC if not from the legislature or a state attorney, we anticipated that problem by obtaining May's written consent to release it.

The *St. Petersburg Times* had reported part of the story—May's visit and the gift of the cheap union cuff links—in December 1974. Letts and the JQC knew also about the alleged bribe, as did the staff of the House Select Committee. By then, Earle was out of money for another expensive JQC trial, out of patience with the court, preoccupied with lobbying for a constitutional amendment to negate the "corrupt motive" precedent set by the Dekle and Boyd decisions, and eager to let the legislature finish what Letts had started.

But the alleged bribe, the most sensational of May's allegations, never became an issue in McCain's impeachment hearing or his eventual disbarment, and a Leon County grand jury that looked into it in 1977 returned a finding of no probable cause for a criminal indictment.[6] It turned out that May had told conflicting stories. When the Miami Strike Force interviewed May about

Nell, May said nothing about any money. If federal prosecutors attempted to turn Nell into a witness against McCain, they failed; Nell preferred to go to prison rather than to cooperate with the Strike Force.[7]

Wanting to hear May's story for himself, D'Alemberte arranged a way that would escape the notice of the capital press corps. He flew to Lee County to be sworn in as a temporary assistant to the local state attorney, Joseph D'Alessandro. (It was D'Alessandro who had prosecuted Nell in the case that the Supreme Court dismissed.) Unlike the House committee's files, the active investigation papers of a state attorney were not vulnerable to public disclosure. May told D'Alemberte essentially what he had told the *St. Petersburg Times:* that Nell gave him a two-inch thick manila envelope that he said contained a book for McCain and warned May not to open it. Disobeying, May cut the envelope open to discover ten bundles of currency, each consisting of $1,000 in $20 bills. He telephoned Nell to beg off the assignment but followed through with it after Nell threatened him. May bought a similar manila envelope, repackaged the money, and delivered it to McCain in his chambers at the Supreme Court. McCain opened it in his presence, dumped the contents on his desk, and said it was what he expected.[8]

Although D'Alemberte believed May, "I found myself thinking I probably would never use this guy as a witness." He was concerned that the young man was visibly nervous, that his personal mannerisms could alienate some legislators, and that the inconsistent accounts he had told under oath would disparage all of his testimony. In that event, the bribery allegation would become a red herring to discredit the entire investigation. Moreover, D'Alemberte thought he had a strong enough case without it.[9]

McCain and his lawyers, James M. Russ and Michael F. Cycmanick of Orlando, tried in every way possible, including a lawsuit in a federal district court, to abort the hearings. Early in the process, Russ objected that it tainted the entire investigation for Tucker to allow the committee's staff director, Mark Glick, to examine the JQC's documents pertaining to McCain. Russ sought to disqualify one of the committee members, Representative John Forbes, because of an unsuccessful suit Forbes had filed the year before for access to all the JQC's secret files. A private investigator working for Russ examined Glick's House personnel file, prompting an unscheduled meeting of the committee to warn the McCain team against badgering witnesses. The investigator's purpose became clear when Russ filed grievances with the Bar against Glick and committee chairman William J. Rish, accusing them of violating rules that restricted lawyers from participating in pretrial publicity, forbade them to use public office for personal gain, and barred false accusations against a judge. If the offensive was meant to discourage the committee, it backfired; Rish and Glick waived the confidentiality that normally cloaked grievance complaints and disclosed them to the press. "There'll be no secrets," said Rish. "I know of nothing I've done unethically in handling this committee. It's a little bit of harassment, but it doesn't bother me." Simultaneously, he and the committee refused Russ's request to subpoena four reporters, Glick, and Earle for testimony that might prove the JQC's secrets were leaking to the press through the committee. Nothing came of the complaints that Russ filed. "I don't think there's enough in that letter for me to send out to a grievance committee," said Norman Faulkner, the Bar's staff counsel.[10]

In ruling against Forbes's suit the year before, all seven justices had conceded that the House speaker or his "designated representative" would be entitled to examine JQC files for a specific impeachment inquiry. The decision was an ingenious compromise between independent branches of government. "In this cause our judicial power must not be used to shield and protect judges guilty of impeachable offenses nor should the legislative power of impeachment be used to conduct broad brush witch-hunts, effectively destroying an alternative means of judicial discipline," Ben Overton wrote for the court.[11] With the McCain hearings pending, Chief Justice James Adkins undermined Russ's strategy by signing a secret order that gave the entire committee broad authority to use JQC material against his colleague. This was disclosed, at the request of D'Alemberte and Glick, only after McCain had resigned a month later.[12] On April 7, the day Adkins signed the order, the court dismissed McCain's petition to bar the impeachment hearings. With all the justices but Overton and England disqualified as potential witnesses, five chief circuit judges joined them in a unanimous decision that the court lacked jurisdiction.[13] A federal district judge, Winston Arnow, reached the same conclusion in an emergency hearing at Pensacola the next day. "It doesn't appear to me you're being denied due process," Arnow told Russ, who had complained that the committee would not allow him to call any witness he wanted. Arnow also emphasized that he did not believe he had jurisdiction in the first place. "A federal court does not exercise its power to enjoin a case of this kind," he said, involving as it did the "right of the people to proceed with the impeachment of their officers."[14]

The McCain hearings began as scheduled the next day without the participation of McCain or his lawyers. Russ appeared only long enough to say that he would boycott them, had instructed McCain not to testify, and would try to find another court to stop the process "just as soon as I can return to my office." By electing not to present McCain or cross-examine other witnesses, Russ conceded to the testimony being one-sided, but he also avoided tipping his hand to McCain's defense in the eventuality of a Senate trial on impeachment charges voted by the House.

McNulty and Mann, a former legislator who was highly regarded in the House, were the leadoff witnesses. In words much stronger than his *St. Petersburg Times* interview, McNulty said he had considered McCain's telephone call unethical and "a personal affront that a judge would think he could influence me on a personal friendship or anything else." McCain's language, as he described it, was a blatant plea to throw the Nell case: "He said, 'Now, Joe, if it's a case that is close on the facts and can go either way, it would be appreciated, and if it is not close, clear on the law, so be it.'" Mann, recounting two telephone calls from Mager concerning the status (but not any requested outcome) of the Nell case, said it had occurred to him "he was not calling on behalf of the attorney general." He suspected that someone might have been orchestrating the telephone calls as a scheme to induce him and McNulty, the two judges voting to sustain the convictions, to disqualify themselves. Mann, who had since left the Second District Court to become a University of Florida law professor, added that he thought the Supreme Court decision in Nell's favor relied on "absurd" precedents and a "hyper-technical" interpretation of bribery.

The committee's decision to survey the entire Florida judiciary, the tactic that appeared to have contributed to Dekle's resignation, led to three other judges reporting out-of-the-ordinary contacts from McCain. He had talked to one of them about terminating the probation of a young man from Miami, the son of a prominent delicatessen owner, who had been convicted of possessing marijuana. The judge did terminate the four-year probation after only one year, a somewhat unusual action considering that it had been another judge's sentence. The judge who had sentenced the young man was C. Pfeiffer Trowbridge of Stuart—McCain's home town—who reported a different case to the committee. McCain had called him to ask why he had revoked a local woman's work-release, sending her back to jail for forgery. When Trowbridge told McCain that she had abused her work release by using a church school's telephone to harass "various former boyfriends, many of whom were married and prominent men in the community," McCain said, "'Thank you judge, that's all I wanted to know and forget we ever had this conversation.'" Trowbridge said that although McCain said nothing that was improper, he was uncomfortable discussing the case with him and tried to end the conversation as soon as possible.[15]

The most damaging witness among the three judges responding to the questionnaire was County Judge LeRoy H. Moe of Fort Lauderdale. He reported a telephone call in which McCain interceded on behalf of a Miami attorney who had applied for a postponement of a hearing for attorney's fees in a probate case. McCain told Moe that the attorney, Burton Loebl, had been his campaign manager for north Broward County. Loebl himself testified that he was merely a campaign supporter. Moe's testimony was as bad for McCain as McNulty's had been because McCain said explicitly, according to Moe, that he would appreciate a favor for Loebl.[16]

Those cases alone might not have persuaded the committee to undertake a potentially ponderous impeachment, but the testimony of four former Supreme Court research aides and clerk Sid White made it all but certain. They portrayed McCain as a judge who rigged the court's decisions for his friends and even boasted that one of them, involving a workers' compensation appeal, was "a fix." The injured worker, Edward Kaplan, was a friend of McCain, who had pledged him to his fraternity at the University of Florida. Kaplan, an electrician, was appealing an industrial claims ruling that had awarded him only 55 percent rather than total disability and less in attorney's fees than his lawyer had requested. Larry Sartin, a research aide who was a roving clerk to several justices, testified that McCain assigned him to write an opinion in Kaplan's favor. "And at some point in the conversation he made the comment, and this is a quote, that 'This case is a fix.'"

Rish asked whether McCain might have been joking. Sartin did not think so. "I will never forget looking at him when he said those words. It hit me so strong,... There was no indication that he was kidding with me, that there was any joking around. I wish I could say that there was, but there wasn't." However, Sartin acknowledged a possibility that McCain meant to say that the case had been "fixed below"—that is, when the industrial claims judge heard it. That benign interpretation—that McCain was merely *undoing* another judge's rigged decision—would be his defense during his disbarment hearing two years later. Still, it was questionable conduct on McCain's part to involve himself in the case of someone he acknowledged as "a very good friend." One legislator asked whether Sartin had suggested to McCain that he recuse himself. "In hindsight, regretfully, no," Sartin replied. But Sartin "thought about it a lot"—the Watergate affair weighed on his mind as a parallel—and he eventually reported the conversation to the JQC. Meanwhile, McCain ultimately cast the deciding vote in a 4-3 decision ordering the judge of industrial claims to grant Kaplan's claims for total disability and attorney's fees. The court said the electric company had failed to prove that lighter duty work was available to Kaplan. Roberts, Carlton, and Boyd concurred only with respect to the legal fees. Sartin, believing there were no grounds to overturn the disability ruling, could not bring himself to write the opinion and delegated the task to another aide.[17]

The other three former law clerks described additional incidents that they believed to be unethical.

William Falck told of having helped McCain finish a dissent in a case that was pending at the Fourth District Court when he was appointed to the Supreme Court. It was one of Joseph Farish's cases, involving a man who had lost his suit against a railroad for injuries suffered when a train hit his milk truck. According to Falck, McCain told him to "be sure to work something in so that we have conflict cert [certiorari] in the Supreme Court." In other words, McCain wanted Falck to write the dissent in a way to make it more likely that the Supreme Court would accept Farish's appeal. When Farish eventually did petition the Supreme Court to hear the case, Falck said, McCain asked him to have the clerk assign it to Carlton so that Falck, who was Carlton's primary research assistant, could "turn your dissent into a majority opinion." Falck thought it would have been as unethical for a law clerk to work on the same case in two different courts as it would have been for a justice to do so. Groping for words, he could only stare at McCain at first. Finally, he said, he told McCain that Carlton knew that he had helped McCain write the Fourth District dissent and that Carlton had decided to recuse himself if the case came to the Supreme Court. "I told Justice McCain it was simply out of the question. I could not do it. He looked at me and I believe he said, 'Well, that seems like a dumb thing to do, but then, all right, if that's what you want to do, okay.' And he got up and walked out." Although Carlton took no part in the court's decision on whether to accept the case, he eventually voted in support of a 4-1 decision by Boyd that reversed the Fourth District and restored a $141,750 judgment for the milk truck driver. McCain was not on the panel.[18]

On another occasion, it appeared to Falck that McCain was meddling in a lawsuit between his brother and David H. Smith, the McCain friend who had become one of the justice's bitter accusers. The Fourth District Court of Appeal had ruled in favor of McCain Sales of Florida Inc. in a dispute with Smith over commissions for selling the McCain firm's road signs. After Smith's lawyers petitioned for Supreme Court review, McCain dropped by Falck's office in Carlton's chambers and said, "This is Willie's case. We are taking care of it." McCain wanted to know whether the clerk's office had assigned Carlton to the case. Falck said he did not know, and McCain left. "I have no idea what he was doing with the file, and I can only report to you the incidents I observed," Falck said. The court denied jurisdiction by a 4-1 vote, with Dekle dissenting and McCain not participating. That outcome favored McCain's brother.[19]

Falck, other aides, and Supreme Court clerk Sid White confirmed rumors of a "McCain technique" that helped to get certain cases before the court faster. One example was a $5,000 contract dispute between Farish personally and Lum's Inc., the restaurant chain. The Fourth District Court of Appeal had overruled a summary judgment in Farish's favor, and he appealed to the Supreme Court. Anne Parker, McCain's first Supreme Court research assistant, read to the committee McCain's recommendation on the document that circulated among the judges for their votes on whether to grant or deny jurisdiction: "Grant certiorari and dispense with oral argument. This issue is not complicated and should clearly appear from the record which Sid asked the DCA clerk to send immediately." Other justices occasionally saw no need for oral argument, Parker said, "but this expediting the record . . . was something that was almost never done, only in cases requiring emergency treatment usually." With McCain, she said, it seemed to generally be in favor of Mr. Farish. The procedure was so unusual, she said, "that it was kind of like waving a red flag in front of a bull." Parker thought it was questionable for McCain to participate in a case that involved his friend as a party rather than just as counsel, and she told him so. "I don't remember exactly what he said," she testified, "but he wasn't impressed by my argument." After accepting jurisdiction, the court restored Farish's $5,000 judgment by a vote of 5-2. The draft of the *per curiam* opinion bore Adkins's initials, but testimony established that it had been prepared at McCain's direction.[20]

McFerrin Smith, another of the former aides, testified that McCain had handed him the file with instructions to write an opinion favoring Farish.

"Did he tell you what theory of law the opinion should reach or did he tell you which party should win?" D'Alemberte asked. "Just which party should win," Smith replied. Smith said he eventually returned the file to McCain, "with a report that I was unable to find any law to support what he wanted me to do." Knowing that Farish was McCain's friend and having seen him visiting the justice's office, Smith "didn't want to go any further to find out why he wanted me to reach that result." Another aide finally wrote the opinion that McCain wanted.[21]

White's testimony was especially damaging to McCain. Referring to dockets the court customarily withheld from the public, the clerk cited nine cases to which McCain asked to be assigned. Four involved Farish; one of them was the Stewart estate case that had aroused Judge Owen's suspicion when McCain asked to exchange oral argument assignments nearly four years earlier. At almost the same time, two other attorneys participating in the case had purchased McCain's Fort Pierce home. White said he considered it "very unusual" for a justice to ask to be assigned to cases as McCain had. The handwritten comments on some of the docket sheets illustrated why the court did not want the public to see them. In opposing a petition to rehear the Kaplan decision, McCain dismissed it as "a melodramatic rehash of the case." Urging his colleagues to review the Stewart case, McCain wrote, "The 4th DCA, prima facie, went haywire." He was the apparent author of the 5-2 Supreme Court decision that overturned an executor's decision to give the $700,000 estate to five charities and awarded it instead to Mrs. Stewart's brother.[22]

The most damaging testimony, or so it seemed at the time, consisted of the allegations that McCain had sought campaign contributions from the two wealthy women, Mary Alice Firestone and Nancy Wakeman, who would soon have highly publicized cases before him. "That shocked my conscience as much as anything else," Rish recalled.[23] David Smith, who had served one term in the House simultaneously with four members of the committee, repeated his allegations of unreported 1968 campaign cash from attorneys Joseph Varon and Steadman Stahl Jr.—Nell's lawyers—who adamantly denied the accusation; of 168,000 brochures that Smith said were illegally supplied by a paint company and supposedly reported on its books as paint can labels; and of an unreported loan of a phosphate company's airplane. Most critically, Smith swore that McCain had often praised Farish as "a great benefactor, a great guy who would always be dear to him," and had talked of soliciting contributions from Firestone and Wakeman. Smith described an occasion at Farish's office where he was excused from the meeting but saw Farish and McCain in the company of a woman whom McCain identified to him as Mrs. Wakeman. According to Smith, McCain told him, "'That was a very interesting conversation we had with Mrs. Wakeman, and she is going to be good for a substantial contribution.'" But Smith admitted that he did not know whether McCain actually received money from her. Referring to a $25 contribution from a lawyer who had been expected to send more, Smith alleged that McCain said, "This guy better not have a case before the appellate bench because he's lost it." McCain made such comments more than once, Smith said.[24]

(The Florida Bar failed to substantiate Smith's allegations in subsequent separate disciplinary proceedings against McCain and Farish. The Bar abandoned its case against Farish, leaving him with an unblemished professional record, but succeeded in disbarring McCain on other grounds. The controversy evidently did the Farish firm no long-term harm, as two members, Rosemary Barkett and Harry Anstead, became judges of the Fourth District Court of Appeal and were eventually appointed to the Florida Supreme Court.)

Committee members were eager to question Farish—"eyeball to eyeball," as Crabtree put it—but they would be disappointed. Appearing under their subpoena the day after Smith's testimony, Farish refused to tell the committee anything but his name. With his lawyer Robert Montgomery repeatedly citing the Fifth Amendment in Farish's behalf, the committee could not get Farish to say even whether he knew McCain. "I am following, reluctantly, the advice of counsel," Farish said. Although the committee maintained that the Fifth Amendment did not apply to matters more than two years old, because they would not have been prosecutable under Florida's statute of limitations, there was another good ground for Farish to decline to testify: no deadline limited Florida Bar proceedings. Moreover, Farish refused to surrender any records to the committee; he and Montgomery cited attorney-client privilege. "I have advised Mr. Farish not to produce any record of any kind relative to any of his clients, period," Montgomery said. Although he would not allow Farish to say anything in his own defense, Montgomery maintained that his client had done nothing wrong. "His ability and his ability alone have led him to the path before you," he said. Farish was let go after only twenty-four minutes. The committee threatened to cite him for contempt—"That was about the surliest lawyer we've had before this committee," complained Eric Smith—but never followed through, probably because

D'Alemberte recognized that the law respected Farish's right to silence. In abandoning the subsequent disciplinary case against Farish, the Bar's counsel conceded that he could not prove that Farish ever "asked for, encouraged, or solicited . . . favoritism" from McCain. Moreover, there was no cancelled check or any other evidence to corroborate Mrs. Wakeman's claim of an unreported campaign contribution to McCain through Farish. The Bar had been unable even to find her. It turned out that she was in the Bahamas, where Farish's agents eventually tracked her down to serve her with a $10 million defamation suit. Farish lost that case; a trial judge dismissed it and the Fourth District Court upheld the decision on grounds that under the "overwhelming weight of authority," testimony to a legislative committee is absolutely privileged. Regardless of the truth or falsity, the witness could not be sued. Farish appealed to the Supreme Court, which refused without comment to hear the case.[25]

The potential weakness of Mrs. Wakeman's accusation was not obvious, however, when she gave what the committee considered clinching testimony against McCain on April 24, 1975. She claimed that, as Smith described, she went to Farish's office to meet McCain, where she was asked for a campaign contribution. She said Farish brought McCain to her home on a second occasion, where she wrote a $1,000 check payable to Farish. She accused Farish of trying to coach her testimony to the committee and said she had retained another lawyer.[26] Minutes later, the committee unanimously voted to impeach McCain, instructing D'Alemberte to prepare articles charging him with "bias and favoritism" to certain lawyers and clients, "undue use of judicial office" to influence decisions, and taking money as either illegal campaign contributions or unlawful compensation. Forbes said he set his mind to impeaching McCain even before Wakeman testified. He thought Sid White's testimony was conclusive. In a dramatic flair, House Speaker Tucker scheduled debate for May 1, an unofficial holiday celebrated by the legal profession as Law Day.[27]

D'Alemberte left early for a speaking engagement in California so that he could prepare the impeachment articles out of sight of the Florida press. Most House members, however, were ready to vote to adopt whatever he wrote. "I know of no one who's going to defend the justice," one legislator remarked. "Just off the cuff, without being committed to it, I think McCain's had it," said another. One who described himself as a friend of McCain's said he thought the justice should resign. A proposal to censure

McCain rather than impeach him evaporated almost as soon as it was float-ed. A succession of House members sought out Rish to assure him that they had not started it.[28]

Russ's calculated boycott had necessarily resulted in an overwhelmingly unfavorable impression of McCain. McCain complained that he had been treated like a "common criminal." Invited to respond, Crabtree snapped, "Not common."[29] But McCain's nonparticipation also left D'Alemberte to guess at the defense strategy for a Senate trial. It seemed to him, however, that McCain was "almost certain to say there was no possibility of corruption because he was on a multimember court, and could not decide cases alone." It would be a good defense unless D'Alemberte could show that McCain had used an insider's advantage to manipulate the other justices. "I really did not underestimate the problems of proving the case," he said. So he sent word through Adkins that every justice who had sat with McCain on *Stewart, Williams, Nell, Lum's, Kaplan, Wakeman,* and other cases that had figured in the hearings would be subpoenaed as a witness for the House. That excluded only England, Sundberg, and Overton, who as the senior of the three would preside over the Senate trial in place of the chief justice, Adkins. It had not occurred to Adkins that he would not be able to fulfill his constitutional role, and D'Alemberte described him as "shaken" on being told he would be a wit-ness instead. "My guess is that a panic went through the court," D'Alemberte said. Among other things, it meant that Roberts and Adkins would have to explain why they did not report McCain's indiscretions to the JQC or do anything outwardly to counter the widespread impression in the Bar that he was biased in favor of certain lawyers. The appearance of impropriety was as much an offense against the Code of Judicial Conduct as actual and inten-tional misconduct. So was the failure of any judge to report what he knew about indiscretions on the part of another. Only one justice would be in the Senate dock if the House preferred impeachment charges, but others would be standing figuratively at his side.

D'Alemberte was in California when he received an urgent telephone call from Marshall Cassedy, the Bar's executive director. Cassedy said Ad-kins wanted to know whether the Bar would agree to disciplinary immu-nity for McCain as a lawyer if he agreed to resign as a justice. Although he was a member of the Bar's Board of Governors, D'Alemberte insisted that he could not make such a commitment and neither could Cassedy. D'Alemberte telephoned Adkins to say, "I would not recommend to the legislature that it suggest what the Bar should do." If McCain resigned, he would have to do so unconditionally. That was tough poker-playing on D'Alemberte's part, considering the historical odds in McCain's favor. There had only been two Senate impeachment trials—both involving judges—and neither resulted in a two-thirds vote to convict.[30]

But McCain had more at risk than his job. He needed just four more months, or so he thought, to qualify for a state pension. D'Alemberte would recommend dealing to that extent, and so would Rish, who reasoned that it would take nearly as long and cost $200,000 or more to complete an impeachment trial. With Adkins as his intermediary, McCain obtained Governor Askew's consent, and on April 28 he resigned, effective August 31. Askew said he accepted the delayed date with "some reluctance," relying on Adkins's promise to assign McCain to no new cases, permit him to write no opinions for the court, and disallow his vote on any case where it would be decisive. Askew's concerns were eased somewhat by Rish's assurance that he would amend pending pension legislation to prevent McCain from qualifying under its terms.[31]

Just one week before McCain's resignation, he and Boyd formed part of a four-vote majority to reject the Bar's petition for rehearing of a decision entitling suspended or disbarred attorneys to work as paralegals for other lawyers. In dissent to the original January 29 decision, Overton objected that it "clearly reduces the effect of any order of suspension or disbarment and is another step to effectively dilute the punishment." To the laity, Overton said, "the difference between mere clerking and the unrestrained practice of law is not apparent."[32] With impeachment still hanging over their heads and disbarment as a potential consequence, it was self-serving for Boyd and McCain to participate in that case. Barely three years later, McCain would benefit from the precedent.[33]

McCain insisted in his resignation letter that his record was "not only defensible but untarnished" and that he was quitting only because he and his family believed that "my present effectiveness on the Supreme Court has been impeded." He told the governor that "without hesitation or equivocation I cannot conceive of any wrong or misdoing on my part" unless "compassion for your fellow man" had somehow become an offense. "I think Florida has had a great thing happen this morning," Rish responded. "It's good for the people of this state."[34]

In Tallahassee, Anne Parker, the former McCain research aide who had avoided my questions for two years, all but slamming her apartment door in my face on one occasion, sent me a dozen red roses.

McCain lost his pension after all. He was anticipating the passage of legislation that would have allowed members of the judicial retirement plan, which required ten years of service, to convert to an elected public-official plan for which his eight years as of August 29 would qualify. He had passed up one chance in 1974 and would not get another because the legislature, with McCain in mind, delayed the effective date to January 1, 1976. It cost him $10,560 a year.[35] Worse things than that lay in wait for him.

⊰ 15 ⊱

The Old Order Is Over

Fred Karl recovered from the surgery that had nearly killed him and applied to the nominating commission for McCain's vacancy. He was easily the best known of the seven lawyers and judges the commission recommended to Reubin Askew, who had served amicably with him in both houses of the legislature. But Karl was somber about his prospects when I called to congratulate him on his nomination and to ask what he could tell me about federal magistrate Joseph W. Hatchett, the other nominee from Karl's home town of Daytona Beach. "Well," said Karl in a melancholy tone, "he's black." I remarked that it would be a problem for Karl. "Don't I know it," he said.[1] There was no doubt in either of our minds how Askew would treat that historic opportunity. One of four "New South" governors elected in 1970, he had prominently opposed racial segregation since his student body presidency at all-white Florida State University in 1951, when his was a lonely voice.[2] As governor, he had shocked many of his own staff by endorsing busing to desegregate public schools; although it was an unpopular position, his reelection was relatively easy. Whenever possible, Askew had appointed African Americans to school boards and other local government vacancies. Toward that end, he required that there be one black (and one woman) on each of his county advisory (i.e., patronage) committees.[3] With respect to the Supreme Court vacancy, he needed to satisfy himself only that Hatchett was qualified—which by definition could be assumed of anyone the commission nominated. With all seven candidates "eminently qualified," Askew conceded, Hatchett's race was a "major consideration."[4] On September 2, Hatchett became Florida's first black justice. Subsequently he was the first black since Reconstruction to win a statewide election in the South, and by President Carter's appointment in 1979 the first to serve on a federal appellate court in the former Confederacy. At an ex-governors' seminar thirty-one years later, Askew declared that Hatchett's selection was his most satisfying accomplishment. "That's what I enjoyed the most, I believe."[5]

LeRoy Collins, the former governor who had hoped to serve on the court himself only to see his application tossed aside without an interview the year before, congratulated Hatchett at his investiture. Hatchett recalled Collins saying, "Now, Mr. Justice, don't you worry about the election. What you need to worry about is making the right decision in every one of the cases that come before you." Collins, who was a fastidious grammarian in his speeches and writings, advised the same of Hatchett. "And when you write opinions, be very careful and take a lot of time . . . about how you write them and make them understandable."[6]

Hatchett, forty-three years old, was the son of a fruit picker and a housemaid, John and Lula Hatchett of Clearwater. Graduating with a political science degree from segregated Florida A&M University in May 1954 at almost the same moment that the U.S. Supreme Court pronounced public school segregation to be unconstitutional, Hatchett was keenly aware of Virgil Hawkins's futile attempts to attend the University of Florida Law School and wasted no time or effort in that direction. He took his legal education at historically black Howard University in Washington, the alma mater of Thurgood Marshall and many other civil rights leaders. Racism still ruled the Florida judiciary when he and classmate Leander Shaw, another future Florida Supreme Court justice, took the Florida Bar examination at Miami in 1959. They were required to sit apart from the white applicants and lodge at a segregated hotel. Hatchett represented civil rights demonstrators on behalf of the NAACP Legal Defense Fund before becoming an assistant U.S. attorney and then a magistrate.[7]

Of the Florida justices who had defied the U.S. Supreme Court by refusing to order Hawkins admitted to the University of Florida law school, only B. K. Roberts remained. Roberts never publicly expressed an opinion on Hatchett's appointment, which had the hugely ironic consequence of contributing to the end of Roberts's reign as *primus inter pares* on the state's highest court.

Adkins's term as chief justice was expiring. By tradition, the position would devolve on the most senior justice who had yet to be chief. That would be Boyd, fresh from the official reprimand and his narrow escape from impeachment, but Sundberg, England, and Hatchett were concerned that Boyd's election would embarrass the court. Overton, who was next in line, agreed with them, but he was unwilling to vote for himself. Boyd, meanwhile, did not intend to step aside. One obvious compromise would be to make Roberts chief yet again. Although the senior justice was hinting that he would not run for a new term, England took it for granted that Roberts would gladly postpone retirement for an unprecedented fourth turn as chief. The younger justices did not care for that alternative either. It seemed to England that the only way out of a stalemate was to demand a vote in public:

> This was designed specifically so that B. K. would not be elected, that the vote for chief justice should be made publicly, in the open courtroom. I said to B. K., "I'm going to insist on an open vote . . . I'm going to make it known that I think it should be in public because of the importance of the office." That's when B. K., I think it was a day later, said, "I will not be a candidate but select Ben." That was the leverage I had. I could not think of anything but sunshine.[8]

Overton became chief justice; it was barely two years after his appointment to the court. The court's placid announcement belied infighting so emotionally charged that by unanimous consent the clerk afterward burned all copies of memoranda written by England, Roberts, and Boyd, who still insisted that he had been vindicated by the multiple investigations. Although Roberts was exempt from mandatory retirement, he decided that it was time to go and did not file for reelection. When Boyd finally became chief in 1984, the last opportunity before his mandatory retirement, the vote was not unanimous.[9]

Roberts's retirement presaged an epochal restriction of the court's jurisdiction, but the more immediate consequence was to alter its calendar. It was a predominantly young court for the first time, with four justices in their forties, each with school-age children. "So the first thing that got changed," Overton recalled, "was the recess period in the summer. The *traditional* recess period, as B. K. kept saying, had always been the entire month of August, but Arthur, Joe, and I said we had to have our children checked in (to school) on August 7 . . . So we started it the second week in July."[10]

Hatchett would need to defend his seat in the 1976 nonpartisan primary merely twelve months after his investiture. He drew a single opponent, but one who seemed formidable: Harvie S. DuVal, a thirteen-year circuit judge in Dade, the largest county, and bearer of one of Florida's oldest family names. DuVal had been one of the substitute judges who voted against reprimanding Dekle. He was a prominent member of Florida's political old guard and it was suspected that Roberts had encouraged his candidacy. DuVal nourished that supposition when he accused Hatchett of neglecting cases to campaign and attributed his information to "a source" on the Supreme Court. From a neighbor who was one of Ed Ball's executives, Ben Overton learned that the archconservative duPont tycoon was supporting DuVal, who attended a Tallahassee party in Ball's honor three days after denying the City of Miami's claim to duPont waterfront land worth an estimated $21.3 million. There were no reported campaign contributions from Ball, who rarely parted with his own money, but he was still presumed to have influence in conservative financial and political circles. It was obviously waning, however, as DuVal managed to outspend Hatchett by only a modest margin, $95,312 to $85,020. Emulating the most recent campaign of the governor who had appointed him, Hatchett limited individual contributions to $100, a tenth of the legal limit. Most of DuVal's money came from Dade and Broward lawyers who had practiced in his court. Among the interesting exceptions were contributions of $100 each from Harvie Belser, a former legislator from Bonifay, and his wife. During the 1950s, Belser had been one of the most strident segregationists in the Florida House of Representatives. Another small but noteworthy contribution was the $100 sent to DuVal by former governor C. Farris Bryant, who had been elected as a strict segregationist in 1960.[11]

The seven-month campaign was the last in Florida in which any statewide candidate appealed overtly to racism. DuVal did so by alleging that Askew had tampered with the nominating commission for the sake of "reverse discrimination." DuVal had nothing to support the claim but the fact that the commission had nominated seven candidates rather than the usual three. In a taped television debate, DuVal contended that Askew had rejected up to six lists from the nominating commission before it finally sent him one with Hatchett's name on it. Askew and the commission chair strongly denied the tampering allegation, for which DuVal offered no evidence. (Askew's archived files reflect no such communications either.) "If they deny it, then I'm in error," DuVal conceded. "I don't know whether I'm mistaken or not."[12]

Although the incident reflected badly on his campaign, DuVal continued to insist that Askew had chosen Hatchett not for his qualifications but for his race. "What in the world is a magistrate?" DuVal scoffed. "He tried the traffic cases in the Naval base, [found] probable cause and set bonds."[13] Hatchett's magisterial duties had in fact been more substantial; they included the responsibility for monitoring the Duval County jail during a lawsuit that contended the conditions violated the inmates' civil rights.[14] DuVal's claim to superior credentials backfired when the Florida Bar and Dade County Bar Association published polls in which the majorities of participating lawyers found Hatchett but not DuVal to be qualified. Moreover, a Dade Bar poll in 1976 had ranked DuVal 40th among 44 circuit judges.[15]

DuVal, as it had turned out, had a reputation like McCain's for favoring a particular lawyer. The attorney in question was Marion Sibley of Miami, who had been Turner's lawyer in the Supreme Court case that stifled the Judicial Qualifications Commission's Market Connection investigation. Sibley's clients included the Flagler Dog Track, on whose behalf DuVal had sent eighteen dog handlers to jail for contempt of his order to end a boycott and resume racing their animals. Two weeks before refusing their attorney's request to disqualify himself, DuVal had been Sibley's guest at an expensive deer hunt in New Mexico. Although he had not disclosed to the other lawyers that he and Sibley were hunting companions, it was known to state pari-mutuel regulators, one of whom mentioned it to me. The *Miami Herald*, which had a working relationship with the *St. Petersburg Times*, assigned Caroline Heck, a former *Times* reporter, to collaborate on the story. DuVal admitted to us that he and Sibley had hunted together and revealed what we did not know: the location. He said that he had "paid my own way" to the hunt at the 137,000-acre Philmont Boy Scout Ranch near Cimarron. What he did not tell us—a fact of which he said later he had been unaware—was that Sibley paid a fee of $500 per person per day for DuVal and fourteen other guests, according to the Scout ranch records. Among the others was a federal judge who, in contrast to DuVal, said he would recuse himself from judging a case involving Sibley or any other similarly close friend. DuVal, on the other hand, not only defended his refusal to step aside but declared that as head of the twenty-eight judges in the civil division he discouraged others from disqualifying themselves when old friends were involved. "If you're going to be a judge, you've got to be a judge. . . . When I don't feel I can rule fairly, I'll get off the bench," he said.[16]

The *Miami Herald* soon challenged DuVal's judicial competence with a report that he had been reversed on appeal in sixty-eight cases, not fewer than twenty as he had claimed. DuVal said he had been counting only the appeals of final judgments, excluding dismissal orders and procedural rulings.[17] It was an unpersuasive excuse, given the decisive importance of many such rulings.

Hatchett characterized the campaign as a referendum on reforming the court. His television commercials and his public speeches stressed the issues of "integrity, impartiality, freedom from special interests." When asked in a friendly manner when the court would overcome its notoriety for political decisions, he replied, "That is part of what this election is all about. Like never before, it's hanging in the balance." Most of the media agreed; Hatchett was the overwhelming favorite of the editorial boards, as well as of the condominium organizations and others that endorsed him in the race.[18]

Hatchett won with 60 percent of the vote, carrying forty-five of the sixty-seven counties including Dade, where DuVal was the hometown candidate, and Duval, the county bearing his family name. All but one of the twenty-two counties that favored DuVal were rural constituencies, predominantly in the northern part of the state, where archsegregationist gubernatorial candidates had run most strongly in the 1960s. Hatchett received more than double DuVal's vote in Pinellas and Hillsborough. Sundberg won the same day, dispatching John V. Russell, a former Fort Lauderdale mayor, in what had been a low-key race with no issues other than a Bar poll favoring the appointed incumbent. Russell, who had gambled on his alphabetical ballot placement advantage, complained, "The real question is not what the organized bar thinks of me or my opponent, but rather what the public thinks of the organized bar." If the public thought about it at all, it was to think favorably of the Bar; Sundberg won with 56 percent. Although Sundberg carried fewer counties, the 37 that favored Russell were, much like DuVal's, small and mostly rural. Running in a three-man race for Roberts's seat with the advantages of having been recommended by the nominating commission and the residual name recognition of having sought the Democratic gubernatorial nomination in 1964, Fred Karl eliminated Richard "Max" Swann in the primary. Swann was a Miami attorney who had served on the Third District Court of Appeal, but he had waited until the next to last day to qualify, and Karl had stolen a march with the editorial boards by then. Karl took 56 percent of the vote in a runoff against Charles R. Holley, a former Republican gubernatorial candidate and former circuit judge from Clearwater. He resigned after only fifteen months, however, because he could not subsist on the salary. The illness had devastated his finances, and he lost a medical malpractice suit that he had hoped would restore his financial health.[19]

Karl was the last justice to join the Supreme Court by election. In large measure because of the election-related misconduct of their predecessors, Hatchett and Sundberg were the last justices who needed to defend their seats in contested races.[20] The Florida legal establishment had lobbied sporadically since the 1940s for the appointment of all judges, who would then stand in so-called merit retention elections. There would be no opponents; should the voters turn out an incumbent, the governor would appoint his or her replacement from among nominees recommended to him. The establishment of nominating commissions by Askew's policy in 1971 and by constitutional amendment in 1972 was a step in that direction, although appointments were to be made through that process only for midterm vacancies.[21] The legislature remained indifferent to a purely appointed judiciary until the succession of scandals at the Supreme Court, all rooted directly or indirectly in the election process, dramatized the case for merit selection. The compromise constitutional amendment, providing for merit selection and retention of only Supreme Court justices and judges of the district courts of appeal, cleared the legislature in the spring of 1976 and was ratified by the voters in November. There was a close call when Republicans in the House tried to change it so that all judges would continue to be elected, with merit-retention votes only for judges who drew no opponents. This was defeated by a 53 to 46 vote to table it. Although Rish's hearings had illustrated why judges—especially the appellate bench—should be insulated from politics, the chairman personally opposed the merit-retention reform. The passage of three decades did not change his point of view. "I still think they ought not to run against their record or run against a ghost, but against an opponent," he remarked in 2006.[22]

Although Hatchett resided at Daytona Beach when Askew chose him, he claimed Clearwater as his home. Following the Overton and Sundberg selections, that meant there were three consecutive Supreme Court appointments from Pinellas County. As that happened to be a Republican stronghold, the majority Democrats did not make it a partisan issue when a Republican representative from Lake County proposed a residency requirement, still in force, for appointments to the Supreme Court. The provision, which Rish supported, states that there must be at least one justice appointed from each appellate district. When a resignation or retirement would leave the court without another justice who had come from the departing member's district, applications are accepted only from residents of that district. This rule mandates inequality of opportunity because the appellate districts vary in population, but the legislature has resisted efforts to change it.

The Constitution Revision Commission of 1978 proposed merit selection for circuit and county judgeships as well, but it failed in a historically close referendum, losing by only 37,162 votes out of 2,154,310 that were cast. There had been relatively little debate on that issue; its failure was a collateral casualty of intense opposition to a casino gambling initiative and another, much more controversial Revision Commission amendment to abolish the elected cabinet.[23] The Bar resumed lobbying the legislature without success, eventually persuading the Senate but not the House in 1992. The Constitution Revision Commission of 1998 proposed and the voters approved an amendment that enables the voters of each circuit and county to opt for merit selection of their circuit and county court judges.[24] However, every jurisdiction rejected the method two years later, with approval averaging only 26 percent and no county more favorable than 39 percent. The provision remains in the constitution, authorizing merit-selection referendums initiated by local petitions, but there is no apparent public interest. The overwhelming rejection was one sign among many of a nationwide conservative backlash against the judiciary.[25]

The Supreme Court scandals had created a once-in-a-lifetime window of opportunity to depoliticize Florida's temples of justice. Without the evidence displayed to the public by his committee, Rish acknowledged, legislators "would have probably been more reluctant to jump on the bandwagon."[26]

⊰ 16 ⊱

The Fugitive

The Florida Bar was not satisfied with McCain's resignation from the bench. It wanted him out of the legal profession altogether. Staff counsel Norman A. Faulkner encouraged the action but presciently advised the Bar's Board of Governors that the disbarment of McCain would be historically "complex, expensive, and time-consuming."[1] It eventually took nearly three years.

At the outset, it was uncertain that the Bar had the power to investigate a former judge for his actions on the bench. Although the Supreme Court had established the Bar in the exercise of its constitutional authority to regulate the admission and practice of lawyers, it had ruled on at least two occasions that judges were subject only to impeachment or to actions initiated by the Judicial Qualifications Commission. There was no Florida precedent for Bar action against a *former* judge for behavior on the bench that would imply unfitness as a lawyer. As McCain had feared, his would be the test case. Responding to the Bar's notice of probable cause in October 1975, McCain's new lawyer, Robert J. Beckham, asked McCain's former colleagues to halt the proceedings. They did.[2]

The court took five months to decide and another six weeks to deny rehearing before finally authorizing the Bar to proceed, and did so only by a 4-3 vote: the Old Guard defeated by the New. The split had been foretold by the tenor of their questions during oral argument.[3] Hatchett, Overton, England,

and Sundberg comprised the majority. Boyd, Roberts, and Adkins dissented, although Boyd straddled both positions. Boyd agreed that former judges could be subject to discipline as lawyers, but said the Bar should file charges only "with prior specific approval of this court." Moreover, he contended that the Bar's requests for authority should be debated and decided in secret. Otherwise, Boyd said, judges would fear reprisal for unpopular opinions or behavior. Writing perhaps with himself in mind, Boyd expressed concern: "Surely everyone everywhere has done something controversial and it would normally be rather easy to find something in any judge's personal or official life about which to file a complaint." He fretted that the majority opinion would tempt the Bar to keep dossiers on all judges, encourage incompetent judges "to remain in office as long as possible," and discourage competent attorneys from seeking judicial service. Roberts and Adkins went further, contending that the conduct of a judge should be off limits to the Bar forever regardless of circumstances. "If a judge serves the judiciary without removal," Adkins wrote, "it must be presumed that he was fit to serve the public as a judge." He complained that the majority was converting the Bar into the "Big Daddy" of the judicial system.[4]

Perhaps fearing how those three would vote, the Bar's special counsel, Bernard H. Dempsey Jr., had advised McCain's lawyers that "certain" of the five justices who had served with McCain were potential witnesses in the Bar's case. But if that was an implied suggestion that Adkins, Roberts, and Boyd should recuse themselves, it went begging. Although they might step aside later, Adkins said, it was better for the elected justices rather than ad hoc replacements to decide an issue as momentous as whether a former judge could be disbarred for conduct on the bench. "We felt that if history is going to be made it should be made by the elected judges of the court," he said.

Writing for the new majority, Hatchett observed that other states were virtually unanimous in allowing former judges to be disqualified from practicing law. What McCain was asking, he wrote, was "tantamount to a claim that a lawyer is immune from discipline for the most egregious ethical improprieties, so long as his misconduct disgraced not only the bar but the bench as well." Hatchett dismissed as premature the fears expressed by Boyd and Roberts. The court would await the Bar's formal complaint before deciding whether McCain was in trouble for unethical conduct or merely for unpopular opinions.[5]

Faulkner warned the Board that the charges would have to be painted with a broad brush, at least at the beginning, because McCain's resignation had stopped the impeachment process, "the only public inquiry into his acts... in mid-stride." The Rish committee had only pointed the way; it would be up to the Bar to probe "each rock or crevice." When Dempsey finally filed the formal charges in June 1976, they largely tracked the Rish committee's hearings fourteen months previously. One new accusation contended that McCain had taken gifts or favors from Nell, although in the end the Bar's prosecutors would be as leery as D'Alemberte of May's testimony about delivering $10,000 in cash to McCain. That left only the nearly valueless cuff links that McCain admitted receiving. The Bar also eventually gave up trying to prove that the elusive Nancy Wakeman had given $1,000 to McCain through Farish. In an entirely new issue, the Bar accused McCain of perjury for "material false statements" in an affidavit he had given in Farish's behalf. The affidavit, designed to counter the research assistants' impressions of McCain's apparent acts of favoritism, denounced Anne Parker, Larry Sartin, McFerrin Smith, and William Falck as upstarts who "considered themselves to be the actual judges," conspired against the justices, and had been "admonished" and in some cases fired because of their conduct. In fact, none had been fired—much to Roberts's regret—but the perjury charge against McCain evaporated because he had not been sworn when he gave the false statement.[6]

The actual trial before Referee Jack Wayman, a Jacksonville attorney, took ten days over two weeks in February 1977. The crux of Beckham's defense was that McCain was "an elected judge in an elected system" when he made the telephone calls that would be difficult to explain away. Conceding possible "bad judgment," Beckham said the Bar could produce no evidence of "moral turpitude."[7] Wayman, who had already dismissed two sets of charges, was impatient with the Bar from the outset over the broad breadth of the allegations, which touched on everything the House committee had heard; the list of more than a hundred proposed witnesses and depositions; and the slow pace of testimony that required several late-night sessions.[8] During tedious proceedings over David Smith's testimony, Dempsey asked McCain to identify W. R. McCain as his brother, and Wayman retorted, "You don't have to prove that to me every day for two weeks."[9] On the third day, during a painstaking interrogation of one of the law clerks, Wayman snapped at Wilson J. Foster, the Bar's assistant staff counsel, "Go ahead. We have a goal, a witness a day. You only have 108 of them listed."[10]

McCain, on the stand for a total of nearly ten hours, contended that he had telephoned Moe about Burton Loebl only because the attorney was "extremely nervous and upset" as to how a Jewish lawyer from Miami Beach would fare before a judge in Broward County, which had yet to complete its metamorphosis into the cosmopolitan constituency that it is today.[11] Loebl, however, testified that he could not recall talking to McCain about his case and had not experienced any prejudice in Broward courts.[12] Moe's allegation turned out to be one of the two charges that Wayman judged to be serious. The referee disbelieved McCain's explanation that he had not tried to argue Loebl's case for him.[13]

Moe's testimony was so powerful that it was quoted verbatim into the Supreme Court's ultimate ruling on McCain.

> My reaction was the call was totally unnecessary, totally uncalled for, but, by the same token, I was a Judge of the County Judges Court, for maybe a little bit more than a year at that time, and here is a man on the Supreme Court of Florida, calling me about a case; as a matter of fact, just a motion for continuance in a case. Now, I had always been taught, through education, through legal training, through custom, tradition, history, what have you, that the Supreme Court of Florida is, let's say, the last repository of all knowledge concerning law, equity, procedure, and certainly ethics, and I didn't know if any other judges were receiving phone calls. I did not know if this stuff went on. By "this stuff," I mean a higher court judge calling another judge about a case pending in front of him. I certainly didn't think it went on. By the same token, it is almost like saying he is on the Supreme Court, he must be right. He must have some kind of reason. There must be some kind of procedural aspect of it that I don't understand. So, my reaction was really mixed. I couldn't see any reason for him interfering with the case before me, but yet, he was a Supreme Court justice and so, it is like I said, I was taught to think, to believe what they do is right.[14]

McCain also claimed that he did not know the Stewart case was docketed when he asked to exchange oral argument dates with Judge Owen at the Fourth District Court of Appeal. He denied asking Parker, his own aide, to draft a memorandum on how it might be appealed. He denied ever saying "We are taking care of Willie's case today." He said that the "this is a fix" remark to Larry Sartin meant that Kaplan "had been had" by the judge of industrial claims, not that he—McCain—was fixing the case. He admitted, however, having asked White to assign him to specific cases—nine, possibly ten, "whatever he testified to"—including *Firestone v. Time,* and said he had stopped doing so after Roberts cautioned him about it. Only four, he said, were Farish's cases.[15] Roberts had also cautioned him, he conceded, that the rumors of a close relationship with Farish could embarrass him. "As a matter of fact it has, hasn't it?," remarked Wayman. "Without any question, your honor," McCain replied.[16]

McNulty's testimony to Wayman concerning McCain's attempt to fix the Nell case was particularly damaging to McCain, even more so than his account to the House committee. McNulty said McCain made it clear to him that he hoped the Second District would overturn Nell's conviction. He said the call angered him so much that he remarked to his law clerk, "I'll be God-damned if I will put my name on a reversal of that case. Now, if I can't conscientiously . . . affirm that conviction, I will get out of the case."[17]

Wayman found McCain guilty on only two of the twenty charges still pending: the telephone calls to McNulty and Moe. The referee recommended only a reprimand and a one-year suspension from the practice of law. Wayman sharply criticized the Bar for relying upon the House hearings to charge McCain with much more misconduct than he thought the Bar had been able to prove, most notably the Wakeman accusation. He was particularly caustic toward the research aides on whose testimony most of the Farish-related issues depended. Wayman considered McCain's aspersions on the clerks "to be corroborated to a substantial extent by the testimony of Justices Roberts, Adkins, and Boyd," and concluded that the aides were "almost totally disloyal to the court and to the various justices sitting on the court. He found David Smith's testimony to be "totally unworthy of belief."[18] With respect to McNulty's evidence, however, Wayman described McCain as "almost totally indifferent concerning, or does not recognize, the unethical quality of his conduct."[19] Alluding to the other issues, Wayman scoffed at the Bar for attempting "to convince me . . . that the Supreme Court was a one-man court under the domination of McCain." But he conceded that McCain "did exhibit very poor judgment from an ethical standpoint" and that "doubtlessly, his lack of good taste did bring about many of the insinuations against him."[20]

Wayman's criticism of McCain's ethical insensibility is difficult to reconcile with the referee's contempt for the only people at the Supreme Court who had been concerned enough to report it. In contrast to the conscientious actions of the research assistants, Roberts—despite all that he had confided to the governor—testified almost proudly that "I've never filed a complaint with the Judicial Qualifications Commission against anybody."[21]

It is the Supreme Court, not the referee, that decides upon the punishment for a lawyer, and McCain would find no sympathy there. The court voted unanimously to grant the Bar's appeal and disbar rather than suspend him. Hatchett, the justice who had replaced him, wrote the decision. It set significant precedents in rejecting McCain's argument that there ought to be a time limit such as the court had invoked to protect Turner, the Miami judge. Hatchett noted that the Bar had begun proceedings as soon as possible once McCain no longer had judicial immunity. Turning to the merits, Hatchett explained why suspension would be insufficient.

> The conduct engaged in by McCain while a Justice of the highest court of this state cuts to the very heart of the judicial system, a system carefully established to insure that equal justice under law prevails in this country for the rich and the poor, the powerful and the powerless. McCain's conduct has done much to erode the public's confidence in the integrity and impartiality of the judiciary and the bar, thus undermining the entire judicial process. . . . McCain's blatant disregard for the integrity of the truth finding process, essential to our notion of equal justice under the law, directly bears on his present fitness to practice law.

The only solace for McCain was the court's agreement with Wayman that the Bar "took an excessively broad approach to this case and failed to early abandon counts that could not be proved." Therefore McCain would not be required to bear the Bar's costs.

Overton, England, and Sundberg concurred in the decision as did three circuit judges sitting in for Boyd, Adkins, and Karl. Writing separately, however, England said he would have found McCain guilty also of impropriety for interfering in the probation case. Sundberg, with England concurring, also wrote separately to emphasize that McCain's case-fixing for campaign supporters was "so inimical to the judicial system that nothing less than disbarment can vindicate the injury done." The public will accept and respect judicial rulings, Sundberg reasoned, "only so long as people have confidence in the institution which renders the decisions under which they must live."[22]

McCain's disbarment did not set the sort of example feared by the Old Guard justices who had voted against the Bar investigation. From 1976 through 2006, thirty-five judges were removed or left office by resignation, retirement, or election defeat with JQC charges pending against them. The Bar sought to discipline only McCain and fourteen others. Seven were disbarred, and another four were allowed to resign in lieu of discipline. The majority of the cases in which the Bar acted against former judges involved criminal convictions.

McCain's disbarment was not the last or the least of his troubles. He was convicted in 1977 of drunk driving. In September 1977, with the court's disbarment decision still pending, he was arrested at Miami on an aggravated assault charge, accused of displaying a handgun to three teenage girls who were talking outside his apartment. McCain pleaded guilty to the assault charge but did not go to jail. His attorney at one point was another disgraced former judge, Alfonso Sepe of Miami, who had resigned from the circuit bench under suspicion of soliciting sex from the wife of a man he had sentenced to prison. Sepe eventually returned to the bench through politics only to be indicted, suspended, and sent to prison for bribery.[23]

McCain entered an alcoholic treatment program, took a job as a law clerk, and began talking about applying for readmission to the Bar.[24] But in September 1982 he was one of seven men accused of an unsuccessful plot to smuggle fifteen tons of marijuana into Louisiana from Panama and Colombia.[25] Under the alias Joe Rico, McCain allegedly arranged to buy a shrimp boat and send it to Colombia where soldiers captured the captain and crew and demanded a $500,000 ransom. When the captain called McCain, he reportedly said, "I'm sorry. I can't help you."[26] McCain was arrested at his Fort Pierce home on Louisiana state charges, released on bond, and rearrested a month later on a federal indictment in the same case.[27] He was freed under an unsecured $1 million bond. In January 1983, McCain failed to appear at a hearing in Louisiana and was declared a fugitive. Facing up to twenty-four years in prison, he had calculated the survival odds for a former judge behind bars and concluded they were not good. His two lawyers were waiting to drive him to Miami International Airport, where they were booked to fly to Houston, but he did not show up.[28] Four months later, he was one of forty-one people accused in a massive state and federal drug bust called Operation Everglades. More than 200 agents surrounded the tiny, remote Gulf coast town of Everglades City in the climax of a two-year investigation that had already seized more than 450,000 pounds of marijuana and thirty-nine boats, but they did not find McCain.[29]

The FBI had already declared a nationwide search for him. There were rumors of McCain sightings in Colombia, Panama, Costa Rica, the Bahamas, and elsewhere, but it is doubtful that McCain ever left the country or that the FBI's pursuit measured up to the bureau's reputation.[30] On November 11, 1986, the 1,390th day of his life as a fugitive, McCain died of lung cancer at the home of a daughter in Jacksonville, where neighbors said he had been living for at least a year under the alias Thomas Sam Mills. The *Miami Herald* reported that he had likely spent the intervening years in South Carolina. In Jacksonville, the four daughters from McCain's first marriage had taken turns caring for him and driving him to doctors and hospital treatments for which they paid cash. He and his first wife, Joyce, had reconciled. Both Joyce and Helen, to whom he was still legally married, claimed his body at a funeral home in Jacksonville, where the state attorney was advised of Thomas Mills's true identity. A few days later, the United States attorney at Miami received a letter in which McCain asked whether he could obtain leniency by turning himself in.[31]

McCain's portrait remains on display with those of other former justices at the Supreme Court building in Tallahassee. It appears to have been painted from a photograph rather than from life.

The Keys to the Courthouse

Campbell Thornal's surgeons at the Duke University medical center found pancreatic cancer and told him he likely had only a year to live. Accepting the prognosis, he worried less about himself than the future of the Florida Supreme Court after his death. Thornal dwelled on it throughout the thirteen-hour homeward journey from North Carolina. Richard R. Swann, a young lawyer and family friend, was driving; the justice rested on the back seat of his ancient green Oldsmobile and reminisced about what he and his closest friends on the Supreme Court had done to make it professional and keep it above politics. But Stephen O'Connell had left for the University of Florida presidency, Elwyn Thomas had retired, Thornal was dying, and soon there would be no counterweight to B. K. Roberts. "His biggest concern was what was going to happen to the court," Swann recalled. "There were other justices that were not as strong. With his dying, the power was going to quickly shift to B. K."[1]

Thornal had long since lost an epic struggle regarding the court's jurisdiction over the district courts. That issue, on which he and Thomas eventually stood almost alone in favor of restraining the Supreme Court's appetite for appeals, had divided the seven justices since the district courts of appeal were established under a 1956 constitutional amendment that Thomas championed as chair of the Florida Judicial Council. Roberts especially chafed under a restricted jurisdiction.[2] The intent was to relieve the Supreme Court's oppressive workload, some 1,300 filings a year, many of which languished fourteen months awaiting oral argument. Congestion "had become almost intolerable."[3] In criminal cases, Thornal recalled, "the bootlegger and bolita peddler" could stay free another two years simply by appealing and posting bond, while the less fortunate "oftentimes remained in jail for months before we could hear their grievance and finally release them."[4] The reform structure, roughly similar to the federal judicial system, anticipated that the three district courts (there are now five) were to have the last word on more than two-thirds of the cases they heard. The Supreme Court's mandatory jurisdiction would be limited to certain specified classes of cases including the death penalty, public utilities, Bar admission and discipline, and the appeals of decisions that passed "directly" on the constitutionality of a law. The court would have the discretion to review decisions that were alleged to conflict with its own precedents or those of other district courts.[5] As with everything else in the constitution, of course, the outcome would depend on the Supreme Court's interpretations; in other words, on the court's self-restraint. That turned out to be thin ice, although it appeared solid at first.

The initial test case resulted in an emphatic ruling that the Supreme Court would refrain from second-guessing the district courts. "It was never intended that the district courts of appeal should be intermediate courts," Justice E. Harris Drew wrote for a five-judge panel in March 1958:

> The new article embodies throughout its terms the idea of a Supreme Court which functions as a supervisory body . . . exercising appellate power in certain specified areas essential to the settlement of issues of public importance and the preservation of uniformity of principle and practice, with review by the district courts in most instances being final and absolute.[6]

The decision denied a second appeal for the owner of a water-filled rock pit who had been sued for the drowning of a child. The man's lawyers claimed that the Third District Court of Appeal ruling against him conflicted in effect with certain decisions of the Supreme Court. But Drew emphasized that there was no "direct conflict." To create direct conflict, he explained, "the decisions must be based practically on the same state of facts and *announce* antagonistic conclusions" (emphasis supplied). Whether the outcome of the most recent case seemed to be fair or unfair was beside the point; the Supreme Court simply lacked the power to decide.

B. K. Roberts, at the peak of his power in his third turn as chief justice, addresses the Legislature. Seated, from left, are House Speaker Richard A. Pettigrew, Governor Reubin Askew, and Senate President Jerry Thomas. *Courtesy of the Florida State Archives.*

The line still held three months later when the court refused to overturn a decision in which the Second District Court of Appeal had upheld a divorce decree with the single word *Affirmed*. The district courts typically relied on these so-called *per curiam* affirmances to dispose of cases that did not seem novel or difficult. Lawyers for the losing spouse in *Lake v. Lake* argued that the facts of the case were very similar to another in which the Supreme Court had approved a different outcome. There was no direct conflict as Drew had defined it, and the Supreme Court properly refused to surmise any. A unanimous five-judge court used the occasion to lecture the legal profession yet again that the district courts *"are and were meant to be courts of final, appellate jurisdiction"* (emphasis in the original). They were not intended to be mere "way stations on the road to the Supreme Court." To make this work, Thomas wrote, would depend largely on the determination of the Supreme Court not to venture beyond the limitations of its own powers by arrogating to itself the right to delve into a decision of a district court of appeal primarily to decide whether or not the Supreme Court agrees with the district court appeal about the disposition of a given case. (*Lake v. Lake*, 103 So. 2d 639 (1958)

Everyone was entitled to a day in court and to a fair appeal, Thomas conceded. "But he is not entitled to two appeals." There would be occasions when the court should second-guess a *per curiam* affirmance, but they should be rare. Otherwise, "if the Supreme Court undertakes to go behind a judgment on the tenuous theory that it must see that justice is done instead of giving to the judgment the verity it deserves and assuming that justice *has been done* the system that has been overwhelmingly approved by the people will be undermined and weakened.[7]

Roberts did not participate in either of the first two definitive decisions on jurisdiction; the reasons why he did not were unreported. But he was plainly unhappy with them, and he did vote a year later in the next important case, which began to turn the tide. In *Harrell's Candy Kitchen, Inc. v. Sarasota-Manatee Airport Authority*, the court accepted jurisdiction over a direct appeal—bypassing the Second District Court of Appeal—of a circuit judge's decision in a zoning case. It acted upon the premise that the judge had "inherently" upheld a state statute. Drew, softening his strong stand of 1958, wrote the majority opinion supported by all the court except Thomas, who dissented, and Thornal, who was disqualified for unstated reasons. Thomas denounced it as "a usurpation of the power of the district courts of appeal."[8] The majority's reasoning potentially qualified every criminal conviction for a direct appeal, since the constitutionality of a criminal statute is almost always an inherent question. A criminal case deluge did not result, but the *Harrell's* case clearly invited "forum shopping" by lawyers who thought their civil appeals might fare better in Tallahassee than at the district courts of appeal.[9]

What little remained of the court's self-restraint vanished in 1965 with a 4-3 opinion written by Roberts that eviscerated the *Lake* precedent. It held that the Supreme Court could examine the original pleadings and decisions in the *trial* courts to find conflict with Florida precedents. This was the landmark case of *Foley v. Weaver Drugs*, a six-year saga that began in a most prosaic way.[10]

Rose Foley suffered a cut wrist when a bottle of reducing pills shattered in her hand as she tried to open it. The Foleys sued Weaver Drugs along with the manufacturer, but the judge ruled that they did not have a legal cause of action against the retailer. The Third District Court of Appeal upheld that finding in November 1962 without a written opinion. The Foleys appealed to the Florida Supreme Court, citing a recent decision of the Second District Court of Appeal that held a retailer responsible for a defective soda bottle.[11] In November 1964 the Supreme Court asked the Third District to write an opinion explaining why it had ruled in favor of Weaver Drugs. "In my humble, and perhaps lonely, opinion," Thomas protested, "such procedure is a distortion of the provisions of the Constitution and an arrogation by this Court of power it does not possess." Thornal concurred in Thomas's "lonely" dissent.[12]

The Third DCA refused to explain, stating that "we do not feel it is essential or appropriate for us now to produce theories and reasons for the decision which we made in November of 1962." The judges objected that it would amount to a second hearing. Turning to the underlying issue that had energized the trial bar in behalf of the Foleys, they pointed out that "omitting opinions in a minority of affirmances is customary with appellate courts. It is a useful, if not essential practice of a busy appellate court such as this. . . . Opinions generally are dispensed with upon affirming cases which do not involve new or unusual points of law." To write more opinions, the judges said, would serve "only to satisfy the parties that the court adverted to the issues and gave them attention, and to add needlessly to an already excessive volume of opinions." If the Supreme Court wanted to know the reasons for the first Foley decision, it was welcome to glean them from the briefs and other parts of the record. The judges remarked with obvious sarcasm that the higher court seemed to have already done that.[13]

The last word belonged to Roberts, who wrote two months later for himself, Drew, Caldwell, and Ervin that the Supreme Court indeed was empowered to look at the "record proper"—that is, everything but the actual testimony—to detect conflict with a precedent and take jurisdiction. "It is the judgment which constitutes the decision in litigated cases, and the opinion merely sets forth the reasons supporting the judgment," he wrote.

Lonely voice of restraint: Justice Campbell Thornal (1955–70), a passionate advocate for restraint in Supreme Court case selection. Thornal's views were vindicated ten years after his death by a constitutional amendment restricting jurisdiction. *Courtesy of the Florida State Archives.*

The consequence was bitterly ironic for the Foleys. Roberts's final opinion upheld the original Third District judgment against them; it reversed the Second District Court's *Canada Dry* decision, which had not been appealed. "We are not persuaded," Roberts wrote, "that considerations of public policy require us to extend to food containers the 'implied warranty' liability of retailers as to the food contained therein; on the contrary, we are of the opinion that it would be unreasonably burdensome to extend liability in this respect."[14]

Although Drew concurred, he had misgivings; he rationalized in a separate concurring opinion that a "short delay in the ultimate disposition of these cases is indeed a small price to pay for consistency and uniformity of decisions throughout the state." Thornal wrote a passionate dissent with Thomas and O'Connell concurring:

> In our apparent anxiety to emphasize the word "Supreme," we can easily overlook the fact that the Courts of Appeal are "Supreme" in certain areas. This is so because the people themselves have said so.... The impact of the majority decision is to create a multiple-leveled appellate system with all of its attendant expense and delay.... With all due respect for the ability and experience of my brethren I find it utterly impossible to locate anything in the Constitution that conveys to this Court the privilege of exploring trial records in order to produce a conflict of decision.... All of this simply means that the District Court decisions *are no longer final* under any circumstances.... If I were a practicing lawyer in Florida, I would never again accept with finality a decision of a District Court."[15]

In the same year that *Foley* was finally decided, the Florida Bar's new assistant counsel, Richard McFarlain, needed Roberts's signature as acting chief justice on an order to produce a state prisoner in a disciplinary case against a lawyer. When McFarlain's eyes fell on an immense stack of files on the justice's desk, Roberts remarked that he was doing title work for Winn-Dixie Stores because the grocery chain thought a justice's opinion was "worth more than that of the average lawyer." Aside from flouting his constitutional obligation to devote full time to his office and to refrain from practicing law, Roberts evidently had a lawyer-client relationship with a corporation that stood to benefit hugely from the holding in *Foley* that retailers were not liable for defective packaging.[16]

Roberts's permissive approach to jurisdiction was reinforced when Carlton joined the court. But by 1977, petitions for discretionary writs of certiorari in district court cases amounted to nearly half the Supreme Court's caseload, which had burgeoned to 2,145 filings compared with merely 482 in 1958. *Foley* "had a tremendous impact . . . .producing an attitude among attorneys that a district court decision was never final," observed a *Florida Law Review* article. "Files in conflict jurisdiction cases circulated to a minimum of five justices' office at least twice—once for a vote on jurisdiction, and a second time either for an often sought rehearing on a denial or, if certiorari was granted, for a decision on the merits."[17]

The case that prompted Thornal's last great protest against *Foley* was on his mind as he rode home from North Carolina four years later. It involved Ed Ball's St. Joseph Telephone Co. and its manager, B. Roy Gibson Jr., who were appealing a $15,000 libel and slander judgment won by *Apalachicola Times* publisher Joseph A. Maloney, a critic of Ball and the duPont empire. With Ball's interest so conspicuous, Roberts would not vote on the case, but Thornal implied to Swann that Roberts had been lobbying his colleagues on the threshold question of whether to review a First District Court of Appeal decision favoring Maloney. The Supreme Court's eventual decision against Maloney described him in strongly unfavorable language that Thornal decried as utterly unsupported by the record. The majority opinion, attributed to Adkins, contended that "the record clearly shows" that Maloney strove to "harass and abuse the duPont interests, apparently for the purpose of convincing the public that these interests were some sort of evil influence in the community . . . and that it would therefore not be a good place to live and do business." That was not what the record showed, but it did echo what Gibson had claimed in a public speech and corporate mailing that blamed Maloney for a decline in telephone company subscribers. In fact, as Thornal observed, the company had more subscribers, not fewer; the difference was that some had simply been transferred to a new exchange. "I do not find the facts to be exactly as stated [by the majority], nor do I find any basis for jurisdiction in this Court which justified consideration of the merits," Thornal protested in a long dissent. "There remains no doubt in my mind that *Foley* was wrong when announced and the error has been compounded by its continued recognition. It should be scrubbed from the books."[18]

Less than ten months later, Thornal was back at the Duke University hospital for surgery that was unable to prolong his life. His death was imminent, but still he wanted to hear how that day's election had come out. "Honey," his wife whispered, "Reubin beat Kirk." Thornal winked at her and smiled. Minutes later, he was dead.[19] Had he lived two months longer, it would have been Askew who appointed his successor. As it was, the choice was Kirk's, and McCain fit himself eagerly into the activist majority, voting liberally to find conflict decisions under *Foley*. *Foley* facilitated the "McCain technique" that the research aides described to the House committee. Rival attorneys were unlikely to overlook the resulting statistic: The Farish firm won conflict certiorari review in ten of eleven successive cases at a time when 85 percent of petitions overall were being turned down.[20]

A few years later, however, it was McCain's departure that tipped the court's balance against *Foley*. Overton, Sundberg, and England were professed conservatives on Supreme Court jurisdiction. Hatchett was of like mind, and it was a unanimous court that called on the 1979 legislature for a constitutional amendment to limit discretionary review. The amendment, in modified form, was ratified in 1980. Among other things, it prohibited review of district court decisions without written opinions. Review based merely on the "record proper" was dead. The Supreme Court would also no longer be required to hear appeals of lower court decisions upholding state laws; it would have jurisdiction only after a lower court *invalidated* a law. Concurrently, the legislature shifted review of workers' compensation cases to the First District Court of Appeal.[21]

The 1980 amendment has been criticized for entrusting less discretion to Florida's Supreme Court than most other states allow to their courts of last resort. Unlike the U.S. Supreme Court, the Florida court cannot take a case simply because it appears to be significant. There must be either a valid point of conflict with precedent or a certification from the district court that it involves a question of "great public importance."[22] Had the Florida court prior to 1980 been as famously reluctant to grant discretionary review as is the U.S. Supreme Court, which accepts only 5 percent of such cases, perhaps there would have been less of an argument, if any at all, for constitutional restrictions on its jurisdiction.

As it became more difficult to get a case into the Florida court, it also became less likely that the court would dare to go where the legislature feared (or refused) to tread. From having been an activist court in the 1970s, "rarely

After the storm. The court in 1978, from left: Joseph W. Hatchett, Arthur J. England, James C. Adkins, Chief Justice Ben Overton, Joseph A. Boyd, Alan C. Sundberg, James A. Alderman. Only Adkins and Boyd remained from the court five years earlier. *Courtesy of the Florida State Archives.*

waiting for the legislature to solve the problems of society that became apparent through the cases on its docket," the court of the 1980s was remarkable for its reluctance to break new ground except in such strictly "in-house" issues as cameras in the courtroom. "The court's attitude changed substantially with respect to societal problem solving," observed scholar Charles S. Lopeman. "The opinions of the 1980s Florida court are replete with appeals to the legislature to establish missing public policy."[23] For example, the court in 1987 refused to make a social host pay for damages caused by an inebriated adult guest.[24] "We cannot find social hosts more liable than the legislature has determined," wrote Justice Rosemary Barkett, whom some considered an activist. Adkins, who had fought and won his own battle with alcoholism, dissented.

A transcendent irony, one that surely would have cheered Thornal, was the contribution of St. Joseph Telephone, through its attorney Ed Mason, in ultimately undoing *Foley* and completely changing the court. But for Mason's *ex parte* memorandum and his visit to Dekle's office, there likely would have been none of the investigations and reforms recounted in this book.

Neither an umpire nor a judge should base his decisions upon his perceptions of public reaction.

—Richard T. Earle Jr., *St. Petersburg Times*, September 5, 1990

⊰ 18 ⊱

Clear and Present Dangers

At a seminar of former Florida governors in March 2006, Reubin Askew needed no time to form an answer to an impromptu question asking what he wished above all that he had done differently as governor three decades previously. Askew said it would be to write the judicial nominating commission membership formula into the constitution, where only supermajorities of the legislature and a statewide referendum could change it. It had not occurred to him in 1971 that any successor would be jealous of the power he had ceded voluntarily to the commissions.[1]

The nominating commissions still recommend between three and six candidates for the Supreme Court, the district courts of appeal, and all midterm vacancies in the circuit and county courts. They do so, however, from a profoundly different perspective. Since 2001 the governor has appointed not just three but all nine members of each commission. One way in which Governor Jeb Bush used his vastly increased influence was to insist on more racial and gender diversity on the trial bench. But he was criticized for making the process much more partisan and for appointing several conspicuously ideological attorneys and politicians to the district courts of appeal.

Askew alluded to this in a subsequent address to the Florida Bar marking his fiftieth anniversary as a lawyer. "For the judiciary to do its job it has got to be independent," he said. "There are those who, within their own right, would try to undermine some of that jurisdiction. I caution them." His service in the other two branches of government, he said, had strengthened his respect for the judiciary: "I came to the conclusion, after all these years, don't look to the executive, don't look to the legislative to protect your rights, you look to the judiciary. For our system of government to function, you have to have the independence of each one and confidence in each one." [2]

Bush was the first Republican governor since Reconstruction to have his own party in command of both houses of the legislature. He was also the first since the modern two-party system took root in 1967 to have none of his vetoes overridden. Until the 2006 session, the last of his eight-year tenure, Bush's control was so virtually absolute that Representative Chris Smith, the House Democratic leader, morosely described the legislature as "Jeb's workroom." Even some Republicans admitted to concern. "When you've got the power to push anything through, and there's nothing they can do about it, I think that's bad," GOP senator Michael Bennett said.[3]

From the outset, the more conservative Republican legislators and some members of Bush's staff intended to use their newfound power to take the Supreme Court in hand. They seethed over decisions that established a privacy right to abortion under the state constitution and nullified a constitutional amendment intended to accelerate executions. Bush implied what he thought of judicial independence when he remarked upon appointing a Supreme Court justice in July 2002: "The increasing power of the courts in our society should not come at the expense of institutions that have *a more legitimate claim to govern our lives*" (emphasis added).[4]

Nonetheless, the judiciary was left relatively unscathed during Bush's first two legislative sessions. There was no appetite for drastic change on the part of House Speaker John Thrasher, Bush's ally in most other matters, or Senate President Toni Jennings. Thrasher's philosophy was rooted in his service as an attorney on the House impeachment committee staff in 1975, where he had seen at first hand how the politics of judicial selection could undermine the judiciary. In 1999, during Bush's first session, the House voted only to allow the governor to immediately replace the former governor's three appointees on each nominating commission. With more than coincidental timing, that bill did not clear the House until the fifty-ninth day of the sixty-day regular session. Jennings then adjourned the Senate at 5:58 p.m. on the final day with six hours and two minutes to spare, leaving the bill dead on the calendar. The bill's sponsor had been on the rostrum a few minutes earlier, pleading in vain to let it come to a vote.[5]

The issue lay dormant in 2000, the last session over which Jennings and Thrasher presided, but returned forcefully in 2001, spurred by the Florida Supreme Court's 4-3 decision the previous December to order a manual recount of Florida's decisive vote in the presidential race between Vice President Al Gore and Texas governor George W. Bush, the governor's brother. Writing in dissent, and doubtlessly with an eye on a legislature that was threatening to preempt any recount by appointing Florida's electors itself, Chief Justice Charles Wells expressed his fear of a constitutional crisis that would do "substantial damage to our country, our state, and to this Court as an institution."[6] Legislation enacted in the final days of the subsequent regular session immediately removed all remaining appointees of Democratic governor Lawton Chiles from the twenty-six nominating commissions and empowered Bush eventually to select all nine members of each panel. The Florida Bar, which previously had chosen three members of each, was reduced to recommending lawyers for the governor to appoint to four of the nine seats. That was a last-minute concession to which there is less substance than it seemed, since it also entitles the governor to reject the Bar's lists time and again until it submits acceptable choices. The House passed the bill on a largely party-line vote, 65 to 50, with ten Republicans bucking Speaker Tom Feeney's intense support for the legislation. Representative Doug Wiles, a Democrat from St. Augustine, recorded his objection in the *Journal* with a quotation from the French magistrate and author Montesquieu: "There is no liberty if the power of judging be not separated from the legislative and executive powers."[7] The Senate approved the bill 29-10, with only one Republican voting no. Three Democrats voted yes, apparently misperceiving that the Bar's objections had been satisfied.[8] Because the Senate acted on the session's last day, amidst frenzied consideration of the annual budget and hundreds of pieces of other legislation, the media gave only passing mention to Bush's momentous takeover of the nominating commissions.

It appeared to former chief justice Gerald Kogan and to some others that the Bar had capitulated due to fear of a greater danger. There was a simultaneous proposed constitutional amendment to drastically limit the Supreme Court's jurisdiction, empower the legislature to license and regulate lawyers, strip the Bar of its power to levy dues and of its appointments to the Judicial Qualifications Commission, and permit the establishment of a statewide court of criminal appeals intended to rubber-stamp death sentences. The truth of the situation was that the court's enemies did not have the votes to pass the constitutional amendment, which languished the entire session in a House committee, but they did have enough to enact the nominating commission legislation with or without the Bar's acquiescence. "They couldn't care less whether we agreed," said Herman Russomanno, the Bar's president at the time. "We were hanging on by our fingernails. . . . They were throwing us a few crumbs." According to Steven Metz, the Bar's chief lobbyist, "We were really faced with the dilemma of not agreeing to the compromise and having no Bar involvement whatsoever."[9]

There had been recurring complaints before 2001 that the commissions nominated too few minority candidates and women for judgeships. The commissions were also susceptible to the influence of large establishment law firms. Justice Richard Ervin once objected that the process would produce only "bland people on the court" and remarked that his own brother, a former Florida Bar president, would not have voted to nominate him.[10] To their credit, however, the commissions rarely defaulted on their fundamental responsibility, which was to vouch for the integrity and ability of the lawyers they nominated. There were remarkably few occasions on which the commissions were accused of recommending poorly qualified people. By one important measure, the commissions performed significantly better than the electoral process. Of the first sixty-nine judges disciplined by the Supreme Court following Judicial Qualifications Commission investigations, 70 percent had arrived on the bench by election rather than appointment. Among the more serious cases ending in removal or resignations in the face of pending charges, 83 percent involved judges who owed their seats to election rather than appointment. To put the statistic in perspective, a 2000 Florida Bar study found that the cohort generating the most offenses, judges chosen by election, accounted for only 42 percent of the trial bench.[11]

One conspicuous blot on the reputation of the nominating commissions involved the panel for Palm Beach County, which tried to stack the deck for the dubiously qualified spouse of a member of the Bar's Board of Governors. Her rival nominees for a circuit judgeship were a county judge poorly regarded by the Palm Beach Bar and a Republican lawyer who had campaigned for Governor Chiles's reelection opponent, Jeb Bush. "It's Bar politics at its

very, very worst in a Bar that's one of the best," Chiles's general counsel remarked shortly before the governor appointed the Republican lawyer. The
highly publicized controversy led to a welcome windfall of applications for
commission memberships, which had gone begging when the governor's office previously advertised for volunteers.[12] In another notorious misstep, the
nominating commission in Dade County in 1987 inexplicably recommended
Alfonso Sepe, an elected county judge, for the circuit court despite his having
resigned from that bench in the face of a sexual harassment scandal twelve
years earlier. Having persuaded Dade County's famously indifferent voters
to overlook the past, Sepe then invoked political influence to return to the
circuit court. He changed his registration to Republican and solicited endorsement letters to Governor Bob Martinez, a Republican, from two leading GOP fund-raisers and a member of the Republican National Committee.
Sepe soon squandered his second chance; in 1991 he was indicted in a state
and federal bribery "sting" known as Operation Court Broom. He resigned
the bench again and eventually went to prison.[13]

Under Bush and the 2001 legislation, the nominating commissions took
on a transparently partisan cast. Applying for membership on the Sixth Circuit Commission, Susan Bedinghaus, wife of the Pinellas County Republican
chairman, wrote that she was "committed to selecting persons who would best
represent Governor Bush's ideals and principles." She got the appointment.
On May 1, 2005, the *St. Petersburg Times* reported in a Law Day editorial that
nearly 80 percent of commissioners statewide were registered Republicans, a
proportion more than twice the party's share of voter registrations. The Bar,
mindful of Bush's ability to reject its recommendations, had chosen deliber-
ately in 2002 to weight them with the governor's party.

The packing of the nominating commissions resulted in several markedly
partisan and controversial appellate court appointments. To the First District
Court of Appeal, whose jurisdiction includes most litigation involving state
agencies, Bush appointed a former Republican legislator, Paul Hawkes, with
no experience in any appeal other than a case in which he was a plaintiff, and
who had lost a close race for a circuit judgeship in 1994. Bush also sent to the
First District a conservative staff attorney, Bradford Thomas, who had been
his leading advocate for the death penalty. On that occasion, Bush's evident
preference for political allies on that court overcame his diversity policies;
both appointees being white men, it left the First District with a roster of
thirteen Caucasian males, one woman, and one black.[14]

To the Third District Court of Appeal, Bush appointed Frank A. Shepherd, a lawyer for the militantly conservative Pacific Legal Foundation, which specializes in opposing environmental and land use regulation and for which Bush wrote a fund-raising endorsement in 2002. Two years later, Bush made another conspicuously ideological appointment to the Third District. Leslie B. Rothenberg had resigned a circuit judgeship, where she had been accused of prosecution bias, to run unsuccessfully for Miami-Dade state attorney in a campaign notable for her written pledge to the Christian Family Coalition to oppose gay marriage and adoption. Her disappointment at losing the Republican primary was consoled with a nomination and appointment to an appellate judgeship. She subsequently won a place on the Supreme Court's Judicial Ethics Advisory Committee.[15]

The Bar nursed its wounds privately for several years until Kelly Overstreet Johnson, its president in 2004, broke the silence by charging that the nominating commission takeover "created the perception that there is no longer independence" from the governor. Johnson also appointed a committee on judicial independence in hope of a different political climate following the 2006 election. At the panel's first hearing, there was testimony that by insisting on six candidates for each judicial vacancy Bush was compelling the commissions to nominate people whom it considered somewhat less than the best. A former member of the Thirteenth Circuit commission, conceding that the former system had been susceptible to local pressures, complained that Bush's commissioners were asking such inappropriate questions of prospective nominees as "'What's your religion?' 'Do you go to church?' 'What religious things are important to you?' 'How do you feel about the death penalty?' Not 'Would you follow the law, whatever the law is?' but 'What are your personal feelings on the death penalty?'"[16] One of the commissioners most controversial in this regard was an African American clergyman, the Rev. O'Neal Dozier, a prominent figure in state and national Republican politics, who reportedly asked judicial applicants whether they were "God-fearing." Bush demanded and received Dozier's resignation after the preacher fomented opposition to the construction of a mosque near his church and was quoted as calling Muslims "dangerous" and "terrorists."[17]

In 2005, Burton Young, the Bar president who had decried the McCain appointment and lauded Askew's decision to establish the nominating commissions, expressed his disillusionment with what had happened since.

Now I'm not so sure. If I had a vote today, I'd vote to elect. . . . If we don't have an absolute merit selection process that is almost guaranteed to produce the best and the brightest, I certainly would trust the electorate more than I would trust somebody like Bush or anybody else who would appoint judges who are politically motivated, not legally motivated. I can't tell you how offensive it is to me. Toying with the independence of the judiciary is one of the worst political crimes anyone can commit."[18]

However, the election process itself has become an increasing threat to the independence and integrity of the judiciary. Florida judicial elections remain nonpartisan, but there is a question as to how long the U.S. Supreme Court will allow that restriction to prevail.

Gratifying social conservatives in a case appealed from Minnesota, the nation's highest court dealt a potentially fatal blow to the American judiciary's fundamental policy that candidates should not comment on issues that might come before them. Although merit retention has spared the Florida Supreme Court from the multimillion dollar special-interest bidding wars that have occurred in some states whose high courts are elected, it is no longer uncommon to see more than $500,000 spent to contest a Florida circuit court seat.[19]

The 2002 campaign, in which 251 circuit judgeships were at stake and 30 were contested in the primary, fulfilled many dismal predictions. The candidates raised $17 million, $8 million of it from sources reported to the secretary of state as lawyers and law firms. Among the 96 competing candidates, who accounted for some $11 million, half were able to put up at least $100,000. One particularly combative Jacksonville race in which two candidates spent more than $600,000 resulted in a Supreme Court reprimand for the newly elected judge for overspending his campaign account and lending it $20,000 at a later date than the law allowed. Concerned over the low quality of the debate, the Jacksonville Bar Association established a fair campaign practices committee to police the conduct of future judicial campaigns in the Fourth Circuit.[20] Circuit Judge John Renke III, winner of a $211,000 Pinellas-Pasco campaign, was removed by the Supreme Court for campaign violations after a four-year JQC investigation.

Campaign finance resembles to some extent the ploys of high-stakes poker: Ten incumbent judges and two lawyers seeking open seats "bought the pot" by putting up at least $100,000 to discourage anyone from filing against them. Half of them made hefty loans to their own campaigns. Two candidates for contested open seats in Miami-Dade and Broward lent themselves more than $350,000 to finance their $400,000 campaigns. Georgetown law professor Roy A. Schotland, an expert on judicial campaigns, calculated that trial-judge campaigns in Florida cost 41 percent as much as candidacies for the legislature, compared to only 5 percent in California. "One big reason: Florida has more judicial campaign consultants," he said. The 2004 elections were a respite of sorts for the legal community's worn-out wallets because fewer circuit judgeships—120—were at stake, and only 18 were contested. Campaign accounts totaled $8.4 million, with lawyers and law firms contributing nearly $4 million.[21]

Nationwide, candidates for state high courts raised nearly $47 million in 2004, almost eight times as much as in 1990.[22] In just one race, two rivals for an Illinois Supreme Court seat collected a combined $9.3 million. The winner, whose fund included more than $350,000 from State Farm, subsequently cast the deciding vote to relieve the insurance company of $456 million in disputed claims. In marked contrast, the 1976 merit-retention amendment has spared Florida's appellate courts the appearance of cash-register justice. There is no fund-raising for Supreme Court or district court of appeal seats except on the infrequent occasions of organized opposition to a retention vote. When conservative critics of the court's abortion decisions mounted serious campaigns to deny new terms to Justice Leander Shaw in 1990 and Justice Rosemary Barkett in 1992, the incumbents were able to win with campaign treasuries of some $300,000 each, significantly less than the norm for a traditionally contested statewide election. Their "yes" margins were approximately 60 percent, ten points or more below the usual merit-retention vote although still comfortable by conventional standards.[23]

Canon 7 of the Florida Code of Judicial Conduct, enforced by the Judicial Qualifications Commission and the Supreme Court, forbids judges and judicial candidates from holding political party offices, making partisan speeches, or endorsing other candidates. They may speak at political party election forums only when all competing candidates are invited. Judicial candidates must appoint other people to raise their campaign money; they are barred from personally soliciting contributions from anyone and even from asking lawyers to speak out in support. The Florida Supreme Court, in ruling that campaign contributions from a litigant should not automatically disqualify a judge from hearing a case, rationalized that the direct solicitation ban "insulates, to the extent possible, justices, judges, and judicial candidates from those asked to make contributions to the campaign."[24]

With respect to people or cases that may come before their courts, Florida judges and judicial candidates may not "make pledges, promises, or commitments that are inconsistent with the impartial performance of the adjudicative duties." There is a twofold purpose for this somewhat ambiguous language: to keep judges from having to disqualify themselves for actual or implied bias and to provide them with a plausible excuse for declining to say what they think about abortion, same-sex marriage, gun control, the death penalty, or any other issue that might animate a single-interest voter. This insulation was weakened significantly, however, by an opinion of the Supreme Court's Judicial Ethics Advisory Committee during the 2006 campaign. The question posed to the committee was whether a judicial candidate could respond to questionnaires "which cover such subjects as same-sex marriage, parental notification, and school vouchers, and whether the candidate agrees or disagrees with recent court decisions." The inquiries were prompted by politically pointed questionnaires issued by the Florida Family Policy Council and the Christian Coalition of Florida. The committee's answer—one virtually dictated by the U.S. Supreme Court's decision in the Minnesota case—was yes, provided that the "scope of such expression . . . should acknowledge the cardinal duty of a judge to follow the law whether the judge agrees with it or not." The candidate "must not furnish answers that appear to bind the candidate if such issues arise once the candidate has assumed judicial office." Four of the committee's twelve participating members—a minority—expressed the view that refusing to answer "might be an ethical imperative, in certain circumstances." Judiciary-watchers noted with interest that a new member of the committee was Judge Leslie B. Rothenberg, the Third District Court of Appeal appointee who had pledged as a candidate for state attorney to oppose gay marriage and adoption.[25]

With the intent that judicial politics should be loftier than other politics, Canon Seven also forbids a candidate to "knowingly misrepresent the identity, qualifications, present position or other fact concerning the candidate or an opponent." Judicial elections are the only forum in which a politician can be punished for being untruthful with voters. Of the seventeen judges the Supreme Court has thrown out of office as of this writing, five were accused of Canon Seven violations, offenses against specific election statutes, or neglect of clients during their campaigns.[26] A sixth resigned from the bench and the Bar after being convicted of concealing his net worth on a campaign financial disclosure statement.[27] Among the seventy-nine judges whom the Supreme Court has publicly reprimanded, twelve came to grief primarily on account of campaign violations of Canon Seven. In the removal ordered in July 2006, the Supreme Court for the first time increased a penalty recommended by the JQC, which had proposed only a fine, suspension, and reprimand for John Renke on the premise that the judge had proved himself capably on the bench. He was accused, among other things, of misrepresenting himself as an incumbent, claiming experience and endorsements that he did not have, and citing support from named "public officials" who were simply officers of the Pinellas Republican Party. The most serious charge was that he had misrepresented $95,800 contributed by his father and law firm as loans to himself in violation of Florida's $500-per-person contribution limit. Regardless of his good service, the court held in a 5-2 decision, "one who obtains a position by fraud and other serious misconduct . . . is by definition unfit to hold that office. . . . Our obligation is first and foremost to the public and to our state's justice system."[28]

It was in 1997 that the court first declared a strict policy against campaign mistruths. In what was thought to be a national precedent for a case with no alleged criminal component, Nancy Alley, a circuit judge for Brevard and Seminole counties, was ordered to appear before the Supreme Court for a humiliating public reprimand broadcast statewide on public television. The court said her campaign propaganda was so "egregious" that it could have justified her removal. Among the allegations: Her campaign mailings implied that a local newspaper had endorsed her rather than her opponent. Playing for Republican votes in a strongly GOP constituency, she also advertised that her opponent—a Republican like herself—had been appointed to the bench by a Democratic governor. The opponent could not refute the inference without violating Canon Seven. The judge also published a photograph of her opponent sitting next to a client identified as a "convicted mass murderer" and "cop killer" who in fact had not yet been found guilty. At the time, the court noted, the judge's opponent was a public defender "observing a duty placed on her as a member of The Florida Bar." The JQC's general counsel, Thomas C. MacDonald, said the decision signified "a very hard line about these election cases."[29] Alley, who accepted blame and threw herself on the mercy of the court, was reelected without opposition five years later.

Only a year after the court made an example of her, a Manatee County judge lost his county court seat to a candidate who promised that he would "always have the heart of a prosecutor" and misrepresented the incumbent's record to accuse him of being soft on crime and absent from court. The JQC charged that the winner, Matthew McMillan, made "explicit promises to favor the state and the police." While a negotiated reprimand and fine were pending before the Supreme Court, the JQC accused McMillan of setting a $100,000 bond for a drunk driving suspect against whom the judge was the complaining witness and of intervening in another case in which he had previously disqualified himself. The Supreme Court removed McMillan, with the opinion remarking acidly that his campaign offenses occurred "well after" Alley's example. To leave him in office, the court said, would send "the wrong message to future candidates; that is, the end justifies the means and, thus, all is fair so long as the candidate wins." Although the case was aggravated by alleged bias on the bench, McMillan became the first Florida judge to be removed over campaign ethics. McMillan contended that he was being punished for defeating an incumbent. "They're afraid that if you win, you'll start a trend," he said.[30]

But in 2002, the landmark U.S. Supreme Court decision in *Republican Party of Minnesota v. White* cast into doubt the future of Florida's Canon 7 and perhaps also the entire concept of a nonpartisan judiciary. The 5-4 decision invalidated Minnesota's "announce clause," which forbade judicial candidates from commenting on abortion, crime, and welfare—Supreme Court candidate Gregory Wersal's pet subjects—or on any other disputed legal or political issue. Justice Antonin Scalia, writing for the majority, mocked the restriction as not only an infringement on freedom of speech but also essentially pointless. "A judge's lack of predisposition regarding the relevant legal issues in a case has never been thought a necessary component of equal justice, and with good reason," he wrote. "For one thing, it is virtually impossible to find a judge who does not have preconceptions about the law." In Minnesota, Scalia reasoned, a judicial candidate could declare right up until the day before election that he considered it constitutional for the legislature to prohibit same-sex marriage, "and may say it repeatedly after he is elected" so long as no litigation is actually pending. As an aid to open-mindedness, "the announce clause is so woefully underinclusive as to render belief in that purpose a challenge to the credulous," Scalia wrote. So long as judges are elected, he said, they must be allowed the same freedom of speech as candidates for any other office. "If the state has a problem with judicial impartiality," Justice Sandra Day O'Connor rationalized in a separate concurring opinion, "it is largely one the state brought upon itself by continuing the practice of popularly electing judges."[31]

Florida's Canon 7, in company with twenty-four other states, is more narrowly drawn along the lines of a 1990 American Bar Association recommendation as a "pledge or promise clause" that prohibits candidates only from appearing to commit themselves on issues they are likely to judge. It was revised from an "announce clause" following a successful lawsuit backed by the American Civil Liberties Union in 1993.[32] As of fall 2006, it had not been tested on appeal to the federal courts, and Florida remained determined to enforce it. More worrisome, however, was a subsequent decision by the U.S. Circuit Court of Appeals for the Eighth Circuit to strike down Minnesota's rule against candidates seeking partisan endorsements or personally soliciting campaign funds from large groups. Because the U.S. Supreme Court declined to review it, that decision is binding (at least for the moment) in only the eight states of the Eighth Circuit.[33]

While that case was pending, the Florida Supreme Court ordered a public reprimand for Judge Carven Angel of the state's Fifth Circuit for identifying himself as a Republican candidate and for campaigning at political events, most of them Republican functions to which his opponent—also a Republican—was not invited. Roy Schotland of Georgetown University described the Florida Supreme Court's decision in the Angel case as the "best thing ever written on judicial elections."[34]

A year later, a federal district judge in North Dakota, ruling in a case precipitated by the North Dakota Family Alliance's highly charged candidate questionnaires, held that even a "pledge or promise" clause is unconstitutional.[35] Should the U.S. Supreme Court eventually uphold that ruling, there would be no prior restraint on judicial campaign promises in Florida or any other state. There would be a corresponding surge in motions asking judges to recuse themselves on issues involving their campaign statements. Socially conservative political organizations have been the only constituency to applaud the Supreme Court's Minnesota decision and its progeny.

The Florida Supreme Court confronted the implications of the first Minnesota case in ordering a $50,000 fine and public reprimand for an Escambia county judge who had defeated an incumbent in a campaign much like McMillan's. "If You Are a Criminal, You Probably Won't Want to Read This," declared one of Patricia Kinsey's campaign brochures. She had "fostered the distinct impression that she harbored a prosecutor's bias," the Florida Supreme Court said. The court acknowledged that candidates are entitled to discuss their philosophies but held that Kinsey had gone too far. "We do not find that these types of pledges and statements by a judicial candidate are protected by the First Amendment," the majority said. Although all seven justices agreed that she should be punished for materially misrepresenting her opponent's record (one justice wanted to remove her), Justices Charles Wells and Peggy Quince dissented on the prosecutor's bias issue, which they said was "directly contrary" to the U.S. Supreme Court's Minnesota decision.[36] However, the U.S. Supreme Court refused without comment or dissent to hear Kinsey's appeal. (The high court's refusal to hear a case means only that it did not care to consider *that* one, not that it would never accept an appeal presenting similar issues.)[37]

The 2006 campaign brought fifty-five new circuit and county court judgeships to the ballot, the result of a legislative compromise that allowed Bush to appoint an equivalent number the year before. In announcing the last of a series of campaign conduct forums under the aegis of the Supreme Court, the Bar, the chief judges of the trial courts, and the Supreme Court's Judicial Ethics Advisory Committee, the office of the State Courts Administrator warned candidates that attendance was not optional. "Just as all judicial candidates are expected to sign a statement when they qualify affirming they have read and understand Florida's Code of Judicial Conduct," the notice said, "so too will they be expected to take part in the forum. And word from the state's highest court is plain: Those who do not participate in this training can and will be judged by what they may refuse to learn."[38]

My mission in writing this book has been to plead the case for preserving the three great reforms of the Florida Supreme Court's most turbulent decade. The disorder at the Supreme Court was an object lesson in the incompatibility of politics and justice. This was such fundamental truth to the architects of the United States Constitution that they gave no thought to electing the judiciary; the question, rather, was whether the integrity of federal judges could be better assured with lifetime appointments or fixed terms. They settled on life tenure subject only to impeachment for cause. "In a monarchy," Alexander Hamilton explained, "it is an excellent barrier to the despotism of the prince; in a republic it is a no less excellent barrier to the encroachments and oppressions of the representative body. And it is the best expedient which can be devised in any government, to secure a steady, upright, and impartial administration of the laws." Implicitly making the case against election of judges, Hamilton observed that "there can be but few men . . . who will have sufficient skill in the laws" and fewer still "who unite the requisite integrity with the requisite knowledge."[39] Although appointment swiftly lost favor to election in the evolving popular concept of American democracy, Hamilton's admonition has been proved true time and again by unfortunate episodes such as the disorder in the Florida Supreme Court three decades ago.

But that accumulated wisdom was unknown or ignored by the legislators who casually allowed Florida's nominating commissions to become the functional equivalents of a governor's patronage committees. This development is a clear and present danger to the nonpartisan judiciary, the second great reform of the 1970s. Although the third reform, merit retention of Florida's appellate bench, appears secure for the moment, it could easily be undone if the public perceives governors exploiting their control of the nominating process to pack these courts of last resort with political or ideological spear carriers.

A fourth great reform, more evolutionary in nature, is that of the Judicial Qualifications Commission itself. No longer is a newspaper's exposé the essential condition for an investigation. Indeed, the JQC became so vigorous as to be accused of being overly aggressive from time to time. Although complaints that do not lead to formal charges must still be kept secret, there have been nearly 150 public cases—as many as 10 in some years—since Boyd, Dekle, and McCain. The majority have resulted in reprimands for a variety of transgressions such as public drunkenness, pulling rank on traffic police and vice officers, conspicuous rudeness to lawyers and members of the public, displaying a loaded handgun in court, and soliciting lawyers for free lunches. Arrogance on the bench has been the most common denominator, a primary or contributing factor in twenty-two cases. One involved a Broward circuit judge who used a device simulating the sound of a toilet flushing to announce his opinion of a lawyer's argument. "To undermine public confidence and respect by such serious violations strikes at the very roots of an effective judiciary, for those who are served by the courts will not have confidence in and respect for the courts' judgments if judges engage in this egregious conduct," the Supreme Court said.[40]

Seventeen judges have been removed, including a district court of appeal judge who pleaded guilty to shoplifting, a circuit judge who was convicted of perjury in a case-fixing scandal, two county judges accused of repeated abusive conduct in court, a county judge accused of sexually harassing her judicial assistant, and a circuit judge who obtained a courthouse job for her housemate and business partner. Seventeen judges have resigned with JQC charges pending. Another seven retired, were defeated, or let their terms run out. Thirteen were involuntarily retired for mental or physical disabilities.

Only five cases have been dismissed after blossoming into formal charges before the Supreme Court. The statistic could be interpreted as proof that the JQC brings to light only the most serious of the complaints it receives, but it could also lend support to the complaints of some lawyers and judges that once the JQC undertakes a case it is like a dog with a bone in its teeth. The truth is concealed by the secrecy the constitution imposes on cases not formally charged.

In 1995, a blue-ribbon panel and the legislature successfully sponsored a constitutional amendment splitting the JQC into two panels: one to bring charges and the other to try them. The amendment enlarged the JQC to fifteen members who rotate between the panels. Significantly, it also authorized the Supreme Court to increase punishments recommended by the JQC. In 1992, the court had remarked in a footnote to which two justices dissented that it could not remove a judge who had been recommended for a reprimand in a hit-and-run auto accident case in which he also misled a police officer.[41] There was almost no controversy over the amendment, and it won nearly 75 percent of the vote in the 1996 general election.[42] It would be another ten years before the Supreme Court used its enhanced power to unseat a judge against the advice of the JQC. Significantly, that case consisted of alleged election violations.[43]

Concurring in 1951 to uphold the Smith Act conviction of Communist Party leaders for teaching (but not attempting) the violent overthrow of the U.S. government, a case that clearly troubled him, Justice Felix Frankfurter penned a memorable definition of the fundamental importance of an independent judiciary.

> Courts are not representative bodies. They are not designed to be a good reflex of a democratic society. Their judgment is best informed, and therefore most dependable, within narrow limits. Their essential

quality is detachment, founded on independence. History teaches that the independence of the judiciary is jeopardized when courts become embroiled in the passions of the day and assume primary responsibility in choosing between competing political, economic and social pressures.[44]

The independence that Frankfurter cherished is inconsistent on its face with the election of judges. But so is the *appointment* of judges if the executive is free to choose them primarily for their politics. Moreover, whatever system a people chooses—election, appointment, or as in Florida a combination of the two—depends for its integrity on the oversight of an informed public. As a journalist for my entire life, I am troubled and chagrined by the contemporary media's increasing disinterest in covering anything about the judiciary other than such "hot copy" issues as abortion, same-sex marriage, lurid crimes, and the occasional U.S. Senate confirmation dispute. Such neglect is not benign. Corruption, like damp rot, flourishes where the sun does not shine. For the sun to shine, there must be a free and fearless press.

The ethical insensitivity of the Florida Supreme Court some three decades ago was exposed by very junior public servants who courageously entrusted the truth to a reporter whom they were confident would not betray them. Thanks to them, and to the stalwart leadership of Reubin Askew, Richard T. Earle Jr., and like-minded reformers of the bench, the legislature, and the Bar, the Florida judiciary regained the trust and respect of the people of Florida. But to the extent that they forget or ignore this history, Floridians are surely condemned to repeat it.

Notes

Chapter 1. Seventeen Equal Pieces

1. Roger A. Schwartz, interview, Dec. 11, 2005; *St. Petersburg Times,* June 8, 1974, Jan. 24, 1975; Joseph A. Boyd Jr., testimony, Florida State Archives (hereafter FSA) series 49, carton 3437.

2. *Gulf Power Co. v. Bevis,* 289 So. 2d 401 (1974); Arthur J. England Jr., e-mail to the author, Feb. 12, 2006.

3. Tracy E. Danese, *Claude Pepper and Ed Ball: Politics, Purpose, and Power* (Gaines-ville: University Press of Florida, 2000), 219, 284; Walter M. Manley II and Canter Brown Jr., *The Supreme Court of Florida, 1917–1972* (Gainesville: University Press of Florida, 2006), 148, 194–95; Allen Morris, *Reconsiderations: Second Glances at Florida Legislative Events,* 3d ed. (Tallahassee: Office of the Clerk, House of Representatives, 1985), 157–63.

4. Diane Roberts, *Dream State* (New York: Free Press, 2004), 229–31; Art. V, Sec. 18, Constitution of 1868, circa 1965; Manley and Brown, *Supreme Court of Florida,* 212.

5. William Durden, interview, Apr. 25, 2002.

6. C. McFerrin Smith III, interview, Feb. 26, 2006.

7. FSA series 19, carton 356.

8. Transcript of testimony in camera, Florida Judicial Qualification Commission (hereafter JQC), Sept. 20, 1974, FSA series 49, carton 3437, folder 46601.

9. *St. Petersburg Times,* Nov. 19, 1974, Feb. 26, 1975; Edwin L. Mason deposition, FSA series 19, carton 355, folder 6; *Florida Bar. v. Mason,* 334 So. 2d 1 (1976).

10. *In re Inquiry Concerning a Judge,* 308 So. 2d 13 (1975); *The Florida Bar v. Edwin L. Mason,* 334 So. 2d 1 (1976).

11. William Falck deposition, FSA series 19, carton 355; Schwartz interview.

12. Schwartz interview.

13. Roger A. Schwartz testimony, Nov. 19, 1974, FSA series 49, carton 3437, folder 7.

14. Schwartz interview.

15. Schwartz testimony.

16. Schwartz interview.

17. Schwartz testimony; Schwartz interview.

18. *Gulf Power Co. v. Bevis.*

19. Schwartz interview.

Chapter 2. Justice Dekle's "Dissent"

1. House Select Committee on Impeachment, chronology, FSA series 19, carton 356.

2. Hal P. Dekle testimony to Judicial Qualifications Commission, Oct. 25, 1954, FSA series 19, carton 355, folder 7.

3. Ben F. Overton, interview, March 31, 2005; *St. Petersburg Times,* July 27, 1973; *In re The Florida Bar—Code of Judicial Conduct,* 281 So. 2d 21 (1973); *In re Inquiry Concerning a Judge (Hal P. Dekle),* 308 So. 2d 5 (1975).

4. Dekle testimony; House Select Committee files, FSA series 19, carton 356.

5. FSA series 19, carton 361; House Select Committee on Impeachment, chronology.

6. House Select Committee on Impeachment, files; Barbara Williams testimony to JQC, Oct. 24, 1974, FSA series 19, carton 355.

7. Roger A. Schwartz testimony to JQC, Nov. 19, 1974, FSA series 49, carton 3437, folder 7.

8. David LaCroix testimony to JQC, Apr. 10, 1974, FSA series 19, carton 355.

9. Vassar B. Carlton testimony to JQC, Oct. 24, 1974, FSA series 19, carton 355, folder 7.

10. Sharyn Smith, interview, Nov. 5, 2005.

11. Confidential source, interview, June 2005.

12. Roger Schwartz, e-mail to the author, Apr. 22, 2006.

13. *St. Petersburg Times,* June 8, 1974.

14. B. K. Roberts testimony, FSA series 49, carton 3563, transcript 8, p. 58; Schwartz testimony.

15. Schwartz testimony.

16. B. K. Roberts testimony to JQC, Nov. 7, 1974, FSA series 355, folder 11.

17. Reubin Askew, interview, Nov. 10, 2005; David LaCroix, interview with Andrew G. Pattillo, counsel to the JQC, Oct. 4, 1974, copy in possession of the author.

18. *Gulf Power Co. v. Bevis,* 289 So. 2d 401 (1974), *Gulf Power Co., et al v. Bevis,* 296 So. 2d 482 (1974)

19. Correspondence quoted in *Florida Bar v. Mason,* 334 So. 2d 1 (1976).

Chapter 3. School for Scandal

1. The Governor's Message to the Legislature, House Journal, Apr. 5, 1955.

2. Department of State, *Tabulation of Official Votes, First and Second Primaries, 1968*, 8–10.

3. Manley and Brown, *Supreme Court of Florida*, 316–20; Department of State, *Tabulation of Official Votes, General Election, 1968*.

4. Manley and Brown, *Supreme Court of Florida*, 316–20.

5. *St. Petersburg Times*, July 3, 1993; Richard T. Earle Jr., interview, July 1994; Ben F. Overton, interview, March 31, 2005.

6. *Carlton v. Carlton*, 104 So. 2d 363 (1958).

7. Manley and Brown, *Supreme Court of Florida*, 311–16.

8. Anne Marshall Parker deposition, Florida Bar files.

9. Clarence Jones, interview, Oct. 14, 2005; David LaCroix, interviews, various dates.

10. *St. Petersburg Times*, Jan. 17, 1974.

11. Richard T. Earle Jr., interview, no date.

12. Sharyn Smith, interview, Nov. 5, 2005.

13. *Hialeah Race Course v. Gulfstream Park*, 245 So. 2d 625 (1971).

14. *Gulfstream Park v. Division of Pari-Mutuel Wagering*, 253 So. 2d 249 (1971).

15. *Hialeah v. Board of Business Regulation*, 270 So. 2d 366 (1972).

16. *State ex rel Hialeah Park v. Board of Business Regulation*, 287 So. 2d 689 (1973); *Gulfstream v. Board of Business Regulation*, 322 So. 2d 919 (1975).

17. Manley and Brown, *Supreme Court of Florida*, 256–59.

18. Ibid., 190.

19. Ibid., 99, 121, 152–53, 191, 194–95.

20. *Florida Handbook*, 2003–2004, 679; *Florida Times-Union*, May 3, 1950.

21. *Miami Herald*, May 9, 1947.

22. *Florida Times-Union*, May 2, 1950.

23. *St. Petersburg Times*, May 1, 1955.

24. *Board of Public Instruction of Manatee County v. State*, 75 So. 2d 832 (1954); Manley and Brown, *Supreme Court of Florida*, 44, 46.

25. Walter F. Murphy, "Lower Court Checks on Supreme Court Power," *American Political Science Review* 53 (Dec. 1959): 1020–21.

26. *State ex rel Hawkins v. Board of Control*, 83 So. 2d 20 (1955).

27. Constance Baker Motley, *Equal Justice under Law: An Autobiography* (New York: Farrar, Straus and Giroux, 1998), 114.

28. *State ex rel. Hawkins v. Board of Control*, 93 So. 2d 354 (1957); 350 U.S. 413 (1956)

29. Lawrence A. Dubin, "Virgil Hawkins: A One-Man Civil Rights Movement," *Florida Law Review* 51 (1999): 937.

30. *State ex rel. Hawkins*.

31. *Tampa Tribune*, Oct. 15, 1957; Harley Herman, "Anatomy of a Bar Resignation:

The Virgil Hawkins Story: An Idealist Faces the Pragmatic Challenges of the Practice of Law," *Florida Coastal Law Journal* 2 (Fall 2000): 84–85; *State ex rel. Hawkins v. Board of Control*, 47 So. 2d 608 (1950).

32. Smith interview; *St. Petersburg Times*, Nov. 20, 1974. The legislature in 2000 reestablished a law school under the aegis of Florida A&M University. See *Palm Beach Post*, Nov. 17, 1998, June 15, 2000.

33. Martin A. Dyckman, *Floridian of His Century: The Courage of Governor LeRoy Collins* (Gainesville: University Press of Florida, 2006), 118–25.

34. *Florida Handbook*, 1969–70, 468–69.

35. Ibid.; *Florida Handbook*, 1971–72, 476–77; Rick Karl, "Electing Supreme Court Justices—for the Last Time." *Judicature*, Jan. 1977, 293.

36. Secretary of State, *Tabulation of Official Votes, Democratic May 28, 1968, Primary Election*, 23–25.

37. Leander Shaw, quoted in Manley and Brown, *Supreme Court of Florida,* 323; David Von Drehle, e-mail to the author, June 9, 2006.

38. *St. Petersburg Times*, Feb. 13, 1968.

39. Manley and Brown, *Supreme Court of Florida*, 302–3, 309–10; Wade Hopping, interview, Jan. 27, 2006.

Chapter 4. David McCain, Eagle Scout

1. Manley and Brown, *Supreme Court of Florida,* 326–30; B. K. Roberts, quoted in William J. Rish interview, June 21, 2006.

2. Wade Hopping interview, Jan. 27, 2006; Manley and Brown, *Supreme Court of Florida,* 304.

3. Manley and Brown, *Supreme Court of Florida,* 327.

4. Ibid., 328.

5. *St. Petersburg Times*, Apr. 18, 1975.

6. *St. Petersburg Times*, Apr. 18, 25, 1975; Feb 6, 1977.

7. *St. Petersburg Times*, Apr. 18, 1975.

8. *Farish v. Wakeman*, 385 So. 2d 2 (1980).

9. *Dobbs v. Petko*, 207 So. 2d 11 (1968).

10. *Weaver v. Stone*, 212 So. 2d 80 (1968).

11. *Wakeman v. State*, 237 So. 2d 61 (1970); *State v. Wakeman*, 343 So. 2d 419 (1971).

12. *New York Times v. Sullivan*, 376 U.S. 254 (1964), *Curtis Publishing Co. v. Butts, Associated Press v. Walker*, 388 U.S. 130 (1967).

13. *Time v. Firestone*, 305 So. 2d 172 (1974), 424 U.S. 448 (1976).

14. *New York Times*, March 3, 1976.

15. *Firestone v. Firestone*, 249 So. 2d 719 (1971).

16. *Firestone v. Firestone*, 263 So. 2d 223 (1972).

17. *Firestone v. Time*, 231 So. 2d 862 (1970); Anne Marshall Parker testimony, Apr. 10, 1975, FSA series 19, carton 361.

18. *St. Petersburg Times*, Dec. 22, 1974.

19. *Time v. Firestone*, 254 So. 2d 386 (1971).

20. *Firestone v. Time*, 271 So. 2d 245 (1972); *St. Petersburg Times*, Dec. 22, 1974.

21. *Time v. Firestone*, 279 So. 2d 389 (1973).

22. *St. Petersburg Times*, Dec. 22, 1974.

23. Ibid.

24. *Firestone v. Time*, 305 So. 2d 172 (1974).

25. William C. Owen Jr., "personal and confidential" to Thomas H. Barkdull Jr., May 14, 1974, FSA series 19, carton 357.

26. *Austin v. U-Tote-M*, 241 So. 2d 186 (1970).

27. Burton Young to Walter Manley, Aug. 6, 2003, copy in possession of the author.

28. Hopping interview.

29. Burton Young, interview, May 16, 2005.

30. Young–Manley correspondence; Young interview; *Jacksonville Journal,* Dec. 9, 1970; Manley and Brown, *Supreme Court of Florida,* 304, 328.

31. Young–Manley correspondence.

32. *State ex rel Pettigrew v. Kirk*, 243 So. 2d 147 (1970); Reubin Askew, interview, Nov. 10, 2005.

33. W. Dexter Douglass, interview, July 1, 2006; Manley and Brown, *Supreme Court of Florida,* 328–29.

34. Ben F. Overton, interview, March 31, 2005; Reubin Askew, interview, March 27, 2006.

35. *Housing Authority of the City of St. Petersburg v. City of St. Petersburg*, 287 So. 2d 307 (1973).

36. Richard T. McFarlain, interview, date unrecorded.

Chapter 5. What's a Politician to Do?

1. Wade Hopping, interview, undated.

2. Manley and Brown, *Supreme Court of Florida,* 331–33.

3. *Sadowski v. Shevin*, 345 So. 2d 330 (1977).

4. *Inquiry Concerning a Judge*, FSA series 49, box 3436.

5. W. Dexter Douglass, interview, Feb. 27, 2006; W.H.F. Wiltshire to Sam Jackowitz, March 22, 1973, FSA series 519, carton 361.

6. FSA series 49, carton 3436; *St. Petersburg Times*, Oct. 7, 1973.

7. W. L. Fitzpatrick to Thomas C. Barkdull Jr., Feb. 12, 1973, FSA series 49, carton 3436.

8. Hal P. Dekle to Thomas C. Barkdull Jr., May 8, 1973, FSA series 49, box 3436.

9. Art. V, Sec. 12, Constitution of Florida as amended, 1966.

10. Thomas H. Barkdull Jr., interview, June 9, 2005.

11. Ibid. Outgoing governor LeRoy Collins promptly restored Dayton to the bench by appointing him to a newly authorized judgeship.

12. Morris, *Florida Handbook,* 29th ed., 127–28.

13. Lucy Morgan, e-mail to the author, June 8, 2006.

14. *In re Inquiry Concerning a Judge*, 238 So. 2d 565 (1970). Kelly was elected to Congress in 1974. He was one of seven members trapped by a 1981 FBI bribery investigation. He was filmed patting jacket pockets stuffed with $25,000 and asking, "Does it show?" Defeated for reelection, Kelly eventually served thirteen months in prison. *St. Petersburg Times*, Aug. 25, 2005.

15. *Turner v. Earle* 295 So. 2d 609 (1974).

16. *St. Petersburg Times*, Oct. 31, 1973.

17. TS, FSA 49, carton 3436.

18. Ibid.

19. *St. Petersburg Times*, Nov. 25, 1974.

20. FSA 49, carton 3436.

21. *In re Inquiry Concerning a Judge 73-6, Hal P. Dekle*, 308 So. 2d 4 (1975).

Chapter 6. Shadows of Treason

1. Reubin Askew, interview, Sept. 26, 2001; Thomas H. Barkdull Jr., interview, June 9, 2005.

2. Richard T. McFarlain, interview, July 19, 2005.

3. *St. Petersburg Times,* June 23, 1999.

4. Mark Hulsey, interview, Jan. 25, 2006.

5. Walt Logan, e-mail to the author, Apr. 30, 2006.

6. Richard T. Earle III, interview, Jan. 24, 2006.

7. *St. Petersburg Times,* Nov. 25, 1974.

8. *Tampa Tribune,* Aug. 16, 17, 1973.

9. Reubin Askew, interview, Nov. 10, 2005; confidential source interview, 2006.

10. *Nell v. State,* 266 So. 2d 404 (1972).

11. *St. Petersburg Times,* Apr. 10, 1975; Joseph McNulty testimony, FSA series 49, carton 3564, transcript 5, 293–341.

12. *St. Petersburg Times,* Aug. 26, 1973.

13. McNulty testimony; *St. Petersburg Times,* Aug. 23, 29, 1973.

14. *St. Petersburg Times,* Aug. 26, 1973.

15. Robert Mann testimony, FSA series 49, carton 3564, transcript 8, 114–40; *St. Petersburg Times,* Apr. 10, 1975.

16. *St. Petersburg Times,* Aug. 26, 1973.

17. Ibid.; B. K. Roberts testimony, FSA series 49, carton 3564, transcript 12, 12–13.

18. *St. Petersburg Times,* Aug. 26, 1973.

19. *Tampa Tribune,* March 23, 1975.

20. *St. Petersburg Times,* Dec. 21, 1974, Apr. 1, 1975.

21. Ibid.

22. Confidential source interview, 2006.

23. *St. Petersburg Times*, Dec. 21, 1974, Apr. 1, 1975; undated memorandum, House Select Committee on impeachment, FSA series 92, carton 5.

24. *St. Petersburg Times*, Dec. 21, 1974, Apr. 1, 1975.

25. *Nell v. State*, 277 So. 2d 1 (1973)

26. Roger A. Schwartz, interview, Dec. 11, 2005.

Chapter 7. Circling the Wagons

1. Reubin Askew, interview, Nov. 10, 2005; *Miami Herald*, Aug. 13, Dec. 6, 1973; *St. Petersburg Times*, March 25, 1973.

2. *State v. Pinto*, 273 So. 2d 408 (1973); *Miami Herald*, Aug. 14, Dec. 6, 1973.

3. *Miami Herald*, Dec. 6, 1973; *In re Grand Jury Investigation*, 287 So. 2d 43 (1973).

4. *In re Grand Jury*; Roger Schwartz, e-mail to the author, Apr. 21, 2006.

5. *St. Petersburg Times*, Apr. 8, 1973.

6. *St. Petersburg Times*, Sept. 19, 1973.

7. *St. Petersburg Times*, Oct. 7, 31, 1973.

8. Gerald Kogan, interview, Apr. 19, 2006.

9. *Turner v. Earle*, 295 So. 2d 609 (1974).

10. *St. Petersburg Times*, Jan. 19, 1975.

11. William C. Owen Jr. to Thomas H. Barkdull Jr., May 14, 1974, FSA series 19, carton 357.

12. *In re Turner*, 573 So. 2d 1 (1990).

Chapter 8. A "Good Old Boy" Court

1. Gary Mormino, *Land of Sunshine, State of Dreams: A Social History of Modern Florida* (Gainesville: University Press of Florida, 2005), 12, 13; Bureau of the Census, <wwww.census.gov/statab/hist>.

2. *St. Petersburg Times*, Jan. 3, 75.

3. *St. Petersburg Times*, Jan. 18, March 14, 1974.

4. Dyckman, *Floridian of His Century*, 255–56.

5. Reubin Askew, interview, Sept. 26, 2001.

6. Ben F. Overton, interview, Mar. 31, 2005; *In re the Florida Bar—Code of Judicial Conduct*, 281 So. 2d 21 (1973).

7. Virginia Ellis, e-mail to the author, Apr. 19, 2006.

8. Gerald Kogan, interview, Apr. 19, 2006.

9. Reubin Askew, interview, Nov. 10, 2005.

10. Overton interview.

11. *St. Petersburg Times*, June 8, 1974; Sharyn Smith interview, Nov. 5, 2005; Roger Schwartz, interview, Dec. 11, 2005.

12. *St. Petersburg Times*, Aug. 12, 1974, Jan. 3, 1975.

13. *St. Petersburg Times*, Jan. 3, 1975; Overton interview.

14. Smith interview.

15. *St. Petersburg Times*, Aug. 12, 1974.

16. *St. Petersburg Times*, Jan. 3, 1975; Smith interview and e-mail to the author, Apr. 20, 2006.

17. *St. Petersburg Times*, Jan. 3, 1975, Apr. 14, 29, 1998.

18. *State ex rel Christian v. Rudd*, 302 So. 2d 821 (1974); *State ex rel Christian v. Austin*, 302 So. 2d 811 (1974).

19. *St. Petersburg Times*, Nov. 6, 1974.

20. Ibid.

21. *St. Petersburg Times*, Nov. 7, 1974, Nov. 10, 2005.

22. *Austin v. State ex rel Christian*, 310 2d 3d 289 (1975).

23. Ed Austin, interview, Apr. 25, 2006; *St. Petersburg Times*, Apr. 29, May 13, 1998.

Chapter 9. A Florida Watergate?

1. *St. Petersburg Times*, Aug. 12, 1974.

2. *Tornillo v. The Miami Herald*, 287 So. 2d 78 (1973).

3. *Miami Herald Publishing Co. v. Tornillo*, 418 U.S. 241 (1974).

4. *St. Petersburg Times*, Dec. 13, 1974.

5. *Tallahassee Democrat*, Sept. 6, 1974.

6. Sharyn Smith, interview, Nov. 5, 2005. In retirement, Ervin joined his brother's law firm and remained there the rest of his life.

7. Smith interview; Arthur England, interview, Sept. 27, 2005.

8. *Board of Trustees of the Internal Improvement Trust Fund v. Ball*, 300 So. 2d 741 (1974). Wakulla Springs is now a state park. The fence remains.

9. *Spector v. Glisson*, 305 So. 2d 777 (1974).

10. Reubin Askew interview, Nov. 10, 2005.

11. England interview.

12. Laurie Hollman, "A New Force Unites Miami's Many Worlds," *St. Petersburg Times*, July 20, 1987.

13. England interview; Department of State, *Tabulation of Official Votes*, Sept. 10, 1974.

14. *St. Petersburg Times*, Aug. 31, 1974.

15. Department of State, *Tabulation of Official Votes*, Sept. 10, 1974, p. 33.

Chapter 10. Like Calling Walter Cronkite

1. JQC testimony, FSA series 19, carton 355, folder 11.

2. Ibid.

3. Ibid.

4. Ibid.

5. Ibid.

6. *St. Petersburg Times*, Feb. 18, 1975.

7. JQC testimony, FSA series 19, carton 355, folder 9.

8. *St. Petersburg Times*, Jan. 29, 31, 1975.

9. FSA series 49, carton 3436.

10. See <www.law.fsu.edu/crc/conhist/1974amen.html>.

11. JQC testimony, Oct. 25, 1974, FSA series 19, carton 355, folder 7.

12. Transcript, JQC Testimony, FSA series 49, carton 3437, folder 46601.

13. Ibid.

14. Ibid.

15. Ibid.

16. Ibid.

17. Ibid.

18. Ibid.

19. Ibid.

20. FSA series 19, carton 355, folder 6.

21. *St. Petersburg Times*, Nov. 16, 1974, Jan. 31, 1975.

Chapter 11. Public Trial, Secret Trial

1. *St. Petersburg Times*, Nov. 20, 1974.

2. *St. Petersburg Times*, Nov. 19, 20, 1974.

3. *St. Petersburg Times*, Nov. 19, 1974.

4. *St. Petersburg Times*, Nov. 19, 20, 1974.

5. *St. Petersburg Times*, Nov. 20, 1974.

6. *St. Petersburg Times*, Nov. 23, 1974.

7. *St. Petersburg Times*, Nov. 25, 1974.

8. Manley and Brown, *Supreme Court of Florida,* 99–100.

9. *St. Petersburg Times,* Nov. 19, 21, 22, 25, 1974.

10. *St. Petersburg Times*, Nov. 20, 27, 1974.

Chapter 12. A Politician First . . . a Justice Second

1. Ben F. Overton interview, March 31, 2005.

2. *St. Petersburg Times*, Nov. 27, Dec. 5, 1974, Jan. 3, Feb. 5, 1975, July 11, 1976.

3. *St. Petersburg Times*, Jan. 3, 1975.

4. *St. Petersburg Times*, Jan. 7, 18, 1975.

5. *St. Petersburg Times*, Jan. 19, 1975.

6. *St. Petersburg Times*, Jan. 18, 25, 1975.

7. *St. Petersburg Times*, Jan. 21, 1975.

8. *St. Petersburg Times*, Feb. 1, 1975.

9. *In re Dekle*, 308 So. 2d 4 (1975); *In re Dekle*, 308 So. 2d 5 (1975); *In re Boyd*, 308 So. 2d 13 (1975).

10. *In re Dekle*, 308 So. 2d 4 (1975).

11. *In re Boyd*.

12. *In re Boyd*.

13. *St. Petersburg Times*, Feb. 5, 6, 1975.

14. *St. Petersburg Times*, Feb. 5, 8, 1975.

15. *St. Petersburg Times*, Feb. 9, 1975.

16. *St. Petersburg Times*, Feb. 8, 1975.

17. *Tampa Tribune*, Feb. 6, 1975.

18. *St. Petersburg Times*, Feb. 11, 1975.

19. *St. Petersburg Times*, March 14, 1975.

20. *Florida Bar v. Mason*, 334 So. 2d 1 (1976).

Chapter 13. Dekle Resigns

1. *St. Petersburg Times*, Feb. 6, 1975.

2. Art. V, Sec. 12(e), 1975.

3. *St. Petersburg Times*, Feb. 11, 12, 16, 1975.

4. Ben E. Hendricks Jr. to Committee on Judiciary, March 6, 1975, FSA series 19, carton 357.

5. *St. Petersburg Times*, Feb. 25, 1975.

6. Art. V, Sec. 12(f)(h), 1977.

7. *St. Petersburg Times*, Apr. 22, 1975.

8. Mark Hulsey interview, Jan. 25, 2006.

9. *St. Petersburg Times*, March 10, 1975; Ben F. Overton, interview, May 15, 2006.

10. Art. V, Sec. 12(g), 1975.

11. *St. Petersburg Times*, Feb. 26, 1975.

12. *St. Petersburg Times*, March 9, 1975.

13. *St. Petersburg Times*, Feb. 26, 1975; Fred Karl interview, May 9, 2006.

14. *St. Petersburg Times*, Feb. 27, March 2, 5, 1975.

15. *St. Petersburg Times*, Feb. 27, 1975.

16. *St. Petersburg Times*, March 9, 1975.

17. *St. Petersburg Times*, March 5, 7, 1975; Karl interview.

18. *St. Petersburg Times*, March 7, 1975; *Pitts v. State*, 247 So. 2d 53 (1971).

19. *St. Petersburg Times*, March 7, 1975.

20. *St. Petersburg Times*, March 11, 1975.

21. *St. Petersburg Times*, March 6, 7, 1975.

22. *St. Petersburg Times*, March 7, 1975; Talbot D'Alemberte interview, May 16, 2005.

23. *St. Petersburg Times*, Apr. 25, 1975; transcript, FSA series 19, carton 355.

24. *St. Petersburg Times*, Apr. 25, 1975.

25. *St. Petersburg Times*, Apr. 28, 1975.

26. *St. Petersburg Times*, May 5, 1975.

27. *St. Petersburg Times*, May 6, 1975.

28. Richard T. Earle Jr., to William J. Rish, June 16, 1975, enclosing medical report dated May 29, 1975, FSA series 19, carton 355, folder 1.

29. Department of State, official canvass, 1980.

30. *Florida Bar v. Crabtree*, 595 So. 2d 935 (1992).

Chapter 14. Appearance of Impropriety

1. Talbot D'Alemberte interview, May 16, 2005.

2. *St. Petersburg Times*, Apr. 24, 1975; document of unknown provenance, believed

to originate with Florida Department of Law Enforcement, in House committee files at FSA series 92, carton 5.

3. *Ft. Lauderdale Sun-Sentinel,* Aug. 6, 1993; *Palm Beach Post,* Aug. 8, 1993; Richard T. Earle Jr., interview, Aug. 1993; *St. Petersburg Times,* Aug. 3, 1993.

4. FSA series 19, carton 357.

5. Gavin Letts to Raymond L. Royce, Apr. 29, 1975, copy in possession of the author.

6. *St. Petersburg Times,* Aug. 11, 1977.

7. Undated document, House Select Committee files, FSA series 92, carton 5.

8. D'Alemberte interview; *St. Petersburg Times,* Apr. 1, 1975.

9. D'Alemberte interview.

10. *St. Petersburg Times,* March 20, 21, 1975.

11. *Forbes v. Earle,* 298 So. 2d 1 (1994).

12. *St. Petersburg Times,* May 12, 1975.

13. *McCain v. Select Committee,* 313 So. 2d 722 (1975).

14. *St. Petersburg Times,* Apr. 9, 1975.

15. *St. Petersburg Times,* Apr. 10, 1975.

16. *St. Petersburg Times,* March 25, 1975.

17. Select committee testimony, FSA series 19, carton 361, 308–22; *Kaplan v. Lowry,* 293 So. 2d 348 (1974); FSA series 49, carton 3564, transcript 4, 55; Larry Sartin, interview, Oct. 2005.

18. William Falck testimony, FSA series 19, carton 361, 157–205; *Williams v. Seaboard Airline Railroad,* 268 So. 2d 459 (1972), 283 So. 2d 33 (1973).

19. Falck testimony; *McCain Sales v. D. H. Smith,* 242 So. 2d 758 (1970); *D. H. Smith & Associates v. McCain Sales,* 250 So. 2d 277 (1971).

20. Anne Marshall Parker testimony, FSA series 19, carton 361, 225–39, 252; *St. Petersburg Times,* Apr. 11, 1975; *Farish v. Lum's,* 267 So. 2d 325 (1972).

21. C. McFerrin Smith III, testimony, FSA series 19, carton 361, 283–303.

22. *St. Petersburg Times,* Apr. 17, 1975.

23. William J. Rish interview, June 21, 2006.

24. *St. Petersburg Times,* Apr. 18, 1975.

25. *St. Petersburg Times,* Apr. 19, July 4, 1975; Bernard Dempsey "confidential" to Michael S. Hacker, Sept. 7, 1976, FSA series 49, carton 3564, box 4; *Miami Herald,* June 23, 1977; *Farish v. Wakeman,* 385 So. 2d 2 (1980).

26. *St. Petersburg Times,* Apr. 25, 1975.

27. *St. Petersburg Times,* Apr. 24, 25, 1975.

28. *St. Petersburg Times,* Apr. 26, 1975.

29. *St. Petersburg Times,* March 27, 1975.

30. D'Alemberte interview.

31. *St. Petersburg Times,* Apr. 29, 1975; Rish interview.

32. *Florida Bar. v. Thomson,* 310 So. 2d 300 (1975); *St. Petersburg Times,* March 27, 1975.

33. *Florida Bar v. McCain,* 361 So. 2d 700.

34. *St. Petersburg Times*, Apr. 29, 1975.

35. *St. Petersburg Times*, March 27, May 22, June 3, 1975.

Chapter 15. The Old Order Is Over

1. Fred Karl, interview, Aug. 1975.

2. Dyckman, *Floridian of His Century*, 50.

3. James Apthorp, interview, Aug. 3, 2006.

4. *St. Petersburg Times*, Aug. 29, 1975.

5. Reubin Askew, "A Day with the Florida Governors," spring 2006 symposium, Lou Frey Institute of Politics and Government, University of Central Florida, March 27, 2006.

6. *St. Petersburg Times*, Apr. 21, 1986.

7. See Hatchett's biography at <www.floridasupremecourt.org/about/gallery/hatchett.html>.

8. Arthur England, interview, Sept. 27, 2005.

9. *Miami Herald*, March 26, 1976.

10. Ben Overton, interview, March 31, 2005.

11. Ibid.; *St. Petersburg Times*, Aug. 29, 31, 1976; FSA series 701, cartons 382, 575.

12. Rick Karl, "Electing Supreme Court Justices—for the Last Time," *Judicature*, Jan. 1977, 293.

13. *St. Petersburg Times*, Aug. 29, 1976.

14. *St. Petersburg Times*, Feb. 19, 1999.

15. *St. Petersburg Times*, Aug. 29, 1976.

16. *Miami Herald*, July 11, 1976; *St. Petersburg Times*, July 11, 1976.

17. *St. Petersburg Times*, Aug. 29, 1976.

18. Ibid.

19. Department of State, tabulation of official votes, Florida primary elections, Sept. 7, 1976, and Sept. 28, 1976; Karl, "Electing Supreme Court Justices," 295.

20. Karl, "Electing Supreme Court Justices," 293–95.

21. Florida Bar, "Merit Selection and Retention," issue paper, July 1993.

22. William J. Rish, interview, June 21, 2006; Senate Joint Resolution 49, *Journal of the House of Representatives*, May 26, 1976, 757–60.

23. Florida Bar, "Merit Selection and Retention," issue paper, July 1993.

24. Florida Bar, "Merit Selection and Retention," issue paper, Sept. 2004; Art. V, Sec. 10(b).

25. Roy Schotland, remarks to California Judicial Council, June 22, 2005, copy in possession of the author.

26. Rish interview.

Chapter 16. The Fugitive

1. Staff Counsel to Board of Governors, undated, Florida Bar files.

2. *Florida Bar v. McCain*, 330 So. 2d 712 (1976).

3. *St. Petersburg Times*, Dec. 12, 1975.

4. *Florida Bar v. McCain.*

5. *St. Petersburg Times*, Nov. 27, 1975.

6. *St. Petersburg Times*, June 23, 1976; Report of Referee, FSA series 49, carton 3563, 8–43.

7. *St. Petersburg Times*, Feb. 15, 1977.

8. FSA series 49, carton 3563, 8–43.

9. FSA series 49, carton 3564, TS 5, 114.

10. Ibid., 12.

11. FSA series 49, carton 3563, TS 3, 203.

12. FSA series 49, carton 3563, TS 12, 64–72.

13. Ibid., 216.

14. *Florida Bar. v. McCain,* 361 So. 2d 100 (1978).

15. FSA series 49, TS 15, 180–81.

16. Ibid., 5–6, 36.

17. Ibid., TS 5, 302–4.

18. Report of Referee, FSA series 49, carton 3563, 10–41.

19. Ibid., 21–22.

20. Ibid., 35, 42–43.

21. FSA series 49, carton 3564, TS 8, 51.

22. *Florida Bar v. McCain,* 361 So. 2d 100 (1978).

23. *Miami Herald*, Oct. 4, 1977, Nov. 14, 1986; *St. Petersburg Times*, Nov. 12, 1991; Associated Press, June 3, 2000.

24. *St. Petersburg Times*, Nov. 14, 1986.

25. *St. Petersburg Times*, Sept. 26, 1982.

26. *Miami Herald*, Nov. 24, 1986.

27. *St. Petersburg Times*, Oct, 17, 1982.

28. *National Law Journal*, Feb. 7, 1983; *Miami Herald*, Nov. 24, 1986.

29. *Washington Post*, July 8, 1983.

30. *St. Petersburg Times*, Jan. 24, 1983, Nov. 14, 1986.

31. *Miami Herald*, Nov. 14, 24, 1986.

Chapter 17. The Keys to the Courthouse

1. Richard R. Swann, interview, Apr. 6, 2006.

2. Manley and Brown, *Supreme Court of Florida*, 259–60.

3. *Lake v. Lake*, 103 So. 2d 840 (1958).

4. Campbell Thornal dissent, *Foley v. Weaver Drugs*, 177 So. 2d 221 (1965).

5. Arthur J. England Jr., Eleanor Mitchell Hunter, and Richard C. Williams Jr., "Constitutional Jurisdiction of the Supreme Court of Florida: 1980 Reform," *Florida Law Review* 32 (1980): 149–51; *Lake v. Lake.*

6. *Ansin v. Thurston,* 101 So. 2d 808 (1958).

7. *Lake v. Lake.*

8. *Harrell's Candy Kitchen Inc., v. Sarasota-Manatee Airport Authority,* 111 So. 2d 439 (1959).

9. England, Hunter, and Williams, "Constitutional Jurisdiction," 151–52.

10. *Foley v. Weaver Drugs,* 177 So. 2d 221 (1965).

11. *Canada Dry Bottling Co. and Food Fair v. Shaw,* 118 So. 2d 840 (1960).

12. *Foley v. Weaver Drugs,* 177 So. 2d 221 (1965).

13. *Foley v. Weaver Drugs,* 172 So. 2d 907 (1965).

14. *Foley v. Weaver Drugs,* 177 So. 2d 221 (1965).

15. Ibid.

16. Richard T. McFarlain, interview, July 19, 2005.

17. Arthur J. England Jr. and Michael P. McMahon, "Quantity Discounts in Appellate Justice," *Judicature* 60 (1977): 445; England, Hunter, and Williams, "Constitutional Jurisdiction," 152.

18. Swann interview; *Gibson v. Maloney,* 231 So. 2d 283 (1970).

19. Manley and Brown, *Supreme Court of Florida,* 227; *St. Petersburg Times,* May 2, 1975; C. McFerrin Smith, interview, Feb. 26, 2006.

20. *St. Petersburg Times,* May 2, 1975.

21. Ibid.; England, Hunter, and Williams, "Constitutional Jurisdiction," 154, 159, 166, 174.

22. Gerald B. Cope Jr., "Discretionary Review of the Decisions of Intermediate Appellate Courts: A Comparison of Florida's System with Those of the Other States and the Federal System," *Florida Law Review* 45 (1993): 67–69.

23. Charles S. Lopeman, *The Activist Advocate: Policy Making in State Supreme Courts* (Westport, Conn.: Praeger, 1999), 92–93.

24. *Bankston v. Brennen,* 507 So. 2d 1385 (1987).

Chapter 18. Clear and Present Dangers

1. Reubin Askew, "A Day with the Florida Governors," spring 2006 symposium, Lou Frey Institute of Politics and Government, University of Central Florida, March 27, 2006.

2. *Florida Bar News,* July 15, 2006.

3. John Phelps, interview, July 11, 2006; Wil S. Hylton, "See Jeb *Not* Run," *GQ,* May 2006, 159–63, 210–11.

4. *St. Petersburg Times,* July 11, 2002.

5. Senate *Journal,* Apr. 30, 1999, 1927.

6. *Gore v. Harris,* 772 So. 2d 1243 (2000), reversed by *Bush v. Gore,* 531 U.S. 98 (2002).

7. House *Journal,* March 22, 2001, 331–32.

8. Senate *Journal,* May 4, 2001, 1505–6.

9. Gerald Kogan, interview, Apr. 19, 2006; Herman Russomanno, interview, June 27, 2006; Steven Metz, interview, June 27, 2006.

10. Sharyn Smith, interview, Nov. 5, 2005.

11. Martha W. Barnett, "The 1997–98 Florida Constitution Revision Commission: Judicial Election or Merit Selection," *Florida Law Review* 52 (2000): 423; Florida Bar position paper "Some Facts and Statistics," Aug. 16, 2000.

12. *St. Petersburg Times*, Dec. 10, 1995; W. Dexter Douglass, interview, July 1, 2006.

13. *St. Petersburg Times*, Nov. 12, 1991; Associated Press, June 3, 2000. For a timeless and penetrating insight into the bizarre theater of Miami-Dade judicial politics, see Joel Achenbach, "Juris Impuris: Is This Any Way to Pick Our Judiciary?" *Tropic (Miami Herald)*, Aug. 28, 1988, 8–15.

14. *St. Petersburg Times*, May 1, 2005; Aug. 20, 2006.

15. *Miami New Times*, Feb. 24, 2005.

16. *Florida Bar News*, Aug. 1, 2005.

17. *St. Petersburg Times*, Jan. 12, July 15, 2006.

18. Burton Young, interview, May 16, 2005.

19. Peter D. Webster, "Merit Selection and Retention of Judges: Is There One 'Best' Method?" *Florida State University Law Review* 23 (1995): 18–22.

20. *Florida Times-Union*, March 31, 2004, Nov. 3, 2005, *In re Gooding*, 905 So. 2d 121.

21. Roy Schotland, remarks to California Judicial Council, June 22, 2005, copy in possession of the author; <http://election.dos.state.fl.us/index.html>.

22. Margaret Ebrahim, "The Bible Bench," *Mother Jones,* May/June 2006, <www.motherjones.com>.

23. Webster, "Merit Selection," 34.

24. *Mary Ann MacKenzie v. Super Kids*, et al., 565 So. 2d 1332 (1990); <www.florida-supremecourt.org/decisions/ethics/canon7.html>.

25. Florida Supreme Court Judicial Ethics Advisory Committee, Opinion 2006–18, Aug. 7, 2006; <www.floridasupremecourt.org/decisions/ethics/canon7.html>.

26. *In re Berkowitz*, 522 So. 2d 843 (1988); *In re Hapner*, 718 So. 2d 785 (1998); *In re McMillan*, 797 So. 2d 560 (2001); *In re Ford-Kaus*, 730 So. 2d 269 (1999); *In re Renke*, 31 Fl Law Wkly 337 (2006).

27. James Berfield, *St. Petersburg Times,* May 8, 1999.

28. *In re Renke.*

29. *St. Petersburg Times*, Oct. 19, 1997; *In re Alley*, 699 So. 2d 1369 (1997).

30. *In re McMillan*, 797 So. 2d 560 (2001); Pat Dunnigan, "Judgment Call," *Florida Trend,* Nov. 2001, 68.

31. *Republican Party of Minnesota v. White*, 536 U.S. 765 (2002).

32. *American Civil Liberties Union v. The Florida Bar*, 999 F. 2d 1486 (1993).

33. *Republican Party v. White*, 416 Fed. 3d 738 (2004), certiorari denied, 2006 Lexis 1050 (2006).

34. *In re Angel*, 867 So. 2d 379 (2004); Roy A. Schotland, e-mail to the author, June 5, 2006.

35. *North Dakota Family Alliance v. Bader*, 361 F. Supp. 2d 1021 (2005).

36. *In re Kinsey*, 842 So. 2d 77 (2003).

37. *Kinsey v. Florida Judicial Qualifications Commission*, 540 U.S. 825 (2003).

38. Office of the State Courts Administrator, e-mail, July 18, 2006.

39. Alexander Hamilton, John Jay, and James Madison. *The Federalist,* 1787–1788 (New York: Modern Library, 2000), 496, 503.

40. *Inquiry concerning a judge (Schapiro),* 845 So. 2d 170 (2003).

41. *In re Fowler,* 602 So. 2d 510 (1992).

42. HJR 1709, 1975; Art V, Sec. 12., <http://election.dos.state.fl.us/elections/result-sarchive>.

43. *In re Renke,* 31 *Fl L Wkly* S 337 (2006).

44. *Dennis v. United States* (concurring) 341 U.S. 494 (1951).

Bibliography

Published Sources

Achenbach, Joel. "Juris Impuris: Is This Any Way to Pick Our Judiciary?" *Tropic (Miami Herald)*, Aug. 28, 1988, 8–15.

Angel, Marina. "Sexual Harassment by Judges." *University of Miami Law Review* 817 (1991): 824.

Baker, Joseph. "What LOOKS Like a Court, TALKS Like a Court, ACTS Like a Court, But Isn't?" *Florida Bar Journal*, June 1988, 12, 14–17.

Barnett, Martha W. "Merit Retention for Trial Judges: It's an Idea That Works." *Florida Bar News*, January 15, 2000, 7.

———. "The 1997–98 Florida Constitution Revision Commission: Judicial Election or Merit Selection." *52 Fla. L. Rev.*, 2000, 411–23.

Caldeira, Gregory A. "On the Reputation of State Supreme Courts." *Political Behavior*, March 1983, 83–108.

Connor, Kenneth L. "Merit Retention for Trial Judges: A Bad Idea Gets Worse." *Florida Bar News*, January 15, 2000, 6.

Cope, Gerald B., Jr. "Discretionary Review of the Decisions of Intermediate Appellate Courts: A Comparison of Florida's System with Those of the Other States and the Federal System." *Florida Law Review* 45 (1993): 62–76.

D'Alemberte, Talbot. "Searching for the Limits of Judicial Free Speech." *Tulane Law Review* 61 (1987): 611–45.

Danese, Tracy E. *Claude Pepper and Ed Ball: Politics, Purpose, and Power.* Gainesville: University Press of Florida, 2000.

DeVault, John S., III. "President's Page: Do We Want Politicians or Judges?" *Florida Bar Journal* 70 (February 1996): 8–10.

Dubin, Lawrence A. "Virgil Hawkins: A One-Man Civil Rights Movement." *Florida Law Review* 51 (1999): 913–56.

Dunnigan, Pat. "Judgment Call." *Florida Trend,* November 200: 68.

Dyckman, Martin A. *Floridian of His Century: The Courage of Governor LeRoy Collins.* Gainesville: University Press of Florida, 2006.

Earle, Richard T., Jr. "Judicial Disciplinary Proceedings: A Constitutional and Sensible Alternative to the Impeachment Process." *Florida Bar Journal,* June 1988, 13–17.

Ebrahim, Margaret. "The Bible Bench." *Mother Jones,* May/June 2006. http://www.motherjones.com.

England, Arthur J., Jr., Eleanor Mitchell Hunter, and Richard C. Williams Jr. "Constitutional Jurisdiction of the Supreme Court of Florida: 1980 Reform." *Florida Law Review* 32 (1980): 147–216.

England, Arthur J., Jr., and Michael P. McMahon, "Quantity Discounts in Appellate Justice." *Judicature* 60 (1977): 442–50.

Hamilton, Alexander, John Jay, and James Madison. *The Federalist,* 1787–1788. New York: Modern Library, 2000. Essays 79–82, 495–530.

Herman, Harley. "Anatomy of a Bar Resignation: The Virgil Hawkins Story: An Idealist Faces the Pragmatic Challenges of the Practice of Law." *Florida Coastal Law Journal* 2 (Fall 2000): 77–111.

Hylton, Wil S. "See Jeb *Not* Run." *GQ* (May 2006): 159–63, 210.

Jacobstein, Helen L. *The Segregation Factor in the Florida Democratic Gubernatorial Primary of 1956.* Gainesville: University of Florida Press, 1972.

Judicial Ethics Advisory Committee. "An Aid to Understanding Canon 7." Tallahassee: Office of the State Courts Administrator, 2006. Also available at <www.floridasupremecourt.org/pub_info/documents/canon7.pdf>.

Kahn, Charles J., Jr. "Judicial Elections: Canon 7, Politics, and Free Speech." *Florida Bar Journal* 72 (July/August 1998): 22–29.

Karl, Rick. "Electing Supreme Court Justices—for the Last Time." *Judicature,* January 1977, 290–96.

Lopeman, Charles C. *The Activist Advocate: Policy Making in State Supreme Courts.* Westport, Conn.: Praeger, 1999.

Manley, Walter M., II, and Canter Brown Jr. *The Supreme Court of Florida, 1917–1972.* Gainesville: University Press of Florida, 2006.

Mormino, Gary. *Land of Sunshine, State of Dreams: A Social History of Modern Florida.* Gainesville: University Press of Florida, 2005.

Morris, Allen. *Reconsiderations: Second Glances at Florida Legislative Events.* 3rd ed. Tallahassee: Office of the Clerk, House of Representatives, 1985.

Motley, Constance Baker. *Equal Justice under Law: An Autobiography.* New York: Farrar, Straus and Giroux, 1998.

Murphy, Walter F. "Lower Court Checks on Supreme Court Power." *American Political Science Review* 53 (December 1959): 1017–31.

Patton, Zach. "Robe Warriors." *Governing Magazine,* February 2006. <www.governing.com/archive/2006/mar/judges,txt>.

Raban, Ofer. "Judicial Impartiality and the Regulation of Judicial Election Campaigns." *Florida Journal of Law and Public Policy* 15 (2004): 205–28.

Roberts, Diane. *Dream State*. New York: Free Press, 2004.

Sample, James. "The Campaign Trial: The True Cost of Expensive Court Seats." <www/slate.com>, March 6, 2006.

Schotland, Roy A. "Comment." *Law and Contemporary Problems* 61 (Summer 1998): 149–55.

Shaw, Leander, Jr. "Florida's Judicial Merit Selection and Retention System: The Better Alternative." *Florida State University Law Review* 20 (1992): 283–90.

Webster, Peter D. "Merit Selection and Retention of Judges: Is There One 'Best' Method?" *Florida State University Law Review* 23 (1995): 1–42.

Interviews Conducted by Author

James Apthorp, Aug. 3, 2006

Reubin Askew, Sept. 26, 2001; Nov. 10, 2005; March 27, 2006

Ed Austin, Apr. 25, 2006

Thomas H. Barkdull Jr., June 9, 2005

Talbot D'Alemberte, May 16, 2005

W. Dexter Douglass, Feb. 27, July 1, 2006

William Durden, Apr. 25, 2002

Richard T. Earle Jr., Aug. 1993; July 1994; undated

Richard T. Earle III, Jan. 24, 2006

Arthur England, Sept. 27, 2005

Wade Hopping, Jan. 27, 2006; undated

Mark Hulsey, Jan. 25, 2006

Clarence Jones, Oct. 14, 2005

Fred Karl, Aug. 1975; May 9, 2006

Gerald Kogan, Apr. 19, 2006

David LaCroix, various dates

Richard T. McFarlain, July 19, 2005; undated

Steven Metz, June 27, 2006

Ben F. Overton, Mar. 31, 2005; May 15, 2006

John Phelps, July 11, 2006

William J. Rish, June 21, 2006

Herman Russomanno, June 27, 2006

Larry Sartin, Oct. 2005

Roger A. Schwartz, Dec. 11, 2005

C. McFerrin Smith III, Feb. 26, 2006

Sharyn Smith, Nov. 5, 2005

Richard R. Swann, Apr. 6, 2006

Burton Young, May 16, 2005

Index

Page numbers in italic type indicate illustrations.

Martin A. Dyckman is a retired associate editor of the *St. Petersburg Times* and author of *Floridian of His Century: The Courage of Governor LeRoy Collins*, which won the Charlton Tebeau Award of the Florida Historical Society and a Bronze medal in the Florida Book Awards in 2007. His series on Florida prison conditions circa 1971 won the distinguished service award of the Florida Society of Newspaper Editors, the Silver Gavel of the American Bar Association, and the Associated Press Managing Editors Association public service award. In 1984, the Florida Bar Foundation recognized his writing on judicial reform with its Medal of Honor Award.

Related-interest titles from University Press of Florida

Counting Votes: Lessons from the 2000 Presidential Election in Florida
Robert P. Watson

Florida's Megatrends: Critical Issues in Florida
David R. Colburn and Lance deHaven-Smith

Floridian of His Century: The Courage of Governor LeRoy Collins
Martin A. Dyckman

Government in the Sunshine State: Florida Since Statehood
David R. Colburn and Lance deHaven-Smith

Government and Politics in Florida, Third Edition
J. Edwin Benton

Land of Sunshine, State of Dreams: A Social History of Modern Florida
Gary R. Mormino

Making Waves: Female Activists in Twentieth-Century Florida
Jack E. Davis and Kari Frederickson

The Myth of Representation and the Florida Legislature: A House of Competing Loyalties, 1927–2000
Eric Prier

Politics and Growth in Twentieth-Century Tampa
Robert Kerstein

The Supreme Court of Florida, 1917–1972
Walter W. Manley II and Canter Brown, Jr.

The Supreme Court of Florida and Its Predecessor Courts, 1821–1917
Walter W. Manley II, Canter Brown, Jr., and Eric W. Rise

The Values and Craft of American Journalism: Essays from the Poynter Institute
Roy Peter Clark and Cole Campbell

For more information on these and other books, visit our Web site at www.upf.com.